D0891832

Franchising in America

THOMAS S. DICKE

Franchising
IN AMERICA

The Development of a Business Method, 1840–1980

The University of North Carolina Press   Chapel Hill & London

© 1992 The University of North
Carolina Press
All rights reserved

Manufactured in the United States of
America

96   95   94   93   92
5   4   3   2   1

Library of Congress
Cataloging-in-Publication Data
Dicke, Thomas S.
  Franchising in America : the
development of a business method,
1840–1980 / Thomas S. Dicke.
     p.   cm.
  Includes bibliographical references and
index.
    ISBN 0-8078-2041-5 (cloth : alk. paper).
— ISBN 0-8078-4378-4 (pbk.: alk. paper)
    1. Franchises—United States—History.
I. Title.
HF5429.235.U5D53   1992
381′.13′0973—dc20   91-43618
                              CIP

The paper in this book meets the guidelines
for permanence and durability of the
Committee on Production Guidelines for
Book Longevity of the Council on Library
Resources.

Contents

Illustrations

Illustration

Acknowledgments

The help and advice of many people contributed greatly to the completion of this book. Several in particular deserve special thanks. My wife, Judy, has been a constant aid. Throughout this project her overall support has been as indispensable as her help in editing and proofreading. Mansel Blackford originally suggested this topic. He then read several drafts, and his comments have improved it immeasurably. Roger Nimps and Kurt Schultz also read and provided insightful comments on various parts of the manuscript.

The administrators of the John E. Rovensky Fellowship in Economic and Business History provided much-needed financial support, as did The Ohio State University and the Hagley Museum and Library. I am grateful.

In the course of my research I also accumulated debts to the staffs of several institutions for their assistance in locating materials. I would like to thank all those at the State Historical Society of Wisconsin, the Edison Institute of the Henry Ford Museum and Greenfield Village, the Ford Industrial Archives, the Hagley Museum and Library, the Domino's Pizza Corporate Archives, and the International Franchise Association library for their help in collecting the information necessary to complete my study. Although everyone at these institutions was very helpful, Darleen Flaherty of the Ford Industrial Archives deserves special thanks for all of her exceptionally able and willing assistance.

Finally, I would like to thank my parents, Dale and Kathryn Dicke.

Franchising in America

Introduction

Franchising became a highly visible institution in the United States during the last half of the twentieth century. At the start of the 1950s franchising was already a considerable and well-entrenched force in the economy. It had dominated such key sectors as automobile sales and gasoline retailing from their earliest years and was well established in lesser industries such as soft drinks and fast food. By the end of the 1960s it was used to sell virtually every type of good or service imaginable, and the franchise outlet had become a ubiquitous feature of the American landscape. Currently, over one-half million individual franchised businesses are scattered across the United States. Together, they account for well over one-third of the total value of all retail sales in the country. That proportion is expected to grow significantly in years to come. The main purpose of this study is to trace the development of the franchise system and explain why it has been possible for franchising to spread so quickly and weave itself so inextricably into the American economy.

The term *franchise* has a long history and a number of meanings. This has caused some confusion among the few authors who have touched on the origins of the system, so the word itself deserves some explanation. Originating from an Old French term meaning "to make or set free" or "to invest with a franchise or privilege," it was used in business at least as far back as the Middle Ages, when franchise referred to government grants of special rights given in exchange for some service, such as tax collection or road construction, that the state subcontracted to private individuals. In the nineteenth and twentieth centuries the term has, until recently, been associated most frequently with grants of incorporation, particularly for municipal services. It was not until the twentieth century that the definition of franchising came to include a method of distribution.[1] Legally and functionally, franchise selling is unrelated to the franchise privileges given by governments. Government franchises were based on the private performance of public services in exchange for special privileges such as limited liability or monopoly rights and form much of the legal justification for the existence of the corporation. In contrast, the franchise method of distribution is a contractual method of organizing a large-scale enterprise that evolved out of the traditional practice of selling through agents.[2]

Standard linguistic and legal reference works indicate that the use of franchising as a method of distributing goods or services—its most common meaning today—is of fairly recent origin. Neither the *Oxford English Dictionary* (*OED*) nor *Black's Law Dictionary* include any mention of franchise selling until the 1970s. The 1972 supplement to the *OED* identifies 1959 as the year the term entered the business lexicon. *Black's Law Dictionary*, which first referred to franchise selling in its 1979 edition, states that franchising developed out of the agency method of distribution. Standard periodical references, a valuable source of information on when terms became popular, first noticed franchising in the late 1950s. The *Business Periodicals Index* and the *Reader's Guide to Periodical Literature* provided headings in 1958 and 1959 respectively. Prior to this time, articles dealing with franchising were indexed under "exclusive agency." Until 1969 the *Reader's Guide* included only a cross-reference to exclusive agency under its "franchise system" heading.[3]

Franchising Defined

Modern franchising can perhaps best be thought of as a method of organization that combines large and small business into a single administrative unit. In a franchise system one large firm, often called the parent company, grants or sells the right to distribute its products or use its trade name and processes to a number of smaller firms. The boundaries of the relationship and the ultimate basis for control are established by contract. Contracts typically either have no fixed term or run from three to twenty years, but once a franchisee signs on, the conditions under which termination or nonrenewal can legally occur are limited as long as performance is satisfactory. Although the contract defines the limits of the relationship, control is based more on the community of interest arising out of the near-exclusive relationship between the involved parties. For the system to work, franchise holders, although legally independent, must conform to detailed standards of operation designed and enforced by the parent company.[4]

There are two general types of franchise organizations. *Product franchising*, the first to develop, remains the most important in terms of the value of total sales. Under this system, a manufacturer markets its output almost entirely through highly specialized retailers, who, in turn, rely on the manufacturer for most of the products they sell. This system first appeared in the mid-nineteenth century, when the makers of costly and complex goods such as farm equipment and sewing machines reached a size where their increased output and expanded markets forced them to modify their agency systems to better coordinate and control the flow of goods from factory to consumer. Today, the automobile dealership is probably the most common example of this type of franchise.[5]

Business-format franchising, the second type to develop, is where the outlet itself—together with a comprehensive package of services to support it—is the product. Business-format franchising emerged in the early twentieth century, when the spread of big business led to the creation of a wide variety of specialized services and managerial tools such as professional advertising and sophisticated accounting systems. These services form the core of the package that business-format franchisers market to the would-be small business owner. By the late 1950s perceptive entrepreneurs realized that, to use a popular example, there was more money to be made selling hamburger stands than in selling hamburgers. Once business-format franchisers understood this and began producing small businesses, they found their success depended on applying the principles of mass production to the bundle of services they provided to their franchisees. When this happened, the franchise industry was born.[6]

Both types of franchising, then, are relatively new. Product franchising, along with better methods of organizing the modern business enterprise, grew out of the changes in technology that led to a national market and high-volume production. By the 1850s, these changes in technology and markets had reached the point where America began to make the transition from a traditional to a modern economy. Unlike more common methods of integrating the activities of the large, multiunit enterprise, however, product franchisers did not rely on the "visible hand" of corporate ownership and direct supervision to coordinate and control the flow of goods through the firm. Instead, they found that since the distribution of their goods required less coordination than their production, they could meet the opportunities and demands of the mass market by converting their independent agents into semi-independent franchised dealers.[7]

Although business-format franchising grew out of product franchising, legally and functionally they are separate and distinct. Business-format franchisers sell the opportunity for business ownership. Product franchisers use the outlets to sell their goods. The profitability of the products sold through the outlets seems to be the most important factor in determining how firms use franchising. The makers of complex goods originally developed product franchising because their goods could not be easily absorbed into normal distribution channels. These products tended to be expensive and durable, like sewing machines or automobiles, and the number sold through any individual outlet was usually low. Their high per-unit profits and their large investments in production facilities gave manufacturers little incentive to consider the franchise as a product, and the relatively limited number of outlets needed to market durable goods further reduced the attractiveness of outlets as products.

On the other hand, the successful sale of services or nondurable goods generally requires closer connections with the parent company since the appearance of the outlet and the service the customer receives there are part of the product the customer buys. These more elaborate franchise packages made it more logical to view the franchise as a product, while the low-profit margins and minimal investments in production facilities gave business-format franchisers additional incentives to convert the outlet into a product in its own right.

Business-format franchisers do more than sell outlets however, and this is where the greatest difference between product and business-format franchisers comes into play. To be successful, a franchise industry firm must produce a wide range of support services in high volume and sell them at a relatively low cost. To do this, franchise industry firms moved big business into the business of creating small businesses. In much the same way that their counterparts in the automobile or sewing machine industry exploited economies of scale or scope to mass-produce consumer goods, business-format franchisers applied the same principles to the production of franchised outlets and associated services.

In addition to my main goal of tracing the origins of the franchise system, I also use franchising to examine the influence of traditional business practices in shaping the organization of the large, multiunit firm and to investigate an important intersection between large and small business in the modern economy. Over the last twenty-five years, the primary focus of business history has been on the institutional development of big business and the appearance of managerial capitalism in the United States. As the work of Alfred Chandler and a number of other scholars has shown, one of the distinguishing features of the modern economy has been the creation of a large body of salaried managers to replace the invisible hand of the market in coordinating the flow of goods and services through the most important sectors of the economy. Large firms were forced to develop bureaucratic organizational structures because the closer coordination required to make mass production and mass distribution work efficiently could not be achieved by allowing market forces to control the flow of goods from raw material to consumer. As the remainder of this study will show, however, in distribution it was often possible for firms to combine the visible hand of management with the invisible hand of the market to coordinate the movement of goods. The makers of automobiles and the refiners of gasoline, for example, developed new administrative structures staffed by salaried executives who controlled and coordinated distribution, but, to actually implement the programs devised by the home office, these firms grafted their new organizational structures onto their already existing network of semi-independent dealers. Ultimately, control came through a combination of administrative fiat, contractual obligation, and economic self-interest.[8]

As to the final goal of my study, it has long been recognized that the place of small business in the modern economy is an underexplored area in business history. The few authors concerned with the relationship between large and small business have tended to stress the existence of a dual economy, where large and small firms coexist much like two noncompeting species who, though sharing the same environment, interact only indirectly. In this view, large firms, which were able to develop technologies and managerial structures to exploit the national market, quickly came to dominate the modern economy and shape its growth. In contrast, small firms, lacking access to economies of scale or scope and the need for managerial innovations, continued to operate much as they always had, except that now they existed on the fringes of the economy, avoiding their larger counterparts by seeking niches where big business could not bring its greater efficiencies to bear.[9]

While this view describes the structure of the economy fairly well, it falls short on explaining how large and small businesses interact in the modern economy. In reality, the relationship between large and small is more complex than is often presented. Small business also adapted to the modern economy, and a major part of this adjustment was learning how to work with, as well as avoid, competition with big business. Just as some small firms have survived by carving out small, specialized areas that fill the cracks in the market left by big businesses, others have found success by tying their fortunes to their larger counterparts. Instead of emphasizing a dual economy where large and small businesses operate in distinct and largely separate spheres, it seems more accurate to think of the modern economy as one where large and small businesses interact constantly, as in the case of the automobile and oil industries, where small firms retail the products produced by big business. Or, to use a more general example, in subcontracting small firms provide all types of services to their larger counterparts. Franchising, which combines large and small business into a single administrative unit, is perhaps the most extreme example of the interconnections between large and small businesses in the modern economy.[10]

Overview

This book is organized around five case studies. The first four examine the evolution of franchise selling, and the final one considers the development of franchising as an industry in its own right. The firms selected for examination either dominated or were representative of their respective industries. Together, they span a 140-year period that begins in the 1840s and ends in the 1980s.

Each chapter is organized in much the same way. A brief sketch of the relevant economic and social conditions at the time franchising was introduced to the industry in question is followed by an overview of that industry as a whole and an examination of how franchising developed in the case study firm. In each instance, the development of franchising is analyzed from its introduction to the time when the franchise organization matured.

Chapter 1 traces the evolution of product franchising out of the agency system using the examples of the McCormick Harvesting Machine Company and the I. M. Singer Company. Both firms turned to agency sales shortly after their founding as a result of wholesalers' inability to sell their products effectively. The cost and complexity of their goods made it necessary for retailers to provide credit, demonstration, maintenance, and repair services. Because most wholesalers lacked the facilities and expertise to provide these services, McCormick and Singer found it necessary to forge direct connections with the dealers who sold their wares. The agency system, already long established, provided a ready but only partial solution to their needs. As long as each firm remained relatively small, the agency system worked well. But as each became a big business, the administrative problems of coordinating the flow of tens of thousands of machines and parts to thousands of dealers forced the firms to standardize relations with their dealers and fashion them into a unified distribution network.

The transformation from an arrangement where agents acted independently of one another and only nominally under the control of the home office to a system where dealers performed as "an organized and responsible army" followed different paths at McCormick and Singer. Because the reaper was a seasonal good and its market was scattered, McCormick was never able to force its dealers to concentrate exclusively on the sale of its products. This made it impossible for the company to gain full control over its dealer network. McCormick could, and did, standardize sales policies and procedures and coordinate the actions of his dealers, but they always maintained a high degree of independence. At Singer, where production was higher and the market was more concentrated, the company ultimately moved toward a dual distribution system, where company-owned outlets handled sales in the high-volume, high-profit urban areas and dealers controlled sales in the hinterlands. Unlike McCormick, Isaac

Singer could establish a high degree of control over his dealers as it was possible for them to concentrate almost exclusively on the sale of his product.

Chapter 2 uses the experiences of the Ford Motor Company to investigate the development of franchising in the automobile industry between 1903 and the mid-1950s. Conditions in the auto industry resembled those in farm implements, and in many ways events at Ford were a continuation of the pattern already established by McCormick. At Ford, however, the shift from independent agents using their best judgment to sell the company's products to a body of semi-independent dealers operating according to uniform policies set and strictly enforced by the company occurred much more quickly and completely than it had at McCormick. Within ten years of its founding Ford was making almost 190,000 vehicles a year, and the greater administrative requirements this placed on the company necessitated tighter control over distribution much earlier in the company's existence than had been the case at either McCormick or Singer. Moreover, the improved communication network of the twentieth century gave Ford the physical means to coordinate and control its distribution system from the earliest days of the business.

Automobile makers in general and Ford in particular also had an additional incentive to change the nature of the agency system they had originally used to market their products. As the number of dealers climbed into the thousands, executives at Ford became increasingly concerned about the possibility of being held legally responsible for the actions of these agents as they carried out their duties for the company.

At Ford, the desire to establish the legal independence of its dealers came at roughly the same time the company was trying to exert more influence over dealers for the sake of administrative coordination. What carmakers such as Ford wanted was a way to tie dealers more closely to the company, while at the same time establishing their legal independence. Franchising proved to be the answer. Even before the introduction of mass production in 1913, Ford's sizable output allowed dealers to make a living specializing exclusively in the sale and servicing of Ford products. This gave the company considerable control over dealers' actions, even as it maintained clauses in the franchise contract that explicitly proclaimed the dealers' legal independence.

Franchise development at Ford was characterized by increasingly close, but not always cordial, relations between the company and its dealers. Administratively, dealers were treated as if they were company employees. Dealers were tied into the company's chain of command, receiving a continual stream of correspondence notifying them of changes in policy or procedure, and factory representatives made regular inspections to see that the directives of the home office were being followed. From its earliest years through the late 1930s, Ford used the threat of cancellation to force dealers to abide by the company's wishes. This policy began to change in the late 1930s, as company officials came to realize that the long-term health of the firm depended on a strong, stable dealer network and that such a network could not be maintained through coercion. Accordingly, Ford revised its franchise contracts to provide dealers with some legal protection from the former abuses of the company and developed institutions to more actively assist them in the profitable operation of their businesses, to arbitrate their disputes with the company, and to give them a stronger voice in company affairs.

Business-format franchising appeared first in the oil industry, the subject of Chapter 3, during the 1920s. The Sun Oil Company, my fourth case, began to use franchised service stations in the second decade of the twentieth century, when the tremendous boom in automobile ownership created an urgent demand for large numbers of conveniently located gasoline outlets. The volatile nature of the product made mass distribution through existing distributors impractical, and the profits that could be expected from a typical outlet were not great enough to encourage independent retailers to establish enough outlets to meet the demand. Therefore, almost by default, petroleum companies were forced to become directly involved in retail marketing. By using franchise systems, oil companies were able to ensure a stable market for their products and reduce the administrative, storage, and maintenance costs associated with retail distribution.

Refiners brought a major expansion of the system in that for the first time franchising was used to market what was essentially a generic good. No obvious physical differences separated one brand of gasoline from another, and it was difficult for the average consumer to notice any variation in how well different brands performed. Because they could not establish a strong brand identity for their product based on its physical characteristics, refiners began to use the outlets where it was sold to distinguish their goods in the public mind. This plan had much to recommend it. By the end of the 1920s most stations carried only one brand, so when motorists chose a station, they also chose a refiner. In addition, the appearance of the outlet and the service the motorist received there were part of the product they purchased with their gasoline.

Once refiners were identified with the outlets that sold their gasoline, it was necessary for them to project a uniform appearance and uniform levels of service at the legally independent stations that sold their products and see that they reflected well on the company. Because legal restrictions made it unprofitable or illegal to control the dealer directly by contract, refiners were driven to create dealer assistance programs that made it in the best interest of the dealer to follow the wishes of the company. Over time this support became quite extensive, covering services such as station remodeling or construction, training, specialized equipment, uniforms, and advertising—all provided free or at a lower cost than dealers could obtain through their own efforts. These services, together with the public preference for branded goods, gave affiliated dealers a significant advantage over independent stations and set the stage for the development of the franchise as a product in its own right.

The final chapter explores the development of the franchise industry and is divided into two sections. The first examines the economic conditions that made the franchise industry possible. People came to prefer branded goods to their generic counterparts and this, along with the host of specialized services that accompanied the rise of big business, gave business-format franchisers a valuable product to sell if they could produce it efficiently in great numbers. Once a few refiners proved that franchising could create a strong brand identity for undifferentiated goods, it was inevitable that others would enter the market. Among the new entrants were firms such as Howard Johnson's; these organizations were not manufacturers and had no significant investments in production facilities. For them it was a short step to where the outlet became a product. A few early "system" franchisers such as Howard Johnson's and A & W Root Beer were active during the 1920s and 1930s, but their owners failed to recognize fully the potential value of outlets as products. The creation of a distinct franchise industry did not occur until the late 1950s, when the press popularized business-format franchising. This, in turn, brought a wave of organizations into the field, the majority of which looked at franchising as a business opportunity rather than as a method of distribution.

Introduction

The second section of Chapter 4 uses the example of Domino's Pizza to trace the institutional development of a typical franchise industry firm. Like many early members of the franchise industry, Domino's began as a traditional retailer, selling its products through company-owned stores. After seven years, Domino's founder, Tom Monaghan, had pushed the business about as far as he could reasonably expect to in terms of size. But Monaghan wanted more and, inspired by Ray Kroc's success at McDonald's, he decided to transfer his expertise in one industry, food services, to another, franchising, where the opportunities for expansion were much greater. Although he realized that he had entered a new business, Monaghan was slow to recognize that it would be necessary to develop a new organization and procedures for the franchisees that constituted his new market. Thus, in 1969, when Domino's began franchising in earnest, the company very nearly collapsed when its informal and underdeveloped franchise service system broke down under the relatively modest demands of producing, servicing, and monitoring the actions of several dozen franchisees.

For the next three years the company hovered at the edge of bankruptcy, but by 1972 Domino's was again fairly stable and Monaghan began to build the internal infrastructure needed to produce franchise services in quantity. Monaghan focused his efforts on three areas: training, outlet standardization, and supply. The process of professionalizing his operations in these areas took most of the 1970s, but by 1979 Domino's was again ready to undertake a major expansion. This attempt was far more successful. Between 1979 and 1985, Domino's opened over 3,500 outlets without seriously straining the company's ability to train, equip, or supply its vastly expanded customer base.

1

Preludes to Franchising

The McCormick Harvesting Machine Company and the I. M. Singer Company

Cyrus McCormick and Isaac Singer started their firms just as America's long-established economic system based on agriculture and small business began to give way to a new economy grounded in industry and controlled by big business. When they began operations in the mid-nineteenth century, their products were new, but they were made and sold much like goods had been produced and marketed since colonial times. McCormick's reapers and Singer's sewing machines were handcrafted in small shops and sold primarily through independent agents who carried them as only a small part of their business. By the end of the century, McCormick and Singer had become large, vertically integrated businesses, where manufacturing and selling were closely linked and administrative coordination, more than market forces, determined the flow of their goods from producer to consumer. In going from small firm to big business, McCormick and Singer acted in response to the economic changes that had begun to reshape America in the 1840s. Like many of their counterparts, McCormick and Singer found that in making this change it was possible to incorporate part of their old marketing structures into their new organizations. This chapter examines the distribution systems developed by Singer and McCormick. Both blended the traditional practice of selling through agents with new organizational techniques to coordinate and control their performance. These marketing systems were important forerunners to franchising.

America's Changing Business System

The changes at McCormick and Singer were hardly unique; they reflected the general alterations in American business that were occurring as a result of population increases and the development of new technologies. Astute business leaders recognized clearly the potentials for expansion inherent in their new world, but they were less sure about how to best exploit them. In general, business people seemed to prefer trying to adapt their existing organizations to the new environment as best they could and resorted to drastic change only when traditional methods failed. Consequently, the initial organizational response to the rise of the modern economy was often evolutionary and piecemeal. This perpetuated the use of traditional business methods, because once accepted they tended to become institutionalized within the structure of the firm.[1]

The growth of the domestic market provided the ambitious with an incentive to develop methods for high-volume production and distribution. Technological changes made this a reality, but only organizational changes made it possible for these new technologies to work effectively. The market had been expanding since the earliest days of European settlement, but because of the great size of the country and the tendency to migrate to sparsely settled frontier areas, it was not until the 1830s or later that many regions possessed a population density great enough to encourage merchants and manufacturers to develop new business methods.[2]

The increase in population and the appearance of large urban centers controlling vast hinterlands of well-settled rural sections encouraged business people to increase the scale and scope of their operations in a few selected areas. But people and cities alone were not enough to alter the basic structure of the American economy. Dense urban and village markets had existed in Europe for centuries and in the northeastern United States for decades without substantially changing the structure of business organizations inherited from the earliest days of European settlement. Until the 1840s, the dominant form of business in the country remained the small firm serving a limited market. Goods flowed from firm to firm in a complex chain, all held together by an intricate web regulated through law, guided by market forces, and driven by the independent actions of countless individuals. Beginning in the 1840s, however, a number of technological changes combined to alter the basic structure of the economy—first by making direct access to large regional markets possible, and second by allowing manufacturers to develop new, more efficient methods of production.[3]

At the heart of these technological changes was the substitution of mechanical power for human or animal power. The introduction of water and, more importantly, steam power, brought about the end of an economy based on handcrafting for local customers and created an industrial economy based on machine production for regional, national, and international markets. The tremendous concentrations of energy provided by water and steam allowed mechanics to develop a galaxy of new machines that previously had been unthinkable owing to the lack of any reliable source with enough energy to power them. In production, the end result was the creation of the factory system, where machines and people were integrated together in ways that permitted high-volume, low-cost production.[4]

The widespread application of mechanical power occurred even earlier in distribution and played a critical role in industrialization by creating conditions that made the development of mass production profitable. The use of steam power to operate the steamboat and the railroad greatly widened the market available to business by dramatically increasing the speed and reliability of the movement of goods throughout the country. In 1800, for example, it took roughly five to six weeks to travel from New York City to the Mississippi River; on the eve of the Civil War, the same trip lasted only three to five days. Due to increased carrying capacity, freight charges dropped as decisively. Inventions such as the telegraph allowed news to travel even faster, and given the fact that information is often the most perishable commodity a business person deals in, this further extended the area a single concern could reasonably hope to serve.[5]

In the early nineteenth century, the two most significant changes occurring in distribution were the ascendancy of the wholesale jobber and the movement of manufacturers into marketing. The increased volume of trade and the broadening of markets created the need for someone to coordinate the movement of goods between makers and sellers. Throughout most of the nineteenth century the wholesale jobber filled this function. For producers, the jobber provided credit and working capital, while relieving manufacturers of the burden of establishing a far-flung distribution system in areas where they were unfamiliar with local conditions. For retailers, the jobber also provided credit as well as contacts for the often-isolated shopkeeper.[6]

The jobber was especially valuable to America's nascent industrialists. As these manufacturers groped toward high-volume production, their primary concern was, by necessity, production rather than distribution. The development of high-volume production techniques was usually a difficult and risky process, and most early manufacturers lacked the time, funds, and desire to simultaneously undertake anything as involved, troublesome, and expensive as the development of their own channels of distribution.[7]

Nonetheless, under certain conditions manufacturers did begin to take over the functions of independent wholesalers as early as the 1840s. In cases where existing distributors proved to be unwilling or unable to effectively market their products, the manufacturers had to fill the gap. In lines where it eventually became more profitable for manufacturers to take over the marketing of their own goods, they generally did so. Changes in the nature of the market often dictated the move into distribution. Improvements in transportation and communication eventually broadened producers' horizons by allowing them to become familiar with conditions outside their locality. A substantial concentration in markets also took place. This change appeared in two areas: first, in the development of large urban centers, which provided the makers of consumer goods with dense and easily accessible markets for their wares; and, second in the development of big business, which gave the makers of producers' goods a small number of customers who took the bulk of their output. In both cases, it often became cheaper for producers to take over the distribution of the products they manufactured.[8]

When manufacturers were forced into distribution, it was generally the goods they made that pushed them into the market. The rapid changes in technology that occurred in the nineteenth century brought new products as well as new production methods. Some of these goods did not fit well into existing distribution channels. When products required special handling (for example, fresh fruit or beer) or needed expert service (such as sewing machines or reapers), manufacturers had to establish their own marketing channels if they wished to sell outside their immediate area. In creating a distribution network, producers faced two choices: they could either build a company-owned system or they could contract directly with independent firms to represent them. When manufacturers discovered it was cheaper to establish their own sales organization, they usually did so. In many cases, however, manufacturers found it more efficient to form direct links with independent retailers.[9]

The choice was not always easy. Direct ownership guaranteed manufacturers complete control over the distribution of their wares and assured the company fairly uniform levels of service and representation in their market areas. Company-owned outlets also made it easier to establish brand identities and to maintain close contact with consumers. On the other hand, with direct ownership came the formidable expense and administrative difficulties inherent in establishing and operating a national sales organization.

The agency system of contracting with independent retailers offered manufacturers a reasonable alternative to direct ownership of retail outlets. Because agents frequently bore selling expenses and assumed credit risks, manufacturers were able to build extensive sales networks quickly at little cost to themselves. The use of agents also eliminated many administrative problems for the parent company, as it could then operate as a wholesaler rather than as a retailer. The primary drawback of agency sales was that it allowed less effective control over sales. Since agents were independent business people, the parent company could not control all aspects of their business. Also, because agents frequently handled the products of more than one manufacturer, they were less apt to push sales as aggressively as regular employees.[10]

The nature of their product mainly determined whether or not producers established a distribution system under their direct control, but the nature of the market and the life cycle of the firm were most important in deciding the type of system a manufacturer was likely to choose. If the firm was new and the market scattered, the owner was more likely to select an agency-based system. When the market was highly concentrated, a manufacturer that had originally used an agent to establish its product frequently found company-owned outlets more effective once its product became well known and its resources were greater.[11]

The experiences of the I. M. Singer Company illustrate the latter type of firm very well. In the early years of the company's existence, Singer's executives chose to market their machines through agents because they could not afford to establish company-owned stores and desperately needed the cash sales generated to and through agents. Later, when the public had come to accept the sewing machine as a consumer good and the company had become more financially secure, Singer began to take over the marketing of machines in cities and towns and used its increased power to bring its remaining agencies so closely under its control that they became nearly indistinguishable from company-owned stores.

The movement of manufacturers into marketing was part of a trend toward specialization caused by the increased volume of trade during the nineteenth century. One aspect of this specialization was the arrival of the exclusive agent. Exclusive agents—those who hold the sole right to sell a manufacturer's products in a given area—first appeared in the United States in the 1830s. In cases where agents were required to make substantial investments in equipment, the nature of the relationship between manufacturer and agent was fundamentally altered. Once agents became dependent on a single manufacturer for the bulk of goods they sold and the expertise they possessed, they lost a great deal of their freedom of action and the relationship shifted from one of principal and agent to that of franchiser and franchisee.

The development of marketing strategies and structures at McCormick and Singer illustrates the divergent paths taken in the evolution of the agency system during the last half of the nineteenth century. Both McCormick and Singer originally marketed most of their output through agents. With various modifications, the agency system established by McCormick continues to be the dominant method of retail distribution in America's farm implements industry to the present day. Singer, on the other hand, quickly moved to establish company-owned branch houses and to reduce its dependence on independent retailers. The remainder of this chapter examines the development of franchising at McCormick and Singer and analyzes the reasons for the divergence of their respective marketing strategies.

Marketing at McCormick

The story of the invention of the McCormick reaper and the development of the McCormick Harvesting Machine Company is fairly well known. In the summer of 1831, at the age of twenty-two, Cyrus Hall McCormick successfully demonstrated the first practical mechanical reaper on a neighbor's farm outside Walnut Grove, Virginia. The machine worked reasonably well but other projects, most notably a partnership in an unsuccessful ironworks, captured McCormick's attention. It was not until 1839 that he made a determined effort to capitalize on his invention.[12]

In the seventy-one years between McCormick's demonstration of the reaper and the formation of the International Harvester Corporation, with McCormick Harvesting Machine Company as its nucleus, the general organization of the McCormick sales force passed through three phases. The first, expansion by licensing agreements, lasted from 1843 to 1849; the second, sales through independent agents in direct contact with the home office, dominated the years from 1849 to 1871; and, finally, the use of a decentralized structure, with the overall sales strategy determined by the home office but administered through a number of branch offices and implemented by retail agents, from 1871 to 1902.[13]

In the first phase of his operations Cyrus McCormick did what manufacturers who wished to go beyond their local markets had done since colonial times: he contracted with others to make and sell his reaper. This allowed him to build a national market out of a large number of more or less individual local markets. McCormick sold his first license to James Hite in 1843 for $1,333. In exchange, Hite received exclusive rights for the manufacture and sale of the McCormick reaper in eight counties in the Valley of Virginia and along the Potomac River for five years. This license, like others later issued by McCormick, was an assignment of patent rights in exchange for a fee. During the next five years McCormick used this as his primary method for expansion. Throughout these years McCormick traveled extensively, often spending six months out of the year on the road, signing up new licensees, overseeing their work, and securing orders for his machines. Although time consuming and cumbersome, this system worked well enough, and by 1844 McCormick had introduced his reaper in ten states.[14]

The terms and territories granted by the inventor varied considerably. McCormick signed up any manufacturer he found to be willing and believed to be competent on the best terms he could get. In 1845, for example, he sold the rights to manufacture and sell the reaper in four Iowa counties for eight years to John Cameron for $1,000. In the same year Henry Bear of St. Louis agreed to pay McCormick a $20 royalty for each machine he manufactured. One of McCormick's more important early licensees was C. A. Brown of Cincinnati, Ohio. In May 1845 McCormick signed a four-year contract with Brown for the rights to sixteen Ohio counties for $1,900. In the first year of his contract, Brown agreed to build approximately 200 machines for the harvest of 1845, and, although Brown's selling rights were limited to Ohio, McCormick allowed him to send agents into Illinois to obtain reaper orders and to produce for the western market generally.[15]

McCormick also expanded his personal reaper sales by contracting with his licensees for the construction of machines on his own account. Typical of these arrangements was his contract of 1845 with Seymour, Chappell & Company of New York for the construction of up to 100 machines at a cost of $55 each. Because records are scarce and the licensees frequently failed to produce as many reapers as expected, it is difficult to be sure exactly how many reapers were built and sold in the early years. In an advertisement in the *Ohio Cultivator*, McCormick claimed to have had 200 machines operating in the West during the harvest of 1846 and 600 under construction for the 1847 season. Whatever the exact number, McCormick's policy of expansion through the sale of manufacturing rights was a clear success.[16]

McCormick had several compelling reasons for his decision to expand by selling manufacturing and sales rights to others. There was such a demand for the mechanical reaper that anyone who could fill even a small part of it could quickly become very wealthy. In the late 1830s and early 1840s, however, the national market was still only a tantalizing possibility. Transportation was so expensive and uncertain that an untested maker could easily destroy his business by selling overpriced machines that might well arrive too late for the harvest. The location of the Walnut Grove shop was particularly poor for taking advantage of the vast potential market of the Midwest. In 1844, for example, McCormick sent a shipment of eight reapers to the Midwest. They began their trip in wagons and canal boats, which brought them to the Atlantic coast. From there they traveled by ship around Florida to New Orleans, then by steamboat up the Mississippi and Ohio rivers for overland shipment to their various destinations. All arrived too late for the harvest of 1844. Moreover, the novelty and cost of the reaper made initial sales difficult, and local manufacturers doubtlessly enjoyed the greater confidence of farmers than did an unknown, distant manufacturer.[17]

McCormick realized that even if he had been able to reach more than a small fraction of his potential market, the Walnut Grove shop would never be able to supply machines for more than local use. And, as early as 1843, it was clear that he intended to sell the reaper as widely as possible. In that year he reported to the *Richmond Semi-Weekly Whig*: "As it is not at all probable that I can always manufacture the reaper to supply the wants of the country[,] I propose to form partnerships for their manufacture and also sell patent rights." Because McCormick lacked the resources to produce his machine, the sale of patent rights to other manufacturers was the best method at his disposal to introduce his reaper to the market.[18]

Finally, McCormick entered the reaper market at about the same time as a number of other manufacturers, and he recognized that success in the reaper business would depend not only on the quality of his machine but also on his ability to become the first to establish his company in the virgin market. It was this desire on the part of McCormick and his competitors that led to the first "reaper war" during the mid-1840s. Historians frequently attribute the victory of McCormick's company in the first reaper war to the marketing innovations developed by the inventor himself. In fact, however, the tools he used involved no radical departure from traditional practice. Whatever innovative behavior he exhibited in marketing was in strategy, not structure. The key to McCormick's success lay in his aggressive policy of marketing the reaper over as wide an area as possible. To carry out this policy McCormick may have pioneered in using national advertising and offering product warranties, but in actually expanding the business of making and selling his machines McCormick relied entirely on traditional marketing structures.[19]

Despite his success in introducing the reaper to the national market, the rapidly changing economy of mid–nineteenth-century America soon dictated alterations in McCormick's strategy of marketing through licensees. First, by the late 1840s transportation facilities had improved to the point where it was possible to ship machines in a timely manner throughout the Midwest from a single well-placed factory. Second, in the eighteen years between McCormick's first attempt to produce and sell the reaper and his purchase of his Chicago partners' interest in the business, the farm implements industry had come of age. In the minds of many farmers, the reaper was no longer a novelty but a necessity. And, finally, as a result of McCormick's original policy of expansion through the sale of patent rights, he was well placed to take advantage of this new situation. Licensees had built up a large market for his reaper and supplied McCormick with the funds to establish his Chicago factory. At the same time, McCormick and his brothers had gained years of experience in shops and sales offices across the United States and Canada, occasionally as paid employees of licensees.[20]

A number of other factors worked against the use of licensees. Despite his best efforts to oversee the production of his machines, McCormick found it impossible to maintain a uniform high quality while relying on a variety of manufacturers. The inventor's correspondence from the mid-1840s is filled with complaints about "worthless" licensees and the problems caused by licensees who used inferior materials or subcontracted their work out to "*other shops* that I [McCormick] consider incompetent and indisposed to do good work."[21]

Regardless of McCormick's concern about the quality of work done by firms not under his direct supervision, when he moved his business to Chicago in August 1847 he once again entered into partnership, this time with Charles M. Gray, a former licensee, to produce 500 reapers for the harvest of 1848. The partnership with Gray differed little from agreements McCormick had with other firms as far as the terms for producing the machines were concerned. Gray assumed full responsibility for the construction and distribution of the reapers, paying for the materials used in building the factory and the first group of machines with his own funds.

The contract also required Gray "to keep full and correct accounts subject to Cyrus H. McCormick's inspection at all times," but from the end of 1847 through June 1848 McCormick was unable to inspect these accounts, as a patent extension case and the need to oversee the work of a New York licensee kept him occupied in the East.[22]

McCormick's relationship with Gray proved to be as unsatisfactory as those with most of his earlier business partners had been and in 1849, after a disagreement over money, McCormick bought out Gray's interest along with that of the two partners Gray had been forced to bring into the business. McCormick now assumed control over the production and distribution of a major portion of his output. The purchase, however, produced no change in either the organization of the firm or in McCormick's policy of expanding sales by granting rights for the manufacture and sale of his reapers in areas he could not reach from his factory. Despite the fact that by the mid-1850s several of his licensees had begun to produce and market their own machines, McCormick continued to sell the manufacturing rights to his reaper as late as 1860. The primary change brought about by his purchase of the Chicago factory was that it greatly increased the number of machines made under his direct supervision. In 1847 Cyrus McCormick produced about 450 reapers; two years later the number had risen to almost 1,500.[23]

From 1849 until the early 1870s, McCormick kept the same general organization that he had inherited from the firm of McCormick, Gray & Company. He continued to use a marketing strategy based on extensive advertising, liberal credit terms, warranties guaranteeing the reaper's performance, and selling directly to farmers through independent agents. The sales organization continued to consist of traveling agents, wholesale jobbers who functioned as state agents, local dealers, and traveling salesmen—all of whom reported directly to the home office and, except for the traveling agents, were under yearly contract to McCormick.[24]

Of the salesmen, the traveling agents were fewest in number, had the broadest duties, and were the only members of the sales organization who were regular employees of the company. These half-dozen or so men were all trusted associates and reported directly to McCormick or one of his brothers. Their duties were essentially the same as those McCormick had performed before moving to Chicago. Travelers were responsible for looking after the general interests of the company and possessed broad powers to do so. They introduced the reaper to new areas, signed up agents, discharged inefficient dealers, reported on the activities of McCormick's dealers as well as competitors, purchased equipment for the Chicago factory, and tracked down lost machines. In exchange for their services, travelers received a salary and, unlike the rest of the company's sales force, were employed year-round, spending the winter months at the factory and traveling through their districts at harvest time.[25]

The company hired wholesale jobbers to act as state agents in the eastern United States and Canada, where the market for reapers was not great enough to warrant complete coverage by local agents but where the firm still wanted to be represented. Aside from personal reaper sales, the duties of the state agents included appointing subagents and supervising reaper shipments in their states. State agents generally worked on a commission varying from 5 to 15 percent for all machines sold in their territories. Once the market for McCormick reapers became well established, McCormick phased out jobbers in favor of local agents. Nonetheless, the company was still using jobbers to handle sales and coordinate the flow of machines through Maryland as late as 1860.[26]

In the Midwest, where over three-fourths of all his machines were sold, McCormick relied on a force of local agents who reported directly to the factory. These agents were usually either established merchants or local farmers who sold reapers only as a part of their larger business. In the early years, McCormick made little effort to oversee the activities of these men or to establish a permanent relationship with them. His company appointed local agents on a yearly basis for the harvest season. Terms of appointment varied, but during the 1850s agents usually received a flat rate of ten or twenty dollars per machine sold and paid for. During the 1860s agents generally earned forty to sixty dollars per month plus expenses while in the company's employ. McCormick probably shifted from commission to salary to compensate agents in the Midwest for the steady reduction in the size of their territories during the 1850s and 1860s. Territories were usually exclusive, and agents were allowed to appoint subagents and make whatever arrangements with them they wished.[27]

Agents were given considerable latitude to handle the company's affairs as they saw fit. Contracts were brief and defined the agents' responsibilities loosely. Specifically, contracts required the agents "to do all the business pertaining to selling reapers" and "to report to said M'Cormick [*sic*] as often as he may desire, say once in two weeks, the number of orders obtained." In addition, agents were expected to keep the company informed about local conditions, such as weather and the amounts of different grains planted, so that managers would have a good idea of how many machines to build and where and when they would be needed. The only areas where the company tried to maintain close control over agents' actions were the price of the reaper and the terms of payment. However, even here the home office was generally willing to accept minor variations if the agents could show good reasons for them.[28]

In this phase of the company's operations, sales agents were agents in the most literal sense of the word. That is, they were independent businessmen who were hired to perform a service that the company was unwilling or unable to provide for itself. The relationship (if not the duties) between both parties was clearly defined by contract. Agents did not take title to the machines they sold, nor did they assume any legal responsibility for repairs after the machines were delivered and set up. When a farmer ordered a reaper, his agreement was with McCormick, not the local agent, who merely forwarded the order to the factory. Thus, agents simply acted as intermediaries between the company and its customers.[29]

Because McCormick placed few demands on his agents and issued new contracts annually, he was able to expand his sales force rapidly. No exact figures exist on the numbers of agents he employed, but by the early 1860s McCormick seems to have had at least one agent in every farming county in Ohio, Illinois, and Indiana as well as extensive coverage in the rest of the Midwest. Aside from his preference for farmers, McCormick was willing to grant an agency to anyone who wished to represent the company, provided there was no other agent in the area and that the applicant agreed not to sell for McCormick's competitors. As an incentive, McCormick also frequently paid his agents' traveling costs and reimbursed them for other expenses incurred in the service of the company.[30]

Cyrus McCormick decided to market his machines at the retail level because of the specialized nature of the reaper and its market, the inability of established wholesalers to provide the company with any services that it could not supply itself more efficiently, and McCormick's desire to create a strong brand identity for his product. The reapers and other implements made by the McCormick company were complex pieces of equipment that underwent regular refinement. Substantial differences existed in the design and operation of the same types of equipment produced by different manufacturers. Marketing these products successfully required demonstrations by salesmen who were thoroughly familiar with their operation. The problems of providing a widely scattered market with a complex product, timely service, and repairs are readily apparent. For a farmer during the harvest, time really was money. Wheat needed to be harvested within about two weeks of when it ripened, so any repairs that could not be made almost immediately meant either lost crops or high charges if some way could be found to finish the job. As a result, any reaper maker who did not also establish and maintain an infrastructure that provided good support services was doomed to failure.

As already mentioned, most wholesalers lacked the expertise and incentive to build the type of marketing system that McCormick required. Farm equipment makers were fortunate in that they had a clearly defined market. McCormick knew exactly who he had to sell to and the types of services he needed to provide. Because of the complexity of the machines he sold, it was vital that he get as close to his market as possible. Repair parts and technical expertise could come only from the factory so, at best, wholesalers would have been an unnecessary link in the chain between McCormick and the farmer. Had wholesalers been able to supply a ready-made string of outlets along with marketing expertise and information, they might have been more of a bridge than a barrier. As it happened, however, McCormick had been forced to build his dealer force right from the start so that when he reached high-volume production, he did not face the choice of creating his own marketing organization or relying on wholesalers. He already had a dealer network in place that was far superior to any a jobber could provide.

Finally, McCormick avoided wholesalers because they could not give him the brand recognition he sought. The inventor's success resulted in large part from his ability to establish a strong following for his product based on a reputation of high quality, continuing improvement, and reliable service. This allowed the company to consistently sell its machines at higher prices than those offered by its competitors. Keeping his own dealer force permitted McCormick to create the illusion of the type of personal, face-to-face relationship that farmers of this era were comfortable with.[31] Much of the company's advertising stressed the fact that when a farmer bought a McCormick reaper, he was dealing directly with the inventor. When ordering the machine during the 1850s, he signed a request that "Mr. C. H. McCormick will manufacture for the undersigned and deliver . . . one of last improved patent Virginia Reapers." When the reaper arrived, the agent sent a notice containing instructions for its assembly and operation. Prominently placed in the upper right-hand corner was a note to the farmer from "C. H. McCormick" asking him to pick up his machine. The home office mailed circulars and catalogs listing prices and terms directly to farmers and encouraged them to write directly to the Chicago factory for parts or advice. It also maintained tight control over the company's advertising so that McCormick—not the agent—was kept in the forefront, even instructing its general agents "to take pains to prevent your local agents from publishing or advertising anything about our business not fully authorized by us."[32]

The sales system worked well when McCormick was a small-sized, regional firm. But as the market for machines and the number of agents grew, the company's loosely structured sales force left the home office unequal to the task of coordinating the flow of machines from the factory to the field. Finally, the chaos generated by the increasingly ungainly sales organization forced Cyrus McCormick to alter his relationship with his agents in the field. The solution he chose was to standardize his dealings with agents. This began the transition from independent agent to semi-independent dealer.[33]

McCormick began to systemize relations with agents in 1859, when his newly created Agency Department started sending uniform instructions and information to all agents in the form of circular letters. The bulk of these letters went out during or just after the harvest selling season. At first, they were more inspirational than informational. Those mailed during the harvest urged the agents to "Sell *all* you have—*new* and *old*" and to "report to the home office the number and type of any machines not needed so that they may be sent to areas where the harvest is later." Letters after the harvest reported the results of the year's efforts ("The battle of '59 is fought—the victory won—and now we look after the *dead* and *wounded*.") and requested an immediate accounting of the machines still on hand.[34]

The company also reminded agents to pursue all collections vigorously, or, as a circular letter of 1859 phrased it, "Sales now over[,] the work of

A typical McCormick advertisement, 1849. (From the Cyrus H. McCormick Collection, State Historical Society of Wisconsin, Madison)

McCORMICK'S
PATENT
VIRGINIA REAPER.

The above cut represents one of M'Cormick's Patent Virginia Reapers, as built for the harvest of 1846. It has been greatly improved since that time, by the addition of a seat for the driver, by a change in the position of the crank, so as to effect a direct connection between it and the sickle, (thereby very much lessening the friction and wear of the machinery, by dispensing altogether with the lever and its fixtures,) by board ribs on the reel, (which operates more gently on the grain than the round ones,) by a sheet of zinc on the platform, (which very much lessens the labor of raking,) by an increase of the size, weight and strength of the wheels of the machine, and by improvement made on the cutting apparatus

D. W. BROWN,
OF ASHLAND, OHIO,

Having been duly appointed Agent for the sale of the above valuable labor-saving machine (manufactured by C. H. McCormick & Co., in Chicago, Ill.,) for the Counties of Seneca, Sandusky, Erie, Huron, Richland, Ashland and Wayne, would respectfully inform the farmers of those counties, that he is prepared to furnish them with the above Reapers on very liberal terms.

The Wheat portions of the above territory will be visited, and the Agent will be ready to give any information relative to said Reaper, by addressing him at Ashland, Ashland County, Ohio.

Ashland, March, 1850.

A typical McCormick advertisement, 1850. At this time McCormick's "Agents" were agents rather than dealers in that they were independent business owners who dealt with the company on a nearly equal footing. (From the Cyrus H. McCormick Collection, State Historical Society of Wisconsin, Madison)

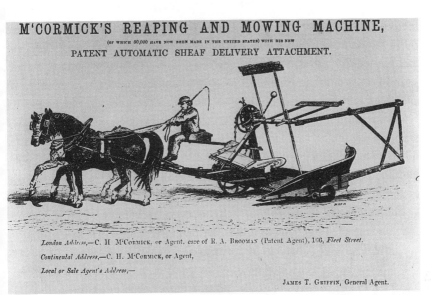

M'CORMICK'S REAPING AND MOWING MACHINE,

(OF WHICH 50,000 HAVE NOW BEEN MADE IN THE UNITED STATES) WITH HIS NEW

PATENT AUTOMATIC SHEAF DELIVERY ATTACHMENT.

London Address,—C. H. M'CORMICK, or Agent, care of R. A. BROOMAN (Patent Agent), 166, *Fleet Street.*

Continental Address,—C. H. M'CORMICK, or Agent,

Local or Sale Agent's Address,—

JAMES T. GRIFFIN, General Agent.

An advertisement to promote the sale of McCormick's reaper in Great Britain. By 1862, the year this ad appeared, McCormick was already well on its way to becoming a multinational enterprise. (From the Cyrus H. McCormick Collection, State Historical Society of Wisconsin, Madison)

collection should be *pressed*. Must we *urge* the necessity of *promptness* in money matters. Without the 'sinews of war' we cannot prepare for the 'struggle' of 1860." The content of these letters did not differ much from the letters the company had sent to individual agents as the need arose, but it did mark a change in the underlying relationship. Previously, the relationship between McCormick and its agents had been on an individual basis. After 1860 or so, the home office began to treat its sales force as part of a team with the Agency Department as its captain, rather than as a collection of independent agents operating on their own behalf as well as the company's.[35]

The systemization of procedures and communications allowed the company to bring some order to its previously chaotic sales organization. By standardizing its relations with agents, or dealers, the home office reduced the number of variables it had to contend with; this made it easier to oversee dealer actions. Establishing a regular channel for universal communication also allowed the company a greater voice in dealer operations, for once these lines were open, the tendency was to use them more and more frequently. This change shows up clearly in the company's general instructions to agents in 1860. Now, in addition to urging agents to sell as many machines as possible, these letters informed them of changes in the sales policy, such as a minor shift in the allowance for cash sales or trade-ins on old machines based on the company's estimate of total demand. Previously, these minor adjustments had been left to the agents' discretion. Routine instructions also informed agents of changes in bookkeeping practices that were designed to bring uniformity to the accounts of McCormick and its dealer force.

The other shift in the relationship between the company and its agents was the expansion of services that the firm provided to the sales force in the field. Cyrus McCormick had always assumed responsibility for advertising his reaper. As the reputation of the McCormick company spread, the task of selling undoubtedly became easier, but until the mid-1850s the company provided little direct support. Because agents were required only to sell machines and make collections, they had little need for institutional support other than advertising. From the start, the company had freely supplied agents with order blanks, pamphlets, testimonials, and other sales aids. In the mid-1850s, however, the factory began sending out a roving force of mechanics to help agents in the field make repairs.

The company's efforts to systemize home office/dealer relations proved to be only a partial solution to one of the problems created by expansion. The number and type of machines produced by McCormick more than doubled between 1860 and 1870, and within this span the home office once again found itself unable to cope with the size of its market. To ease the strain, the firm decided to delegate some of the responsibility. After the Chicago fire of 1871, the sales department continued to formulate overall marketing strategy but shifted accountability for its implementation and routine operations to approximately forty general agents scattered across the United States and Canada. Over time, these agencies developed into company-owned branch houses, and their agents became managers rather than independent businessmen. In retail distribution, however, the agent remained supreme. The main effect of McCormick's move toward decentralization was to increase substantially the contact between agents and the company and to bring the agents under the company's direct control. By decentralizing control over the sales force, McCormick could institute closer supervision and coordination of local agents and provide them with better delivery and repair services.[36] For the most part, McCormick's sales organization was similar to those used by his larger competitors. The nature of the market for farm implements, the particular needs of the product, and the original success of the agency method were largely responsible for the type of sales force that ultimately developed in the farm equipment industry. The market for farm implements was widely scattered and seasonal, and it required an extensive knowledge of local conditions. For these reasons manufacturers found it too expensive to establish a large number of company-owned outlets. Yet, due to the complexity and high price of farm equipment and the need for immediate access to parts, manufacturers could not hope to succeed without them. Particularly in the early years, farmers were unwilling to buy reapers that they had not had a chance to inspect closely and see in operation.[37]

For many reasons, implement makers initially turned to the agency system. After manufacturers modified their channels to accommodate the independent retailer dealer, another factor, institutional inertia, further strengthened ties between companies and their agents. By the early 1870s, McCormick's agents were so deeply embedded in the company's organization that they could exert considerable pressure to discourage the sale of machines unless through independent retailers. The best evidence of McCormick's reliance on his dealers and the company's commitment to the agency system was the firm's reaction to the Granger movement of the 1870s. Despite the repeated efforts of state Granger organizations to eliminate the agent from McCormick's distribution system, the McCormick company refused to sell outside its established dealer network.[38]

Agents further strengthened their grip on the retail trade during the 1880s when associations of dealers started to appear, first in the grain-producing regions of the West and later across the nation. Adopting the slogan "to the retail dealer belongs the retail trade," dealer associations in the early years of the twentieth century began to work closely with manufacturers to protect their mutual interests. Because these associations were not widely influential until after the formation of International Harvester in 1902 and because their activities paralleled those of similar organizations in the auto industry, examination of the role of dealer associations has been deferred to the next chapter.[39]

The distribution system developed by McCormick and the farm implements industry generally was a blend of traditional small business and
the modern, vertically integrated firm. The independent dealer has dominated the retail trade in the farm implements industry from the 1840s
to the present. As the development of the McCormick company shows,
large-scale production required close coordination between production
and distribution. But at McCormick this coordination could be achieved
without owning the entire distribution system. McCormick's volume eventually forced the company to establish branches to oversee the activities of
dealers and to coordinate the flow of machines from the factory to agents.
This increased control strengthened the ties between the producer and
the distributor but did not lead to the direct ownership of retail outlets.
Instead, the sales agent evolved into the factory dealer.

What the case of McCormick in particular and the farm implements
industry in general suggests is that when the limits of vertical integration are reached, a symbiotic relationship develops between a few large
manufacturers and many small retailers in the same industry. Because the
seasonal nature of the market for farm implements did not allow McCormick's agents to concentrate solely on the sale of the company's products,
this relationship did not become close enough to bring independent dealers
completely under the influence of the company. As a result, the relationship
between farm implements dealers and manufacturers stood somewhere
between that of agent and franchise operator.

Marketing at Singer

The sewing machine had already drained the fortunes of a number of
inventors when Isaac Merritt Singer entered the fray in the summer
of 1850. To any impartial observer it would have seemed that Singer had
chosen a project unlikely to succeed. Four years earlier Elias Howe had
patented a sewing machine, and, heartened by Howe's success, a number
of other inventors, infringers, and improvers were devising new machines
and improvements on existing models. Problems, however, existed. None
of these machines, not even Howe's, worked well. Moreover, in order to
construct a workable machine in 1850 it was necessary to use the patented
features of several different inventors. The result was a legal tangle that

left potential customers wary and made it impossible for any single manufacturer to market a machine without the fear of long and costly patent
litigation. In addition, it was by no means certain that a legitimate and
workable machine would be a commercial success. Its high price and complexity made it unsuitable for the mass market. And tailors and seam-
stresses, the machine's most obvious customers, had serious doubts about
the workability of a mechanical sewer and feared for their jobs should such
a device be perfected. In 1850 the slim profits in the industry were being
made in patent suits, not in the sale of machines.[40]

Desperation and chance drove Isaac Singer to the sewing machine. In
the summer of 1850 he was a failed actor and a sometimes inventor, with
an invention no one wanted and a wife and four children to support. After
the collapse of his theater company, the Merritt Players, in 1844, Singer
decided to return to his earlier career as a mechanic and inventor. Over
the next six years, he achieved modest success operating a shop that made
wooden type and signs. But Singer was not the sort of person to be content
with the life of a mechanic and shop owner. He wanted success on a grand
scale and so turned his efforts to invention as the way to gain the wealth
and fame he sought. In 1849 Singer moved to New York to perfect and
market his carving machine. His arrival was the first link in an unlikely
chain of events, including an explosion and fire that destroyed his shop
and carving machine, that would eventually bring Singer and the sewing
machine together. Because of his misfortunes in New York, he and his new
financial backer, William Zieber, left for Boston in 1850 in an unsuccessful
attempt to find customers for the carving machine.[41]

In Boston, Singer and Zieber rented space in the shop of Orson C. Phelps
at 19 Harvard Place. It was this chance occurrence that introduced Singer
to the sewing machine. At the time Singer and Zieber took up residence at
Phelps's shop, Phelps had just begun manufacturing the recently patented
Blodgett & Lerow machine. Like most early sewing machines looking for
a place in the market, the Blodgett & Lerow worked well enough to give its
inventors hope that it could be perfected with a few minor improvements
but not well enough to be a commercial success. Of the approximately 120
machines manufactured by Phelps in 1850, only 8 or 9 could endure regular
use by the tailors in Blodgett's factory upstairs from Phelps's shop.[42]

At the urging of Phelps and Zieber, Singer, having no market for his
carving machine and having used up Zieber's resources, turned his hand

to the sewing machine. Perhaps because he had no familiarity with tailoring, Singer quickly grasped the basic problem with the Blodgett & Lerow machine: it was designed to stitch as a tailor would. Like Howe, Singer realized that a machine did not need to duplicate the motions of a tailor in order to sew. After carefully inspecting the machine for a few days, Singer sketched out a new mechanism to hold and sew cloth. On September 18, he signed a contract with Zieber and Phelps to produce and patent his new mechanism. According to the agreement, Zieber would supply the last of his ready cash, forty dollars, and Phelps would provide a staff and equipment. The three men were to share equally in the profits from Singer's creation. After almost two weeks of constant effort, the inventor succeeded in building the machine he had chalked out on a spare board for his partners. On the following day he left for New York with the machine to have patent papers drawn up, and the firm of Singer & Phelps was soon in business.[43]

Singer quickly discovered what Elias Howe and other industry pioneers already knew: inventing a workable sewing machine did not guarantee a ready market. Apparently, in the beginning Singer and his partners did not plan for any particular market or method of distribution. In the first advertisement of his machine, placed on November 7, 1850, Singer announced: "An Agent (with whom exclusive arrangements will be made) is wanted in every city and town in the United States." The company was slow to appoint agents, however, and in the first year the partners themselves made the majority of sales to firms in New York and New England. Throughout that year the problems of just keeping the doors open and Singer's constant disagreements with his partners prevented the firm from developing a coherent marketing plan. At any rate, production was so low that no extensive sales network was needed.[44]

Beginning in the summer of 1851, the condition of the I. M. Singer Company, as the firm was now known, improved to the point where the partners were able to develop an organized sales plan. Edward Clark, a new partner, was the man most responsible for shaping the early sales policies of the company. Clark was a New York attorney whom Singer met while working on his carving machine; Clark became a partner in exchange for his legal services, which were needed for patent battles. Under Clark's guidance, the Singer company began to follow the practice common among sewing machine manufacturers in the 1850s of expanding its market through the sale of territorial distribution rights.[45] Like Cyrus McCormick, Edward Clark instituted a policy of growth through the assignment of patent rights for exclusive territories primarily because the company could not afford to establish direct representation. However, at Singer and in the sewing machine industry generally, the sale of territorial rights resembled commodities speculation more than a serious attempt to build a distribution system. At the same time McCormick was using exclusive agents to expand the production and sale of his reaper, Isaac Singer was relying on income from the sale of exclusive rights to gain enough cash to keep his firm in business. The rights to sell Singer's machine could be had for a few hundred dollars, and apparently most investors purchased them in hopes that the firm would do well and the value of their exclusive selling rights would increase.[46]

Between 1851 and 1856, when the company ended the practice, Singer sold dozens of exclusive patent rights ranging in size from a single city to entire states. In some years the profits from patent rights actually exceeded the profits from the sale of sewing machines. The rights assigned by Singer and Clark usually were the same. In exchange for a fee ranging from a few hundred to a few thousand dollars, the assignee received "the sole and exclusive right to use, and vend to others to be used (but not to build or make) . . . *Singer's Straight Needle Perpendicular Action Sewing Machines.*" Singer agreed to sell sewing machines to rights holders at between $55 and $70 when the retail price of the machine was advertised at $125. Contracts ran for the term of the patent, and, when improved machines appeared, the company usually agreed to sell new models to rights holders at a price of $10 more per machine.[47]

Although not a perfect arrangement for selling sewing machines, the use of territorial rights did hold several attractions for the company. The most important was that it was the only available method for meeting Singer's two most pressing needs: working capital in the short run and a national market in the long run. As a reliable source of cash, the sale of patent rights was a godsend. In the particularly grim years of 1851 and 1852, rights holders actually paid Singer almost $12,000 for the privilege of introducing his machine to the market. They also paid for the machines themselves in either cash or short-term notes. In addition, agents absorbed virtually all the costs of selling and of providing consumer credit. Moreover, because an assignee's rights were based on Singer's patent, the rights holders were willing to align themselves with Singer in his legal battles with Elias Howe.[48]

Despite the short-term advantages of marketing through territorial rights, the company's top managers had a number of reasons to be dissatisfied with the system. Singer and Clark personally had always disapproved of the practice and used it only as an necessary expedient. Their main objection was based on the belief that, unlike the machines of their competitors, Singer's worked well enough to be a commercial success. Therefore, more profits would accrue from the sale of the machines than from the sale of patent rights.[49]

The most significant problem with the way Clark had organized Singer's marketing system centered around the contract, which was designed to stimulate the sale of territorial rights, not Singer's machines. Unlike McCormick's use of exclusive rights, Singer's contract lasted for the life of the patent and gave the company almost no control over the assignee's business operations. The early contracts, for example, did not stipulate the number of machines an agent needed to buy or the price he could charge. Dealers purchased their machines at a 40 to 60 percent discount from the advertised price, and Singer was helpless to prevent his rights holders from underselling him along the border between his and their territories. With all these difficulties, it was obvious to Singer and Clark that the long-term health of the firm required a change in the sales organization.[50]

Two events in 1856 acted as catalysts for an aggressive policy of buying out assignees. The first was the formation of a "sewing machine combination." The combination grew out of a meeting held in October 1856 in Albany, New York, that brought together representatives of the four firms holding all the major patents needed to produce a workable machine. The purpose was to find some way to stop the seemingly endless litigation that threatened to destroy the industry. The solution was the creation of a patent pool that controlled all major patents to the machine and sold licenses back to members for the manufacture and sale of the machines. The pool eroded the old marketing system in two ways. First, it removed the control of individual firms over basic patents, and, second, it ended the industry's speculative period by allowing the unhindered production of workable machines. After 1856 sales through agents and through company-owned branches became the dominant methods of distribution in the sewing machine industry.[51] The second event was Singer's movement into the consumer market. In 1856 Isaac Singer introduced the "turtle-back," his first machine designed specifically for the domestic market. The turtle-back was smaller and less expensive than his earlier models and came packed in a wooden crate that doubled as the machine's stand. The decision to concentrate on the consumer market was a logical one. The sewing machine had been perfected to the point where it was durable enough for home use, the potential market was huge, and the formation of the combination finally allowed manufacturers to concentrate on making and selling machines. Before the sewing machine could be marketed as a consumer good, however, a new method of selling was required. Ways had to be devised to provide consumer credit, supply reliable instructions and service to customers, and clearly distinguish Singer's machine from that of his competitors. To meet these needs, the company adopted a policy of establishing company-owned outlets and selling through exclusive agents on short-term contracts. The results of these two changes showed up clearly in the annual sales tallies. From 1853 to 1855, the firm sold about 850 machines per year; in 1856, the number soared to over 2,500.[52]

Singer had always used agents and company-owned branches to market its products. The company granted its first agency contract in 1851 and opened its first permanent branch house in Boston a year later. After buying out long-term patent assignees in 1856, Singer began to build a sales organization around company-owned branch houses or general agencies in cities and large towns and local and traveling agents who sold short-term contracts in the hinterlands. Edward Clark made the local branch-house managers or general agents responsible for developing the surrounding area and gave them the freedom to cover their districts as they thought best. To carry out the actual job of selling machines through the branches, the company relied most heavily on "canvassers," who visited potential customers in their homes and made arrangements to demonstrate the machine. In rural districts the company depended on local merchants and traveling agents to demonstrate the machine, sell it, and market accessories such as needles and thread. The New York office invoiced machines to branches and general agencies at a set discount, typically 25 percent for branches and 25 to 40 percent for general agents, or sold the machines directly to local dealers at the same discount as general agents. Agents received a larger discount than branches because they usually paid all or most of their selling expenses.[53]

While the Singer company was still experimenting with its branch system during the 1850s and 1860s, it continued to rely on local agents to promote its machines outside the branch cities. At this time, when production was rising rapidly and the market was still largely virgin, company executives were more interested in expanding their sales force than in exercising tight control over dealers. As a result, the conditions placed on agents were flexible. In most cases, Singer refused to hire anyone who already represented a competitor's products but was willing to employ merchants who sold noncompeting goods. The company preferred people in the garment trade for their experience and connections or ministers' wives for the aura of respectability they projected, but it would accept anyone of "good character" who wished to sell in an unrepresented area.[54]

The agency contracts from the 1860s illustrate the tenuous connection between the home office and its sales organization. These contracts were one page long and contained only four clauses. Contracts were open-ended and could be terminated by either party for any reason. They gave the company no right to monitor the performance of agents or examine their books. In theory, agents bought all machines for cash and assumed full responsibility for credit and repair services. In fact, once the company entered the consumer market, Singer found it necessary to provide credit to agents who typically sold machines on time but lacked adequate resources to offer customer credit. This kept agents indebted to the company and forced Singer to become more closely involved with agents than originally intended.[55]

The system of appointing agents more or less indiscriminately allowed Isaac Singer to introduce his machines to a large market quickly, but it failed to sustain their sale. Sewing machines were expensive and unfamiliar, requiring manufacturers to provide retail customers with a wide range of services before they could be successfully marketed. Some of these services—such as assembly, minor adjustments, and instructions on how to operate the machine—could be done by agents with a minimum of training. Others—such as repairs and financing—required extensive and continuous contact with the home office to be performed effectively. By the mid-1850s sewing machines were fairly durable, but they did occasionally need repair, and as the number of models increased, repairs must have been increasingly difficult for agents who were not in close contact with the company. By 1860 smaller agents were sending machines to the nearest branch for service. Although necessary, this was not the type of policy that encouraged consumer loyalty or faith in the local dealer.[56]

In the 1870s the McCormick Harvesting Machine Company and the makers of other farm implements established wholesale branch houses to coordinate the flow of machines to dealers and to provide assistance in sales and repairs. Singer and other major sewing machine makers set up branches for the same reason, but they had the additional incentive of a highly concentrated market that made company-owned branch houses profitable sales offices and valuable advertising tools to develop the reputation of their machines. From the 1850s through the 1880s, major sewing machine manufacturers such as Singer and Wheeler & Wilson maintained large, elaborate showrooms in their principal branches to give the appearance of style and stability. In its description of the opening of Singer's New York office in 1857, the *I. M. Singer & Co.'s Gazette* captured the image sewing machine makers were trying to project: "There is no place in the city more beautiful and attractive than this. A palace of white marble, tasteful and elaborate in the architecture and decorated interiorly with all the splendor of modern art; it forms an appropriate temple for the exhibition and sale of the most useful invention of the present century." Singer did not require his agents to be as extravagant in setting up their own businesses, but he did expect their offices to be "located on some good and convenient street where ladies would not hesitate to visit."[57]

Historians agree that the "tight central control" that Singer maintained over its sales organization was an important factor in the rapid gains the company made after the formation of the patent pool. In the 1850s, however, Singer actually had slightly fewer branch houses than Grove & Baker, one of its major competitors, and Singer's branches probably received less direction from the home office than did those of its competitors. Just as McCormick had in the farm implements industry, Singer achieved the appearance of uniformity and control by setting the retail price of its machines and making extensive use of national advertising to promote its product rather than the seller. Singer was careful to require that "all business should be done in the name of the company," as the "names of our agents on signs, circulars, cards, and the like . . . are considered rather

Like his competitors, Singer tried to create an elite image for his machines through the use of elaborate showrooms, such as this one in the New York City office. (From From the American System to Mass Production, 1800–1932, *by David A. Hounshell [Johns Hopkins University Press, 1984], p. 84)*

injurious to our business." The company was far less concerned about how the agents actually ran their business affairs.[58]

From 1856 to 1877 Singer's agents and branch managers operated relatively free from direct home office supervision. But in 1877 Edward Clark, who had become first president of the newly incorporated Singer Manufacturing Company following the death of Isaac Singer the year before, started to bring the entire sales force under the tighter control of the home office. He hoped that greater supervision would lead to lower selling costs. During the 1860s and 1870s the price of sewing machines fell steadily. Whereas Singer's original machines retailed for $125, by 1866 the price had dropped to $60 for cash sales and by 1877 the basic model cost $30. As the price of the machines decreased, the selling expense per machine rose proportionally, because the company's sales cost per machine remained fairly stable. Even when the company sold to agents at a set discount, expenses remained about the same, as agents demanded and got extra discounts to compensate them for the reductions in price.[59] Clark's program took seven years to complete. During that time, the extremely decentralized structure of the sales department was replaced by one with tight central management. In terms of relations between Singer and its agents, the reorganization had two effects. First, it resulted in the conversion of independent agencies to company-owned outlets, except in areas where the volume of sales was too low to warrant the expense of a regular company store. Second, in areas where Singer continued to market through dealers, the company established such strict controls over their actions that they became nearly indistinguishable from regular company employees.[60]

The model for Singer's reorganization was the system developed by George Baldwin Woodruff, the company's general agent in England. As a result of heavy competition from imitators, Woodruff had been forced in 1876 to lower the price of Singer's basic machine to about $25. Despite this reduction, he was still able to send to the New York office approximately $146,000 from the sale of about 50,000 machines. Woodruff did so by moving away from the practice of selling through wholesalers. Instead, he established a system of small retail outlets—both independent and company-owned—throughout the country to provide intensive market coverage. This plan not only allowed him to maintain a high level of sales but also lowered selling costs, as it removed the wholesaler from the distribution chain. In comparison, Singer's German agent, George Neidlinger, who relied heavily on wholesale jobbers, showed a profit of only $95,000 for about the same number of sales.[61]

Inspired by Woodruff's success, Singer's top executives called a general meeting of their American agents in April 1877 to discuss the possibility of implementing the English system in the American market. In November 1878 they passed on the results of this meeting to the dozen or so branch houses and general agents in a confidential circular entitled "Suggestions to Central Offices as to General Organization and the Small Branch System." This circular provided criteria for establishing various types of offices within central districts, including how they should be organized and the types of records they should keep. Under this plan, the central offices, as the old branch houses and general agencies were now called, would open company-owned branch offices in the county seat or largest town in their territory, excluding the central office city. If the branch city had a population between 10,000 to 20,000, a building could be leased as long as the rent did not exceed $300 per year, although the company expected it to range from $50 to $200, "being graded by the population and probable sales."[62]

In keeping with the goal of reduced selling expenses, the company had rescinded its policy of maintaining elegantly appointed offices. By 1877 the sewing machine's image had settled into the public consciousness as a machine that offered utility and economy for the masses rather than luxury for the elite. Perhaps recognizing this fact, Clark gave up the idea of the sewing machine palaces and recommended to the branches that their furniture "be as plain as possible, the cost to range from $25 to $75" and that the office provide "a good display of plain signs" with "some representation of our TRADE MARK."[63]

The remainder of the November 1878 circular consisted of equally detailed instructions for establishing and staffing smaller branches and descriptions of the duties of employees. Although Singer's executives believed that the general system outlined above was "as a rule, necessary to the future success of our business," they presented the plan only as a series of "RECOMMENDATIONS" and requested merely that central office operators "use their best judgment in working GRADUALLY into it." The company was vague about the status of independent agents, perhaps because of conflicting desires. Clearly, top management wanted greater control over its sales force and believed that direct ownership of outlets was the best way to achieve it. But the main goal was to reduce selling expenses and in marginal markets agents had already proven to be more economical than company-owned stores. The tentative nature of the suggestions indicates that the company understood the trade-off involved and was willing to leave the details of the small branch expansion plan to central branch managers, who were, after all, closest to the scene.[64]

The only area where the company demanded rather than suggested compliance was in financial reporting. In December 1877 Clark sent two long circulars to all central and branch offices detailing new accounting practices that were designed to provide New York with a more accurate picture of the number of machines on hand, on consignment to agents, and actually sold in central office territories. Unlike the suggestions for the small branch system, there was no room for variation or delay in implementing changes in bookkeeping practices. All central and branch offices were to institute the required changes immediately and to see that all company representatives in their territories did the same.[65]

Perhaps because the price of the sewing machine continued to drop or because the company now had more complete and comparable data about sales expenses, the concern over sales costs resurfaced within a few years. Disparities between branches led home office executives to make another change in its sales organization. In 1881 the directors of the company, with an eye toward equalizing costs, established a force of traveling examiners to visit the central offices, branches, and agencies and "carefully and minutely inspect into the books of accounts, receipts and expenditures of money, bills receivable, notes, liens and evidence of debt of every kind, and to report in detail in regard to the condition of the business, and the merits or faults which may appear in the methods of conducting the affairs at each particular office examined." Despite their broad mandate, the inspectors were not given the formal power to alter the branch policies. They still wielded significant influence, however, as the concern this time was with disparities in selling expenses. The directors stressed that, because examiners would be "well acquainted with the best methods of conducting our business, as practiced and systematized by our best agents, . . . their advice and suggestions as to changes which may be required, will be entitled to much consideration."[66]

The examiners submitted detailed reports, typically running from eight to twenty pages per branch, and a final report of similar length on the central district as a whole. These reports provided what appears to have been an accurate picture of the organization and performance of offices and personnel in the sales territories; estimates of current and future sales prospects based on personal observations, interviews, census data, and crop conditions; and anything else of interest to the company.[67]

The examiners' reports show that by the early 1880s the central offices had already organized their sales territories about as far along the lines suggested by the company as they profitably could. Central office managers cited the same reasons for not opening company-owned offices in villages and satellite shops in urban areas: the low volume of sales did not justify the expense, and established agents preferred to sell on their own account. In the end, concerns over cost won out. As long as managers kept expenses down and sent in complete financial reports on time and in the proper form, the main office was content to leave organizational details in the hands of the branches.[68]

Little information exists on why agents were reluctant to give up their agencies or what became of them after they did, but one examiner's report provides some insight. In January 1880 a Mr. Baar, who had been an agent in the Washington Branch of Singer's Baltimore office for over ten years, sold his business to Singer and was retained as manager of the branch. Although the business had prospered with Baar as agent, it floundered after he became the manager. By March 1881, when the examiner's report was written, the office was only breaking even, and relations between the company and Baar had become strained. Baar blamed Singer for placing too many restrictions on his actions, whereas the examiner believed that the reason for Baar's unsatisfactory performance was his regret over having sold his business. As the examiner put it, the former agent had "lost his independence"; this made him surly and slow to carry out the wishes of his superiors. To solve the problem, the examiner recommended "a change of management."[69]

Once Singer established a system to monitor the actions of its twenty-some branch offices, through frequent and uniform reports supplemented by regular and detailed inspections, it was finally able to achieve its twin goals of effective control and reduced selling costs. In 1877 Clark had attempted to establish control through the direct ownership of the bulk of the sales system. He quickly found that this plan interfered with the goal of lowering selling costs and reduced the flexibility of the sales organization by making it more difficult to cut costs when sales fell off. By 1885, when the company perfected the organization of its selling force, Singer's management had come to realize that complete ownership was neither profitable nor necessary for adequate control of the sales organization.[70]

In the reorganization of 1885, which was essentially a continuation of the process started in 1877, corporate executives recommended strongly to central office managers that supervising canvassers, who were in charge of the lowest level of the sales force, be paid either a "nominal rent" or a "nominal salary in lieu of the office rent" along with their commissions. A supervising canvasser was expected "to pay all expenses, except freights, hire his own help, if any, and machines [were to be] consigned to [from?] the company in his care." The terminology of this reorganization plan and the contracts under which supervising canvassers operated show a growing awareness by top management that ownership was not the only, or the most profitable, way to build its marketing organization. The organization set up in the 1870s and 1880s was designed to "create a system which will utilize the magnificent organization and unequalled facilities of this company." One of the key parts of this system was the use of company-owned and operated branches to oversee the activities of nominally independent dealers.[71]

Although technically independent in the sense that they owned their own shops, hired and controlled their staffs, and relied on profits rather than salaries for the bulk of their income, agents were under such tight control that Singer's managers could claim success in their goal to "*own and run* our canvassing force." Elaborate contracts gave Singer complete control over the actions of its agents and provided for their immediate dismissal if they did not carry out all of the terms.[72]

Singer's contracts of the 1800s reflected an awareness of its new needs and powers. In the first place, the company's emphasis in marketing was no longer to sweep the home market before the competition had a chance to become established; rather, it was to "secure every good sale and no bad ones." To do this, Singer redesigned its sales organization to give it "entire control of our men, perfect knowledge of their work, the power to so direct and control them that each knows his work and will do all he can without loss of time and without interference; all working intelligently and systematically together as an organized and responsible army." Top management expected some resistance because "the older and smarter canvassers will see that this plan puts them in the Company's power as its servants with no chance to threaten or defy it." Nevertheless, top management reasoned, the benefits of being associated with the Singer name ensured that no matter how rigid the control, the company would always be able to find agents.[73]

Conclusion

The experiences of the McCormick and Singer companies illustrate two extremes in the adaption of the agency system to the needs of manufacturers operating in a national market. At McCormick, the agency system required little modification because the peculiarities of a huge, thinly scattered, and seasonal market made it impossible for the company to control its agents closely. On the other hand, Singer could almost eliminate traditional agents within a relatively short time, replacing them with company-owned outlets managed by regular employees in dense urban markets and a tightly controlled dealer force in less populous locations.

Although the evolution of the agency system was quite different at Singer and McCormick, there are some notable similarities in the reasons both firms originally turned to agency sales and later modified their marketing organizations. For both companies, selling through agents was a very effective method of introducing their products to the national market. It cost them little, was easy to administer, and could be done quickly. Once this task was completed, both firms tried to gain more control over the actions of their sales force. In their drive for greater influence, there was a tension between the desire to extend effective controls over sales and the desire to reduce selling expenses. Equilibrium was reached at the point where company ownership stopped and agency sales began. At McCormick, the tension was resolved at the wholesale level. The company never made any significant attempt to take over the outlets of its independent retailers, for in almost all cases it would have been prohibitively expensive to do so. On the other hand, much of Singer's market was concentrated inside urban areas, making it practical for the company to phase out dealers.

In creating their sales organizations, both companies became increasingly aware that it was possible to have control without ownership, and both were successful in tightening controls over agents without assuming the ownership of their businesses. This step was at the heart of the evolution of the independent agent into the semi-independent dealer. Companies such as McCormick and Singer were able to increase their power over agents because the development of oligopoly in manufacturing severely limited the number of firms with which an agent with special expertise could do business.

In many ways, the developments at McCormick and Singer antedated opposing views on the franchise system that would become popular in the 1960s. The appearance of a few large manufacturers in the farm implements industry provided employment for thousands of small businessmen. The advantages of support and assistance from the factory made the job of retailing both easier and more secure than it otherwise might have been.

n this case, the appearance of big business stimulated small business by reating a need for large numbers of independent retailers to handle the elling of farm equipment. At Singer, the company's development into a modern, vertically integrated big business encouraged the appearance of a large group of nominally independent retailers. These dealers stood in an awkward position: they enjoyed few of the personal benefits of small business ownership, yet were still subject to most of its risks. Writers in the 1960s often saw franchising in one of these lights. For some, franchising was the last and best hope for the survival of small business in an economy dominated by big business. For others, the system represented a cruel hoax, promising economic freedom but in reality only creating a new type of "wage-slave."[74]

At the close of the nineteenth century, franchising was still in its infancy. Companies clearly recognized the limitations of the agency system as a method of distribution for complex brand-name goods in the national market. They modified agency sales to suit their needs, but neither McCormick, nor Singer, nor any of the other firms using various modifications of the agency system fully understood the potentials of franchising. Similarly, the courts had yet to recognize that the rise of big business had substantially changed the nature of the relationship between large firms and their sales representatives. The full impact of these alterations would become more apparent as large firms gained greater experience in selling nationwide through outlets they did not directly own. In the twentieth century, the burgeoning automobile industry led to the fuller development of franchising.

2

From Agent to Dealer

The Ford Motor Company,

1903–1956

At the Ford Motor Company the transition from independent agent to franchised dealer occurred more quickly and completely than it had at either McCormick or Singer, mainly because Ford became a truly big business much sooner. Ford produced for the national market almost immediately. Consequently, it experienced the same general pressures that led McCormick and Singer toward franchising much earlier in its existence.

Changes in the economy allowed Ford to expand quickly. When Henry Ford began operations in 1903, it was relatively easy to get goods to and information from the national market. Ford organized his company with this in mind. Like other innovations created to serve big business, franchising reflected the increased capabilities of the economy and the growing sophistication among business leaders for organizing a large-scale enterprise. In the modern economy, quick and reliable communications made it practical for manufacturers to try to coordinate and control the actions of thousands of dealers. Mass production allowed dealers to specialize in the products of a single firm. This, in turn, bound makers and sellers in a special relationship that was controlled partly by market forces and partly by administrative fiat. The remainder of this chapter uses the experiences of the Ford Motor Company to examine the development of this special relationship and its evolution into the franchise system.

America's Maturing Economy

Between the founding of McCormick and Singer and the beginning of Ford, the United States nearly completed the shift from developing country to industrial nation. In production, and to a lesser extent, distribution, a technological explosion allowed firms to produce and sell more efficiently, but only if they could do so at high volume. Those that could exploit economies of scale or scope expanded rapidly. As they did so, they altered the basic structure of the economy and society. The economic dominance of big business was at the center of this change. The rise of the large-scale commercial enterprise touched off another round of change as the next generation of business leaders sought to adjust to the new environment built by their predecessors. Thus, starting in the late nineteenth century the focus in economic development shifted from creating big business to making it more efficient. In general, the process of building an infrastructure suitable for big business fell into two broad classes: (1) organizational or managerial innovations such as franchising or bureaucratic management, and (2) specialized services, such as professional advertising or market research, to serve big business and take advantage of its needs and abilities.[1]

The basic elements of the modern economy—a national market, high-volume production, large-scale business enterprises, and a host of services to meet its needs—were in place and expanding by the start of the twentieth century. The national market, in particular, was highly developed. By 1880 the basic structure of the rail system had been completed, and by 1900 interfirm cooperation by the major roads made it possible for manufacturers to move their goods quickly and cheaply over more than 250,000 miles of track. Beginning in the second decade of the twentieth century, the widespread availability of the motor truck and a rapid increase in the number of surfaced roads fleshed out this system by allowing fast and cheap transportation within and between cities and main rail lines. By 1910, for example, over 10,000 trucks were registered in the United States. Ten years later the number had risen to over 1 million, while at the same time the amount of surfaced roadways increased to well over 350,000 miles.[2]

In manufacturing, the greatest change by far was Henry Ford's introduction in late 1913 of true mass production of a complex good. By employing an extreme division of labor, using specialized machine tools extensively, and allowing machines to set the workers' pace rather than the other way around, Ford brought about a truly revolutionary increase in output and decrease in price for the Model T. Although he did not invent the automobile, by discovering a way to mass-produce it he became, in a very real way, the father of the industry. Because of the obvious advantages of Ford's system and his willingness to allow others to copy his methods, mass production spread quickly to other industries engaged in the manufacture of complex goods.[3]

The tremendous increase in the size of the market and the amount of goods available caused a number of basic shifts in the ways goods were distributed. In the first half of the twentieth century, the most significant change was the emergence of the mass retailer. The department store, the chain store, and the mail-order house all represented retailers' attempts to seize the opportunities of the modern economy. All had their beginnings in the last half of the nineteenth century, but none reached their full development until the early years of the twentieth.[4]

Department and chain stores derived their efficiencies from the sale of relatively small and inexpensive consumer goods to urban customers. The great variety these stores offered attracted the steady flow of customers needed to ensure a high rate of stock turnover. This high turnover, coupled with the advantages of bulk purchasing, produced greater economies, allowing chain and department stores to sell at prices below those of their smaller competitors. To tap the vast rural market created by improved rail and postal services, entrepreneurs built mail-order houses such as Montgomery Ward, established in 1872, and Sears & Roebuck, which opened in 1887. Through the use of centralized distribution hubs similar to those used today by the national package delivery services, mail-order houses could approximate the economies of scale achieved by high-volume producers and combine them with the benefits of bulk purchasing.[5] Like the traditional merchants they to a degree replaced, the new mass retailers were ill-equipped to market complex goods that required regular service and frequent repairs. Consumers' increasing technological sophistication and the appearance of independent repair facilities did eventually enable mail-order houses to market a few well-established nongeneric goods, but the service requirements of specialty goods such as the automobile did not allow for distribution by either mass retailers or their more traditional counterparts. Thus, even in the early twentieth century, the maker of any new complex good still had to develop a distribution system if he or she wished to sell in the national market.[6]

For mass distribution to work, however, it was not enough to simply move goods out of the factory. It was also necessary to get information from the market to the home office, develop the means to process it into a useful form, and act upon it. For innovators, this became possible even before the turn of the century and meant that they could design their operations around the assumption that they would have easy access to markets and information on a national scale. By the second decade of the twentieth century, the flow of information was swift enough and deep enough that businesses could formulate coherent plans and policies on a national scale and establish methods to monitor their implementation. As early as 1915, for example, Ford routinely collected daily reports from branches located in every part of the country. These branches could, in turn, communicate with hundreds of dealers with nearly equal speed. The practical result of this change was to reduce home office reliance on the independent judgments of local managers and to allow big businesses to greatly increase the levels of standardization and control over their operations.[7]

Before big businesses could take full advantage of the expanded communications network, they needed more efficient methods of processing and organizing the information they received. In terms of office technology, the typewriter and the vertical file cabinet—in widespread use by 1900—were by far the most important technological changes, which allowed the now greatly expanded administrative staffs to process the tremendous volume of information businesses received into a useful form. Big businesses also developed elaborate bureaucratic structures to organize, standardize, and coordinate the movement of information. To perform this work they created a new class of employee, the clerical worker, whose job was to neither make nor manage but to coordinate the flow of information between these two groups.[8]

As executives gained greater experience with big business, they also began to develop more efficient managerial tools and organizational structures and to create a host of services designed specifically to meet the needs of big business. Among the mechanisms used to replace the invisible hand of the market with managerial coordination were improvements in accounting procedures, particularly the ideas of standard volume and flexible budgeting, devised during the 1920s. These gave managers a powerful tool not only for determining costs but also for measuring performance. To help project future demand, managers also began to make extensive use of market forecasting, derived primarily from information made available by improved communications.[9]

To help coordinate the operation of their far-flung and often diverse operations, many firms, particularly those making a variety of products, turned to the decentralized structure pioneered by executives at duPont and General Motors in the early 1920s. The chief advantage of this system was that it delegated responsibility for overall operations to the various division heads, thus freeing up the home office to concentrate on issues of policy and coordination of the various units for the benefit of the company as a whole.[10]

The support services comprising the infrastructure created to make big business operate more efficiently are too numerous to mention, but several, such as professional advertising and market research, stand out. Most of these services were developed in-house as a result of the specialization and professionalization made possible by the size of big business. Together, they produced an array of incremental improvements to operations and facilities by giving the firm access to experts in these areas. Some, such as professional advertising or management consulting, eventually developed into industries in their own right, serving a relatively small but prosperous clientele of large-scale enterprises. Whether provided in-house or purchased from outside suppliers, these support services often meant the difference between industry leadership and mediocrity.[11]

Just as the new economy produced new methods of business organization and support services, it helped create a society with different wants, needs, and attitudes that required different products and approaches to marketing. This new society was composed mainly of an urban-industrial population that, if still suspicious of the power of large-scale industry, had at least reached an accommodation with big business and recognized its centrality to their lives.[12]

The greatest social change brought about by the creation of a modern economy was a basic shift in where and how the majority of people lived. As one historian has noted, the "United States was born in the country and has moved to the city." Industrialization made the shift possible. In 1860 not quite 20 percent of the country's population lived in urban areas. By 1920, when the modern economy was firmly established, just over one-half of all Americans lived in towns or cities. The magnitude of this change is even more striking if one considers the decline in the portion of the population that obtained its livelihood from agriculture. In 1860 over 40 percent of the work force earned its living away from the farm; two generations later, 73 percent did so.[13]

The rapidly expanding urban centers, which drew both native and new-comer, were not just larger and more numerous copies of preindustrial cities. Industry and technology combined to fashion new cities that differed considerably in terms of their physical layouts, living conditions, and working environments. The most noticeable physical change was the appearance of "streetcar suburbs," created when interurban transportation allowed cities to expand by reducing in-town travel time, thereby enabling people to settle farther from the city center. The coming of the automobile intensified the expansion and specialization of the city, as people gained the ability to separate themselves even more from their workplace. This resulted in sharp divisions between commercial, residential, and industrial sections of the city. At the same time that technology was building a more stratified city, it was also contributing to the development of a national culture as the level of isolation that had made smaller cities "island communities" broke down under the homogenizing influence of mass production, national distribution, and national advertising.[14]

Of the new attitudes created by the modern economy, one of the more noticeable was the appearance of a consumer culture based on an assumption of abundance and characterized by mass consumption. In this so-called culture of abundance, society's worldview was grounded in an assumption of virtually limitless material wealth and consumption was viewed as a type of pleasant obligation. Two complementary changes were responsible for the new consumer culture. The first was the increase in real wages created by industrialization. The second was the increase in the volume and variety of consumer goods made possible by an expanded technological base, affordable through the efficiencies of mass production, and desirable through professional advertising.[15]

The relationship between the culture of abundance and business showed up clearly in the auto industry. The rise in real income caused by the first wave of industrialization made it possible for the automobile to become a common consumer good, as the car was an expensive item no matter how efficiently it was produced. Before automobiles could be mass-produced, it was necessary that a significant portion of the population either have enough money to afford a car or be willing to borrow the funds to buy one. As Ford discovered in the 1920s, people may have considered the automobile a necessity, but it was best marketed as a luxury. Once the virgin market for cars disappeared, consumers had to be persuaded to buy what they wanted but did not need. The success of this approach signaled a shift in attitude: consumption became an end in itself and consumer goods were valued beyond their practical use. Perhaps more than any other fictional character, Sinclair Lewis's George Babbitt represented the contemporary awareness of the hold of the automobile on the popular imagination and the spread of the consumer culture during the interwar years. For Babbitt, "whose god was Modern Appliances," the automobile was a good deal more than a form of transportation: "To Babbitt as to most prosperous citizens of Zenith, his motor car was poetry and tragedy, love and heroism." Lewis's grim portrayal of Babbitt as an empty man who based his beliefs on his neighbors' and his sense of self-worth on his possessions shows that there was serious concern about the diffusion of the consumer culture in America. Whether one sees Lewis as a reactionary lamenting the passing of his good old days or as a prophet of some of the less desirable parts of the future, it is clear that the society he wrote about was undergoing tremendous change.[16]

Although manufacturers developed the franchise system to meet the requirements of the modern economy, the economy and society were interrelated and franchising meshed well with both parts of the new order. By combining large and small business, manufacturers were able to largely avoid the lingering concerns about the implications of the spread of big business. Moreover, the low cost of establishing franchise outlets made it possible for manufacturers to set up large numbers of conveniently located and fully equipped outlets that promoted a strong brand identification among consumers who increasingly demanded more goods, more convenience, and more reliable service.

The Automobile Industry Develops

The automobile industry developed in an economy and a society that were far different from the ones that had existed when McCormick and Singer began their operations. The industry's growth and form were deeply influenced by these changes. By 1900 the United States was well on its way to becoming an industrial nation. This more than anything else explains the rapid spread of the automobile. By the time the Ford Motor Company opened its doors in 1903, most of the innovations in transportation and technology discussed above were already a part of the business environment. Companies like Ford created their organizations at a time when such prerequisites to big business as high-volume production technology and a national market were already available; they were not forced to adjust to these changes after they occurred. Henry Ford could begin with the idea of operating in the national market and build his business around this idea. Within two years of the company's founding, for example, Ford already had branch sales offices in Boston, Chicago, New York, and St. Louis.[17]

The auto industry was a small, but growing, part of the economy at the start of the twentieth century. In 1900 roughly 300 companies were producing automobiles, but their total output amounted to only slightly over 4,000 "exciting but undependable cars," most of which were expensive, experimental, and aimed at an upper-class market. Within twenty years the car changed from "a rich man's toy" to a possession that most middle-class families could hope to own. At the same time, automobile makers moved from craft production to mass production.[18]

In its early years two characteristics—rapid expansion and instability —typified the industry. By 1900 only one manufacturer, Ransom E. Olds, had reached commercial levels of production. Nevertheless, by 1923 automobile manufacturing ranked first in terms of the value of output of all

American industries, with over 4 million units produced and $2.5 billion in sales for the year. The obvious appeal of the product, a large virgin market, the existence of a technological base capable of mass production, and the ease with which automakers were able to build their own distribution networks combined to bring about this rapid expansion.[19]

Instability came principally from the technological problems inherent in a new and highly complex product, the lack of any established method of production or distribution, and the shortage of capital available to most firms. The lure of tremendous profits for anyone able to make a practical car doubtlessly also drew incompetent manufacturers into the industry. In any case, the failure rate of automakers in the first decade was remarkably high. According to one study, in 1902 only about a dozen firms were producing cars on a commercial scale; by 1910 the number had increased to 52. In the intervening eight years, however, over 600 firms had entered the field. Nearly 90 percent either never reached the production stage or disappeared after making cars for only a few years. After about 1910, when high-volume production was widespread, the industry began to stabilize as a small group of firms established themselves as leaders in the national market. Few successful firms were organized after this time, given the cost of building manufacturing facilities capable of commercial production and the competitive advantage possessed by firms already operating nationally. From about 1910 to the early 1970s, the American market was largely the preserve of domestic automakers that increased in size while decreasing in number.[20]

At the time the automobile made its appearance, the United States possessed a technological base that was capable of providing the services needed to produce cars in volume. By 1900 the "American system" of manufacturing, which was ideally suited to the high-volume production of complex mechanical goods using interchangeable parts, had spread from a few New England arms producers to new industries such as sewing machines, farm implements, and some aspects of bicycle making. The large and well-developed machine tool industry, created to serve these manufacturers, had the capability to build the equipment required to mass-produce the automobile, while professional schools and industry provided a large number of highly trained and experienced engineers to design the needed equipment.[21]

The rapid increase in automobile production and potential market areas led to an equally swift modification of the agency system. The basic method of distribution through a few company-owned branches controlled by the home office and responsible for coordinating the actions of hundreds of retail dealers was in place at Ford within five years of the company's founding.

In contrast, both McCormick and Singer, which were formed before the full development of the modern economy, took years longer to create similar organizations—in part because their initial output and markets were small enough that they did not require close control over marketing, but also because the lack of quick and reliable communications made such control unfeasible. Ford, on the other hand, was able to achieve considerable power over its distributors almost immediately because the company's enormous production enabled it to require its dealers to specialize while improved communications enabled it to monitor the actions of thousands of dealers spread across the country.[22]

Early Franchising at Ford

The change from agent to dealer still lay in the future when Henry Ford, at the age of forty, helped establish the Ford Motor Company. From its start, the company bore the unmistakable imprint of Ford's personality and ideas. He built the firm around his idea of a "universal car," and he controlled its direction from 1903 until his retirement in 1945 at eighty-two. The company's early success and later decline can be attributed to the ideas and prejudices of Henry Ford.

The Ford Motor Company was founded on June 16, 1903, by twelve stockholders, who contributed a paid-in capital of $28,000. Ford, who supplied his patents, engine, and knowledge, received a 25.5 percent interest in the firm and complete control over the design, production, and assembly of the company's products. Like most early automobile makers, Ford began as an assembler rather than as a manufacturer of cars. Operating out of a small plant off Mack Avenue in Detroit and following the common practice of the time, he contracted with various manufacturers who shipped components to the plant for assembly.

Detroit proved to be a good location for the company. Nearly half of the automobiles produced in the United States in 1903 were made in Michigan, and Detroit was the most active automobile manufacturing center in the state. Thus, Ford could contract with capable and experienced firms, such as the Dodge Brothers, which already had a good reputation for producing engines and running gear. Ford's first car was the Model A, an eight-horsepower, two-cylinder runabout with a base price of $750. Sales for 1903–4 totaled 1,700 cars and, except for a slight dip to 1,599 units in 1905–6, rose fairly steadily after that. For the next four years Ford experimented with different models at different prices, ranging from the 1907 Model K, priced at $2,800, to the Model N, introduced in 1905 at $500.[23]

Like most of his competition, Ford soon made the transition from assembler to manufacturer. In 1904 he moved his assembly plant to larger quarters on Piquette Avenue, and in 1905 he established the Ford Manufacturing Company to produce the engines and running gear for the Model N. In 1907, when he gained a controlling interest in the stock of the company, the two firms were merged, and Ford was at last in a position to carry out his original goal of manufacturing a reliable, low-priced car for the masses.[24]

Ford pursued his idea with a vengeance. Running counter to the conventional wisdom in the industry and the opinions of his fellow stockholders, he decided in 1907 to concentrate on producing and marketing a single car, the Model T. The wisdom of his decision was soon apparent. Between 1908 and 1923 over one-half the cars produced in the United States were Fords. By the mid-1920s, however, times had changed and the Model T, despite continued improvements, was obsolete. Ford was slow to make the changes required to remain competitive, and the company experienced a downturn.[25]

The decline of the Ford Motor Company from the late 1920s through the mid-1940s illustrates well the limits of mass production and the importance of developing a full range of subsidiary institutions to support a large-scale business in the modern economy. From 1907 to 1927 Ford built his company around one idea: to produce a single type of car as well and as cheaply as possible. From a strictly economic point of view, the project was a remarkable success. Ford's production and distribution system were generally recognized as the most efficient—if not the most effective—in the industry. "Fordism," as his mass production techniques were labeled, became the standard by which the efficiency of other producers was measured. Personally, Ford's success with the Model T made him a folk hero and an international celebrity and provided him and his descendants with an immense fortune. As Ford never really understood, however, in an economy of abundance efficiency alone does not ensure success. By the mid-1920s it was apparent that simply mass-producing and distributing a limited line as cheaply and efficiently as possible would no longer guarantee the continued dominance of the Ford Motor Company. Once the virgin market for automobiles disappeared, market research, dealer support, consumer credit, and model changes for marketing purposes all became important for success in the industry. Under the leadership of Henry Ford, the Ford Motor Company moved very reluctantly to develop these services.[26]

Ford introduced the Model T in October 1908, and within a short time it revolutionized the industry and catapulted his company into a position of dominance. He originally built the Model T at his two Detroit plants and planned to turn the as-yet-uncompleted Highland Park factory over to construction of the Model T. It was at Highland Park, which was officially completed in 1910, that Ford first achieved true mass production late in 1913. The coming of mass production to the automobile industry provided the final push needed to complete the change from agent to franchise dealer.[27]

From 1903 to 1907 Ford's distribution system resembled McCormick's during the 1880s. The automobile itself was, like the reaper, still largely sold as a seasonal good. Sales in many parts of the country fell sharply in the winter, and the car was so undependable and produced in such limited quantities that few dealers could specialize in automobile sales, much less the cars of a single manufacturer. Also, because the investment required in specialized equipment and facilities was still small, dealers felt little need to tie themselves to a single company. Finally, in these years Ford's total production was not great enough to call for close coordination with dealers. At this time Ford sold his cars through agents, branch offices, and traveling salesmen, as well as directly from the factory through advertisements.[28]

The first marketing problem most automakers faced was how to reach the public when they typically lacked adequate funds to meet the costs of production, much less distribution. The most common solution was to shift the burden to someone else. In production, this took the form of buying components on time and forcing suppliers to carry the needed inventory. In distribution, automobile makers generally chose to concentrate on wholesaling to agents. Agents were forced to include a deposit with each order and to pay cash on delivery. Agents thus relieved makers of the burden of carrying a large inventory of finished cars while at the same time supplying them with the funds to continue production.[29]

Ford followed this general pattern. The experience of William Hughson, Ford's first agent, illustrates the importance of wholesaling through agents in the early financing of the firm. Hughson first met Ford in 1902 at a bicycle show, where he was so impressed with both the man and his automobile that he advanced the company $5,000 on the first shipment of six cars, a shipment that did not arrive until some months later. Agents typically paid 10 to 50 percent down when they ordered cars, with the rest due on delivery. Charles H. Bennett, an original stockholder in the Ford Motor Company, later recalled: "Mr. Ford estimated that it would cost him $20,000 or $25,000 at the most to get the Company started. He told me afterward that it actually took less than $14,000 to get it going. It must have been because of [James] Couzens's [Ford's business manager] policy of collecting in advance; you couldn't do it any other way. What man steps in and buys $20,000 or $50,000 worth of goods and says, 'Here's a check for half of it!' And it wasn't even made! You've got a profit included in that and not only that you've got the cash to make it!"[30]

Considering that dealers paid cash on delivery, absorbed all the selling costs, and allowed Ford to concentrate on production, the standard discount of 15 to 25 percent on cars and 25 percent on parts made this a very advantageous system for Ford. Thus, in the early years there was little need to be concerned with the operation of the dealer network. Although agents were independent businessmen who operated under few restrictions from the company, Ford was still able to market its complex product successfully by relying on dealer self-interest to promote sales and service.[31]

Like most carmakers, Ford was so anxious to establish itself in the market that, as one early sales manager recalled, the company had "no stipulations or qualification for a dealership. It could be a blacksmith shop, a garage or a good livery stable." Contracts, when they existed at all, were simple documents whereby Ford agreed to sell and the agent to buy the company's products. Dealers, for their part, were fairly easy to recruit, even at Ford's slightly lower-than-average discount, because the investment in special tools, facilities, and training was so limited.[32]

At this time Ford left the recruitment of agents largely to the branch managers or larger agents. The company provided little guidance other than instructions to appoint "good men." Like agents for McCormick and other farm implement makers, Ford dealers typically sold other products or other makes of automobile. For example, C. C. Housenick, a typical small-town dealer, already owned a clothing store in Bloomsburg, Pennsylvania, when he began to sell "Stutz, Hudson, Overland, International, and many others [including Ford] from the shirt counter of Housenick & Co." in 1909. Although Ford discouraged agents from handling other products or at the very least competitors' cars, it was powerless to halt the practice until around 1911, when the growing reputation of the Model T increased the value of a Ford agency and the volume of production had reached the point where larger agents could reasonably be expected to concentrate exclusively on the sale of Ford products.[33]

In keeping with Ford's emphasis on production during the pioneer period, the company made no consistent effort to provide dealers with assistance or use them as sources of market information. As early as 1904 the board of directors voted to hire several mechanics to help dealers with training and repairs, but no system of regular visits for assistance and evaluation existed until after 1907, when Norval Hawkins became the first head of sales. Similarly, the company did not maintain regular contact with its agents or institute regular meetings between either dealers or branch managers to get feedback on problems of selling or on public response to the product. This is not to say that it discouraged dealers from suggesting improvements to Ford cars or from informing the company of public attitudes. But such information was not expected and no formal system existed for its collection or analysis. After 1907 dealers were required to send in regular sales reports, but apparently Ford made no use of this information for forecasting purposes. Until 1916 production was based largely on the number of cars a dealer was bound to take by his contract.[34]

Ford's informal system, where "nothing [on dealer contracts] was standard with the exception of discounts" and no coherent system existed to coordinate and control distribution, worked well enough when total output

Barry Motors Sales, 1914, dealers in Ford and Overland. Despite Ford's preference for exclusive dealers, some, like Barry, still managed to carry more than one make of car even after the introduction of the Model T. (From the collections of Henry Ford Museum and Greenfield Village, Negative no. 4925, Dearborn, Mich.)

was still relatively small, the market was large, and an automaker's main concern was getting enough cars to the public. However, the long-term health of the industry demanded closer coordination between manufacturers and dealers if the automobile were ever to become a practical consumer good. The high attrition rate for manufacturers and the increasing consolidation in the industry drove the point home that automakers would have to devote greater attention to marketing if they wished to survive. Henry Ford, like most of his competitors, recognized this. And as his company solved production problems, he turned his attention to developing a marketing organization that would promote his business over the long term.[35]

To improve its marketing position, the Ford Motor Company increased control over its dealer force. The spurs behind this goal were the twin needs of service and repair for the automobile and standardization and organization for the rapidly growing firm. Henry Ford's belief in the importance of uniform facilities, levels of service, and pricing accelerated this process. From the start he had recognized the importance of his dealer network, even though, because of production concerns, he initially took little interest in its operation. As Fred Rockelman, a mechanic at the Mack Avenue plant recalled: "Mr. Ford from the very early days pressed that dealers should be able to give service to their cars. . . . He always said that a car was never complete, that it was 75 percent complete when it left the factory and 25 percent of the completion was done by the dealers. It needed gasoline, it needed tires, it needed tire repairs, it needed washing and it needed tuning up."[36]

The man most responsible for reorganizing Ford's distribution system was Norval Hawkins. Ford hired Hawkins, an accountant and efficiency expert, in the fall of 1907 to act as commercial manager. Hawkins immediately set out to standardize Ford's sales. His first step was to expand the branch organization and provide branch managers with closer guidance from the home office. Because Ford's sales organization already marketed the automobile nationally, Hawkins had a good base from which to work. By the start of 1907, Ford had sales branches in Boston, Chicago, New York, and St. Louis. By the end of the year, Hawkins had eleven sales branches operating.[37]

The branches formed the organizational core of Ford's sales department. They acted as storage points for cars and parts and maintained their own retail sales force. Originally, the company treated branches "practically the same" as agencies by providing them with little guidance from the home office. Managers were responsible for recruiting agents, overseeing their progress, and providing them with assistance in repairs. Ford gave managers the authority to negotiate the best terms they could get with agents, provided the discount did not exceed 20 percent, as well as a free hand in canceling agents and establishing the limits of their territories. The home office retained control over pricing but had no formal apparatus for checking up on dealers. After Hawkins reorganized the system, policy-making became more centralized in the home office and the branches were left with the responsibility for implementing the wishes of the sales department. One practical result of this change was that branch managers were forced to increase their supervision of dealers but lost the ability to negotiate contracts and appoint or cancel dealers without home office approval.[38]

Below the branches were the dealers, who formed the bulk of Ford's marketing organization. One of Hawkins's first moves to bring uniformity to the dealer network was to introduce standard yearly contracts that were secured by a cash deposit based on the number of cars purchased. The two most important types of contracts were the dealer's and the subdealer's agreements. The dealer's contract was a standard agreement made directly with the company. The subdealer's agreement, which gave the firm representation in lightly populated regions, was made between the dealer and his agent but on a contract written by Ford. This agreement assigned the dealer responsibility for supplying and overseeing the subdealer's operation according to standards established by Ford.[39]

The new contracts gave the company substantial control over distribution without the financial and organizational burdens of ownership. Contracts established the resale prices of cars and parts, responsibility for service, and the number of cars and parts that dealers were required to take and the prices they would have to pay. Although the specifics have changed to better define the rights and obligations of each party and some provisions have been nullified by legal changes, the basic relationship between the company, the dealer, and the agent—as defined by the contract—remains much the same today as it did in 1908.[40]

Considering their importance to both the company and the dealer, the contract was a simple affair. According to its terms, a dealer agreed to purchase a set number of cars each month at a discount of 15 to 25 percent and to sell them only at prices established by Ford. The company reserved the right to cancel any dealer who failed to take his monthly allotment but in practice rarely did. To promote sales, Ford required each dealer "to keep in stock at all times . . . at least one automobile . . . for the sole purpose of demonstration and exhibition to intending purchasers" and to "maintain a salesroom and properly equipped repair shop." Dealers were also bound "to keep on hand at all times a Standard Stock of the Parts of The Manufacturer's products" and "to make repairs on all automobiles made by The Manufacturer, whether sold by him or not, and to perform this work promptly and in a good and workmanlike manner."[41]

Buel Motor Company, ca. 1918. Despite its reputation for economy and utility, the spartan Model T often appeared in very elaborate showrooms. (From the collections of Henry Ford Museum and Greenfield Village, Negative no. 6074, Dearborn, Mich.)

In exchange for meeting the terms of his contract, the dealer received the exclusive right to sell Ford products in a clearly defined area. Outside urban areas, Ford preferred to grant individual dealers a fairly large territory, typically one in which they could expect to sell one hundred or more cars per year, and then leave it to the dealers to cover their territories with subdealers. However, company officials retained the right to determine where and when subdealers were needed and did not hesitate to require dealers to appoint them if they thought it necessary. In order to protect the territories of dealers and subdealers, Ford reserved the right to fine and/or cancel any dealer who engaged in cross-selling, that is, selling to customers who lived outside the dealer's territory, or "bootlegging," as the wholesaling of cars to unauthorized dealers was called.[42]

Of the remaining contractual provisions, the most important were those dealing with cancellation and advertising. Either party had the right to cancel the agreement for any reason, and termination became effective on the receipt of written notification. Because substantial investments in specialized facilities and equipment were still rare during this time, sudden cancellation worked no real hardship on most dealers. In the event of termination, the company could be required to repurchase most new parts on hand, but it did not have to buy back demonstrators or any other cars the dealer might own; however, the dealer did have the option of filling orders received prior to termination and purchasing all cars consigned to him at 10 percent below their list price. Advertising was required. After 1911 the company demanded that all dealers "conspicuously display" signs identifying themselves as Ford dealers and advertise regularly in local papers using materials provided by or modeled after those supplied by the company.[43]

Conspicuously absent from dealer contracts during this time was any discussion of the company's right to monitor a dealer's operations. The company could inspect dealers' parts inventory to see that they were maintained at the level required by contract, and dealers were required to give the home office a complete accounting of all sales, including the names and addresses of purchasers, on a regular basis, but until the end of 1938 dealers were not compelled by their contracts to provide any information on the internal workings of their businesses. In practice, however, after about 1907 branch managers supervised dealers closely by sending representatives or "roadmen," as they were called, to inspect and evaluate a dealer's establishment to ensure conformity with company standards.[44]

The contractual obligations placed on dealers would have classified them as exclusive agents were it not for the fact that their contracts specifically denied the existence of an agency relationship. As Ford's "Dealer Agreement" for 1908–9 stated, "It is hereby expressly agreed and understood by and between the parties hereto that The Dealer is in no way the legal representative or agent of The Manufacturer, and has no right or authority from it to assume any obligation of any kind, expressed or implied, on behalf of it or to bind it thereby." Ford and automobile makers generally sought to establish the legal independence of their dealers for two reasons. The first and most important reason was the desire to relieve the company of legal responsibility for the actions of its agents. The second was the fear that if the courts recognized agents as the legal representatives of the

manufacturer, then automakers would run the risk of being sued "in every nook and cranny of the nation where they had a franchised dealer" rather than just in the states where they were registered to do business.[45]
The final phase in Ford's early marketing efforts was its adjustment to mass production. Faced with a strong demand for cars and a steadily increasing output as a result of mass production, the sales department followed a two-pronged approach of opening additional sales outlets and strengthening home office control over their operations. Between 1913 and 1916 the number of company-owned branches rose from twenty-one to thirty-four, and each branch came under increasing pressure to hire more dealers for its territory. As the dealer network expanded (Ford had nearly 7,000 agents in 1913), the relative importance of retail sales through the branches declined. It was now clear that the dealer would, as Hawkins noted, remain the "foundation upon which our business operates."[46]

Ford entered the era of mass production with a well-developed marketing system already in place. At the top was the sales department, which determined policy and oversaw the operation of the rest of the system. Below the home office level, a number of branch offices and a few large agencies implemented the policies of the sales department, monitored dealer operations, acted as assembly and distribution centers, and handled retail sales through their own showrooms and a few subbranches. Below them were the thousands of dealers who served as the main point of contact between the company and the public. Thanks to Norval Hawkins, dealers operated under standard yearly contracts, but many still did not sell cars full-time and some did not yet specialize in the products of a single maker.[47]

The truly revolutionary increase in output and the decrease in price resulting from the introduction of mass production makes it easy to overlook the importance of distribution to the success of Ford. It has been said that automobile makers developed the franchise system by default. This is misleading. What automakers found was that with slight modifications, traditional methods worked quite well. Ford and the rest were not inattentive to distribution; it was just that in the beginning, distribution did not need a great deal of attention. At Ford, the coordination of mass production and mass distribution required no dramatic innovations in either the organization or the methods of the sales force. In the early years, the company successfully marketed its increased output by expanding rather than seriously altering its sales organization. The most important change—the loss of equality between factory and agent—was neither intentional nor immediately obvious; rather, it was a result of the tremendous power that mass production gave manufacturers.[48] Automobile makers had good reasons for originally turning to independent agents. Agency sales allowed them to cover the national market quickly, cheaply, and thoroughly. When the industry was in its infancy, dealers provided manufacturers with most of the capital for expanded production while at the same time relieving them of the expense and trouble of building and staffing a national distribution network. Agency sales have long been recognized "as a form of pioneer distribution to give way to the manufacturer's selling force or to factory branches after adequate distribution has been built up." The question of why the automobile industry moved from agency sales to franchising rather than to the direct ownership of retail outlets or to some other hybrid form of distribution can be answered by looking at the advantages that franchising provided. The inherently unequal relationship between the factory and dealers allowed manufacturers to exert a high degree of control in the field; therefore, automakers were able to build unified distribution systems without the expense of ownership or the legal problems associated with agency sales. This, along with greater flexibility and potential for growth, led automakers to rely almost exclusively on franchising.[49]

By 1916, however, the pressures of distributing Ford's incredible output were great enough to be a problem even for the company's adaptable marketing system. In 1909–10 Ford sold less than 20,000 cars. In 1913–14 the number rose to almost 250,000 and by 1916–17, to over 700,000. Beginning in March 1916, when production methods were well in hand, Ford's executive and operating committees turned their attention to improving distribution. There seemed to be two possibilities: Ford could either expand its own retail sales network and use agents only in underdeveloped markets, much as Singer had decided to do in the 1880s, or it could follow the path chosen by McCormick and concentrate entirely on wholesaling its products through dealers tied closely to the company.[50]

Committee members originally favored a Singer-like system of company-owned outlets in major markets coupled with franchised dealers in the hinterlands. At the initial meeting of the operating committee, held

The Ford Motor Company

*Timmerman Motor Sales Company, 1923. By the 1920s dealer invest-
ments had risen to the point where loss of the franchise could work a real
hardship on the dealer. Notice that the dealer offered help in owner financing. (From the collections of Henry Ford Museum and Greenfield Village,
Negative no. 833.36400, Dearborn, Mich.)*

on March 7, 1916, the first topic of business, after defining the scope of
the committee's powers, was the question of retail sales. Norval Hawkins
advocated establishing company-owned branches in cities with a population of 100,000 or more "not only as a profitable venture but as an indemni-
fication against some of the practices of the larger agents which mitigate
against the service which the Ford Company is anxious to give owners
of Ford cars." The meeting records do not elaborate on which practices
Hawkins found objectionable, but even a casual reading of dealer contracts
and sales department directives reveals that the company had a potent
means of ensuring dealer compliance with its service requirements. Cancellation or nonrenewal was a serious threat to any dealer as the Model T
still "sold itself" in 1916, but the consequences would be especially devastating for the larger dealers, who by now had significant investments in

facilities and equipment. It is most likely that Hawkins was more interested in expanding retail profits from branches located in high-volume urban markets.[51]

At first, the committees responded favorably to Hawkins's proposal, and on March 20 the executive committee approved a plan to establish twenty-three new retail branches to be opened by August 1, 1916. By July, however, the executive committee had reversed its thinking and decided that "the Ford Motor Company could not continue to do both retail and wholesale business in the future owing to the company's great growth." The main reason given was Ford's inability to open enough subbranches to provide convenient service in cities with branch sales outlets. On August 1, the day the newly established retail branches had been scheduled to replace dealers, the executive committee officially ended the retailing of cars by the Ford Motor Company.[52]

No detailed records exist of the internal debate over the question of retailing, but the decision probably came from Henry Ford. Ford was the only person with the influence to bring about such a significant change in policy in so short a time. By August many of the retail branches were in operation and agents in the affected cities had been canceled. Although implementation of the new policy was gradual, the change still must have produced a considerable amount of confusion, unnecessary expense, and dealer animosity. Moreover, the decision to specialize in wholesaling fit into Ford's ideas of efficiency through specialization, which had proven very successful in production, so it seems likely that on reflection he would not have wished to dissipate the company's energies by moving into the distribution side of the business.[53]

The poor performance of branch retail sales may also have played a part in the decision. For years the correspondence of the sales department had been filled with complaints that selling expenses were "altogether too high" and instructions to fire all "deadwood." Hawkins's letters to branch managers (for example, "Our retail business at some points during the past season was certainly a joke") indicate that branch sales frequently failed to live up to home office expectations. One part of the problem was the branch store's inability to sell on credit because of Henry Ford's prejudice against the practice and his wish to keep the company out of the banking business.[54]

Despite the temporary upheaval it caused, the elimination of retail sales brought no major changes to the sales organization. In many cases former branch employees simply became dealers, and in at least two instances Ford apparently leased former retail branches to new dealers. In the long run, the decision to concentrate exclusively on wholesaling probably worked to the company's benefit by allowing it to concentrate on production and giving it greater flexibility to deal with changing market conditions through easy entrance and exit from markets.[55]

Adjusting to the Modern Economy

Henry Ford soon needed the greater flexibility that his dealers provided. Over the next forty years market conditions changed dramatically, and the fortunes of the Ford Motor Company changed with them. Into the early 1920s the demand for cars exceeded their supply. From about 1922 to 1942 the capacity to produce exceeded demand. Then, as a result of curtailed production brought about by depression and war, demand again exceeded supply through the early 1950s, when a glut once again plagued the industry. In 1916 Ford was still in the early stages of its phenomenal rise, which lasted through the mid-1920s. Beginning about 1926, however, the company entered a twenty-year decline caused by its failure to adjust to the new market. As soon as supply exceeded demand in the early 1920s, the focus of the automobile industry shifted from production to marketing. Henry Ford was reluctant to introduce new models simply to increase sales, to expand the role of his distribution system to include market research, to supply consumer credit and other auxiliary services, and to recognize the company's reliance on its dealer network. The results were disastrous. In a little over twenty years, the Ford Motor Company not only lost its position as the undisputed leader in the industry, but it declined to the point where its very survival was problematic by the time Henry Ford retired in 1945.[56]

Notwithstanding Ford's inability to change with the market, in terms of structure, the company's distribution system closely resembled those of its more successful rivals. In keeping with the industry trend, relations between Ford and its dealers became increasingly close between 1916 and 1956. Where Ford did differ from the other firms was in its *attitude* toward dealers. While other automobile makers, most notably General

Motors, had been developing institutions "based upon the recognition of the community of interest between the corporation and its dealers," Ford continued to act as if dealers were considerably less than junior partners and moved only hesitantly to aid its dealer network. In matters of finance, Ford continued to treat its dealers as if they were independent business owners with whom the company should drive the best bargain it could. Weaknesses here contributed significantly to Ford's decline after the mid-1920s.[57]

Given the tremendous power Ford held relative to any individual dealer, this attitude ensured that when times were hard, the dealer network would be prone to resentment and defections. Because the relationship between the company and its dealers was symbiotic, any serious weakening of the dealer network ultimately weakened Ford as well. The belief that sales were the dealers' problem also made it more difficult for the home office to understand that cars no longer "sold themselves" and that to remain competitive Ford would have to give its dealers more assistance and rely on them more heavily for market information.[58]

Between 1903 and 1937 management assumed, or at least acted as though, a ready market existed for the company's products. Therefore, the main thrust of its sales policies was to blanket the country with outlets, establish uniform levels of service, and educate dealers on the proper methods of selling. Because of the widely recognized value of a Ford franchise, the company found it easy to expand rapidly and exert a high degree of control over its dealers. Few reliable figures on the exact number of dealers tied to Ford before the mid-1920s, but the general trend was upward until the late 1920s. In 1913 the company had nearly 7,000 dealers. By 1924 that number had increased to roughly 9,500 dealers and 8,500 subdealers, and by 1928 there were over 8,800 dealers and 20,000 subdealers. Beginning in the late 1910s the company also contracted with garages to furnish "Ford authorized Parts and Service." In 1928 almost 45,000 service dealers were under contract with Ford.[59]

With the rapid expansion of the sales organization came the need for increased control and supervision by the home office. Clearly, its dominant position in the industry gave Ford the ability to forge its dealers into a unified and controllable sales force. The franchise contract, and the threat of its cancellation, provided the ultimate basis for control, but as a practical matter dealer actions were regulated through periodic policy letters issued by the home office and company inspection. Thus, Ford administered its dealer network as if it were actually owned by the company.

As part of its general program to standardize selling operations in 1916, the operating committee decided that since all form letters originating from the home office "were of necessity policy letters . . . all branches should be instructed to keep copies filed numerically as well as under subject . . . so that they might have full instructions and enlightenment on policies current." Although originally directed toward the branches, many of these letters dealt with dealer operations and by 1920 the company required all dealers to have a similar system. Thus, these letters formed a continuously updated operations manual for dealers. Letters were organized by subject, such as "Sales," "Legal," and "Parts and Accessories," and covered all aspects of a dealer's business—from the number of salesmen he should have to procedures and equipment needed for various types of repairs.[60]

Similarly, after the company's decision to market exclusively through franchised dealers, branch inspections became more frequent, thorough, and systematic. Beginning in 1922 the company instituted a uniform dealer rating system, grading each dealer on "Sales," "Service," and "General." These categories were further subdivided under various headings, allowing roadmen to simply check off a dealer rating in each area. This sheet supplemented the detailed written accounts of a dealer's operations and photographs of the dealer's facilities. In 1927, in an effort to gain a better understanding of dealers' financial well-being and to facilitate comparisons between dealers, Ford also introduced standardized accounting practices at all dealerships.[61]

Despite the fact that Ford administered its dealerships as if they were part of the company, sales to dealers were handled as if dealers were a captive market to be exploited for the company's benefit. The latter view shows up most clearly in Ford's actions during the recession of 1920. A sudden drop in demand in 1920 caught Ford, like a number of other automobile makers, offguard. To make matters worse, Ford was already overextended due to the huge expenses incurred from building the massive River Rouge manufacturing complex outside Detroit and Henry Ford's attempt to buy up all available shares in the company. For a time it appeared that Ford's fall might be as dramatic as his rise, but as usual he surprised his rivals. To meet this unexpected and pressing need for cash, Ford returned to his original tactic of shifting his financial burdens to dealers and suppliers. By shipping dealers unusually large numbers of cars with sight drafts attached, he converted a sizable portion of his inventory to cash. Unlike the early years, however, in 1920 dealers did not want most of these shipments and could only be forced to accept them under threat of cancellation when their yearly contracts expired. This attitude went beyond crisis management. Until the mid-1930s Ford frequently reduced the prices of cars with little or no notice to dealers and frequently failed to compensate them for cars purchased under the old price but sold under the new.[62]

Despite the inequality of the franchise relationship, dealers received many benefits from their association with Ford, particularly when times were good. For all the restrictions the company placed on their actions, dealers still had more freedom than regular employees. They enjoyed the good profits derived from close affiliation with a well-established firm, sold a product with an excellent reputation for quality and value, received a high degree of technical support for service and repair work, and obtained proven advice in business management and sales methods. Although its managers could be arbitrary and sometimes treated dealers as servants rather than partners, Ford's primary concerns were that dealers sell cars at prices set by the company and provide honest and reliable service. As long as dealers were effective in those areas, they ran little risk of cancellation.

Even if the risks of cancellation remained low, the damage it could do to a dealer's livelihood increased greatly after 1913. Mass production made it profitable for dealers to specialize in the output of a single manufacturer and make large investments in related facilities, equipment, and training. By 1915, for example, the average dealer had a capital investment of almost $20,000 and over seven employees. This was a substantial amount to have sunk into a business whose existence ultimately rested on a single manufacturer's willingness to continue the franchise.[63]

As dealers became specialized, they also became organized. Regional associations of new car dealers had existed since before World War I, but it took the threat of a government-ordered curtailment of passenger car production to bring about the formation of the National Automobile Dealers Association (NADA) in 1917. NADA survived the successful resolution of that problem and quickly became a powerful political force. Ford originally took little notice of NADA, possibly because it was uncertain

hat approach to take. Throughout the 1920s the company was generally
ostile to dealer associations, probably because such groups presented a
ocal point for organized action against the company. On the other hand,
ealers and makers had a number of common interests, such as promoting
ood roads, and here groups like NADA represented the whole industry.
)uring the late 1930s Ford also discovered that these associations could
e a valuable tool for coordinating dealer actions and mobilizing public
pinion.[64]

The End of the Model T Era

The Great Depression started early for Ford. By 1922 or 1923 potential
supply far exceeded demand and anyone hoping to sell low-cost trans-
ortation needed to contend with stiff competition from the used car. In
ddition, by the mid-1920s the Model T, despite significant improvements,
as obsolete. Ford ceased production of the T in 1927, but the depres-
ion set in before the company could iron out production problems with
s successor, the Model A. In the face of this crisis Ford, in 1928, tried
o stimulate sales of the more expensive Model A by setting up its own
nance company, the Universal Credit Corporation (UCC). Consumer and
ealer financing was already an established practice in the industry, and
ord dealers had long been unhappy about the lack of any formal company
ssistance in this area. Recognizing the need for consumer credit of some
ort, Ford's sales department had, since 1916, helped prospective dealers
btain credit from local banks, but there was no uniform policy of finan-
ial support. Ford lagged behind other automakers in financing not only
ecause of Henry Ford's distaste for banking but also because he believed
hat the low price of the Model T made consumer credit unnecessary in any
ase. Ultimately, it was the desire to stimulate Model A sales that pushed
ord into financing, but regardless of the motive, Universal Credit was a
oon to dealers. With UCC, a dealer could finance 90 percent of the cost
f car purchases, while consumers were able to obtain financing with as
ttle as one-third down.[65]

The formation of UCC did not, however, mark a new attitude toward the
ealer force. Overall, Ford used two basic approaches to cope with the de-
ression. The first, from 1932 through 1937, was basically a continuation
f past policies. Ford tried to increase sales by expanding a dealer force

that had been badly damaged by the depression and erratic supplies of new
cars resulting from retooling problems with the Model A and the V8 en-
gine. Faced with the obvious and continuing failure of a policy based on
the assumption that more dealers automatically meant more sales, Ford in
1938 adopted a new strategy that recognized the importance of a healthy
and content dealer network. To this end, the sales department began to
give its dealers more support. Whether intentional or not, the programs
concerned with dealer well-being proved to be more effective than coercion in increasing Ford's control over distribution as these programs were
designed and supervised by the home office.[66]

Ford's first organizational change in response to the drop in sales caused
by the depression was to move back into retailing. Reportedly established
"to maintain its dealer organization, and particularly its service organization at the desired high level," Ford organized the Ford Motor Sales Company late in 1932. Like its early attempt at retailing, this foray targeted
major cities as locations for company stores. But unlike Ford's venture in
1916, the Ford Motor Sales Company was never envisioned as a replace-
ment for the dealer network. Despite Ford's assurance that its new retail
branches were "primarily in your interest" as "models from which our
dealers may gain benefit," dealers were quick to "register their objection
most forcefully" to what many viewed as an attempt to drive them out of
the most profitable market areas.[67]

Overall, dealers need not have feared the change. Ford established only
sixteen branches in twelve cities, and their total new car sales barely
topped 5,000 units in the best year. Ford's excursion into retailing was
also short-lived. The Ford Motor Sales Company had ceased operations
at all but three branches by the end of 1937 and was liquidated in 1943.
While its exact motive is unclear, Ford may have wished to use the retail
branches as a yardstick to measure dealer performance and possibly to
intimidate an increasingly dissatisfied dealer force. In any case, the sales
company was a failure financially, and from the small number of outlets
opened it is apparent that Ford never intended to replace even its urban
dealers.[68]

Ford's brief experiment with retailing notwithstanding, the main thrust
of the company's sales efforts during the early 1930s lay in increasing
the dealer force while decreasing the number of branch personnel. Given

Stark Hickey Sales, 1932. In the early 1930s Ford put tremendous pressure on dealers to take cars. These rows of new Fords must have been very difficult to sell in 1932, the worst year of the Great Depression. (From the collections of Henry Ford Museum and Greenfield Village, Negative no. 833.57173.1, Dearborn, Mich.)

the uncertain nature of the times, it is difficult to measure the success of Ford's expansion program. From 1933 to 1940 the number of Ford dealers fluctuated between about 6,750 and 7,150, which was less than the number operating during the 1920s but approximately equal to the number of dealers the company had during the 1950s.[69]

Just as it had during the depression of the early 1920s and the slack times of 1926, the company used its power during the first part of the 1930s to force dealers to absorb the factory's surplus. In a letter explaining the plan for a major sales campaign in July 1933, for example, the sales department expressed clearly the home office's attitude toward dealers when it informed all branch managers: "The most effective 'sales pressure' we know of is a good supply of new units in dealers' hands. In fact a thirty day stock, based on current sales[,] is absolutely essential to a vigorous merchandising program. So irrespective of alibis, objections, or resistance of one kind or another, we must have an adequate supply of cars and trucks in the hands of our dealers—not in September or October but RIGHT NOW."[70]

By the late 1930s it was apparent that Ford's earlier policies were not working as well as the company had hoped. Most of the dealer force was stretched to its financial limits, the annual dealer mortality rate was 14 percent, and, probably because of the company's reputation for autocratic treatment, good dealers were hard to find. Something needed to be done. In 1937 Ford finally began to significantly alter its relationship with the dealer force by strengthening dealer support services and providing checks against arbitrary action concerning dealers. A lengthy memo to J. R. Davis, Ford's head of sales, dated December 23, 1937, identified the main "problems confronting dealers, on which they look to us for assistance" as "Unsatisfactory profit, "Insecurity of investment," "Inability to obtain adequate working capital," and "Difficulties in merchandising used cars" and summarized what the company could do to correct them. The company took its new commitment seriously and within a year had begun to assist dealers in all four areas. In the case of unsatisfactory profit, for example, Ford raised the dealer discount on some models and began to provide even more advice on improving dealership management. In one of its greatest policy shifts, Ford now assumed some responsibility for helping dealers market used cars. Beginning in 1938, Ford introduced a number of special programs such as "Used Car Week," which the company organized, coordinated, and partially funded. It also liberalized its franchise contract.[71]

After careful study of the General Motors franchise, Ford introduced its new contract in December 1938. As the first major revision of Ford's selling agreement since it became standardized in 1908, the 1938 contract signaled the company's new attitude toward its dealers. Most of the changes were designed to protect dealers from earlier abuses. Of the new provisions, the most important were a ceiling on the number of cars that dealers could be required to stock (between 8 and 12 percent of the previous year's sales), a guarantee of 60 days' notice prior to termination, a guarantee that the company would repurchase any new cars and parts on hand at the time of cancellation, and a proportional rebate on the price of all cars purchased within 60 days of any reduction in advertised car prices. These changes brought Ford into line with the policies of its major competitors.[72]

As already indicated, the franchise contract established the boundaries of each party's rights and obligations but had little impact on how the system worked on a day-to-day basis. The contract could guarantee a more equitable relationship between the factory and the dealers, as Ford's new contract did, but how well this relationship actually worked depended on the multitude of policies, procedures, and organizational structures developed to carry out routine business. Ford also made substantial changes in these areas. In the case of cancellation, for example, the contract guaranteed dealers 60 days' notice before termination, but to reduce the number of unwarranted terminations, Ford also revised it policies so that—at least for larger dealers—the home office received notice of the recommendation to terminate from the branches before the dealer was formally notified. This gave home office officials, who were farther from the scene and therefore less likely to be affected by personal considerations, a chance to head off a termination recommendation that they might otherwise feel compelled to accept for fear of undermining a branch manager's authority. In cases where formal termination requests were forwarded to the home office, managers were now also required to give more extensive justification.[73]

World War II postponed further development of the increasingly elaborate relationship between the company and its dealers. When passenger car production stopped in 1942, normal relations were suspended until the end of the war. But, in keeping with its new policy of dealer assistance, Ford did make a few attempts to aid its dealer force during the war years. The company subcontracted some of its war work to larger dealers in the Detroit area and passed along opportunities for the sale of alternate products, such as animal feed, but in the main dealers were left to their own devices.[74]

Henry Ford II's assumption of leadership at Ford and the reorganization he began in 1945 marked the beginning of the company's rebirth. A major part of his restructuring involved an overhaul of the franchise system. In carrying out this reorganization, the company extended but did not radically change the course set in 1938. Emphasis continued to be placed on improving relations with dealers, increasing the flow of information between dealers and the company, and the creation of programs to give dealers better support in sales and the overall operation of their businesses.[75]

J. R. Davis, who survived the reorganization, began his work even before war's end. Recognizing the need for a healthy and efficient dealer network to ensure postwar prosperity, Davis, in January 1945, announced some of the company's plans for improving dealer relations after the war. One of the more important mechanisms, dealer councils, was introduced later that year. Under this system, the dealers in each of Ford's thirty-three marketing zones elected two dealers to represent their interests and express their views to district officials. In turn, two of these dealers were elected to represent their compatriots in each of Ford's six regions, while each region sent two dealers to the national council. All representatives served for one year. Although these dealers had no power to set policy or settle grievances, they did provide clear channels of communication for dealer concerns to all levels of management.[76]

After establishing the dealer councils, Ford launched a variety of programs, large and small, that illustrated the company's new concern for its selling force. In 1946, for example, a short but intensive training program for branch and region personnel was designed to give company representatives who came into regular contact with the dealers a broader, more detailed knowledge of dealer operations and sales techniques. Dealers had long complained that the people who oversaw their business for the factory did not always understand it. Taught at the Ford Rotunda near the River Rouge plant, the course lasted two months and was divided into twelve sections covering most phases of dealership management and operation. One year later, Ford began a similar program for dealers and their employees. To help calm dealer fears about their ability to sell their businesses or pass them on in the event of their death or retirement, Ford instituted a training program for dealers' sons shortly after the war and liberalized restrictions on the sale or transfer of dealerships.[77]

The most important change in the structure of the marketing system was the formation of a Dealer Policy Board in 1956. Created in the wake of two congressional hearings into factory/dealer relations in the auto industry, the board was expected to "work for improvement of the relations between Dealers of the Car and Truck Divisions and the Company." Its specific duties included serving as a type of ombudsman empowered to hear all dealer complaints, acting as the final review body in the company's nine-step termination process, and generally looking into all matters affecting company/dealer relations. Positioned outside the regular chain of command, the Dealer Policy Board reported directly to the board of directors and the executive committee. No dealers sat on the policy board, but any dealer had access to it and could thus bypass both the dealer councils and regular internal channels if necessary. More importantly, the policy board had no responsibility for sales and was less directly hindered by potential conflicts. Contrary to the fears of some congressional investigators, this board was not created, nor did it perform, as window dressing. Its first head was Benson Ford, Henry's brother, who took a lively interest in the job. The board reviewed all terminations and during its first ten years, it reversed the decision to cancel in about one-third of the cases.[78]

Another important function of the Dealer Policy Board was to monitor legislation affecting factory/dealer relations. To do this the board established very close relations with NADA and local dealer associations, and it is here that Ford's new attitude toward its dealers showed up most clearly. Although openly hostile to all dealer associations until the early 1930s, company representatives throughout the 1950s regularly attended dealer association meetings either as speakers or observers and worked closely with NADA and other dealer groups in promoting legislation beneficial to the industry generally.[79]

Ford acquired a keener interest in monitoring legislative activity that might affect its relationship with dealers as a result of two separate congressional hearings, one in late 1955, which was directed toward General Motors, and the other in early 1956, which examined conditions in the auto industry as a whole. These hearings investigated factory/dealer relationships with an eye toward protecting dealers from coercive practices. The catalyst for the hearings was NADA, whose members faced short-term problems created by oversupply and pressure resulting from a fierce battle for supremacy in the low-priced field by Ford and Chevrolet. Underlying this was the more fundamental concern that dealers' livelihoods were based on contracts giving manufacturers ultimate control over their ability to continue operations.[80]

Some of the most interesting testimony from the 1956 hearing came from Henry Ford II. Ford had the unenviable task of defending his company's franchise system to a Senate committee that was obviously aware of the company's past abuses and the current inequities of the franchise agreement. One of the senators had worked for a number years for a Ford dealership. Although he clearly admired Henry Ford II and his company, the senator was troubled by Ford Motors's power over dealers. Ford freely acknowledged the company's often-harsh treatment of dealers in the past but stressed that, since the end of the war, it had come to see the importance of a healthy dealer network and had made vast improvements in factory/dealer relations.[81]

Ford's command of detail in explaining dealer services and contract termination was impressive, but his most perceptive comments were those on the nature of the franchise relationship. He compared his company's arrangement with its dealers to a marriage. His analogy was apt in many ways. The relationship between the company and dealers was certainly built on the assumption that it would be close, long-lasting, and exclusive. It also entailed a host of obligations not spelled out in the contract. Finally, as representatives from both parties stressed, how well it worked depended far more on trust and goodwill than on the specific terms of the agreement, since the form of the contract remained fairly stable while the nature of the relationship shifted with events.[82]

From the dealers' point of view, the most important change affecting the balance of power was the increased cost of establishing a dealership. Since the 1920s dealer investments had been substantial, yet they had no formal guarantee that manufacturers would permit them to sell their products over the long run. Ford's 1955 contract, which was typical, had no fixed term but allowed the company to cancel the agreement for any reason with ninety days' notice. Although few dealers were canceled (out of a force of over 6,300, Ford terminated eight dealers in 1954 and twenty-eight in 1955), the average dealer had much to lose and the fact that it could happen left most dealers uneasy about their relationship with the factory.[83]

Congress responded to this problem in 1956, when it passed the Federal Automobile Dealers Franchise Act. The law accepted the inequalities inherent in the franchise system but attempted to safeguard dealers by ensuring that contracts were fair even though they were unequal. Thus, it responded to the dealers' greatest fears: unfair cancellation and intimidation based on the threat of cancellation. The new law gave dealers the right to sue for damages any automaker who terminated or failed to renew the dealer without just cause or who acted in bad faith. This, combined with the community of interest that already existed, went a long way toward stabilizing the industry.[84] Much of the rhetoric surrounding the 1956 law and the Senate hearing that preceded it emphasized the question of dealer independence, but equity—not independence—was the real issue. By definition, the franchise system moved the relationship between dealers and makers out of the free marketplace. Auto dealers had not been independent business owners since before mass production, but they had gained from their special relationship. In the auto industry, the franchise represented an extremely close and lasting (sometimes for generations) connection. To sever it would bring high costs to both parties. For this reason franchise negotiations since the 1930s had focused on making agreements as fair as possible. Here, the disproportionate power of the manufacturer was the source of the problem. In 1956 Congress moved to protect dealers not by dissolving the franchise relationship (because neither party sought such a change), but by allowing dealers a close and now somewhat sheltered relationship with manufacturers.[85]

Conclusion

The franchise system in the automobile industry evolved in three phases before stabilizing in the mid-1950s. From the start of the industry until about 1907, automakers used a wide variety of methods to market cars, including exclusive agents, who were the forerunners of the modern franchised dealer. At this time, Ford's agents were independent business people who frequently sold other products as well as automobiles and who as a rule required no close or lasting association with the manufacturer.

From about 1907 to 1937, Ford dealers were subordinate to the company, which was successful in establishing tight control without actually assuming ownership of retail outlets. The relationship during these decades can best be described as master to servant. Dealers no longer bargained with the company on roughly equal terms. Contracts became take-it-or-leave-it affairs and, as Ford became more powerful, terms became increasingly lopsided. Finally, beginning in 1937 at Ford and about ten years earlier at most other major producers, the realization that the relationship between dealers and makers was symbiotic began to alter the operation of the system. Both parties began to stress the idea that the long-term health of the industry required more equity between makers and sellers. At this point, the system started to move toward an equilibrium whereby manufacturers maintained dominance over dealers, but dealers gained some protection from manufacturers' arbitrary exercise of power and received assistance from them in the form of financing, special training, and arbitration of disputes.

3

Expanding the System

The Sun Oil Company,

1919–1959

Petroleum refiners turned to franchising for the same general reasons as other business people. The pull of the market combined with the lack of any suitable channel of distribution or the reasonable expectation that one might develop independently drew refiners into retailing. As others before them, refiners also found franchising to be the most inexpensive and effective way of establishing sales outlets and maintaining control over their operations. Unlike earlier franchisers, however, oil refiners sold a product that was essentially generic. This marked a major expansion in the system. Until then, franchising had been used only by the manufacturers of complex goods, where extensive service and repair needs required close connections between maker and seller. Refiners turned to franchising when they found that it was a powerful tool for building a distinct identity for their gasoline, a previously generic good. This, in turn, led to the creation of a new type of franchising and set the stage for its evolution from a method of distribution to an industry.

The franchising of generic goods appeared first in the oil industry because gasoline had special storage and handling requirements. Oilmen quickly discovered that due to the highly flammable nature of their product, as well as the great size and mobility of its market, gasoline had to be sold through specialized outlets. Filling or service stations, as these outlets came to be called, appeared in the first decade of the twentieth century—as soon as the demand for automotive gasoline reached a point that made specialization possible. The service station soon displaced other more generalized types of retail outlets.

It was the need for special handling that originally led refiners into retailing, but it was the realization that their gasoline sold better if they could give it a distinct identity that accounts for refiners' continued efforts to control distribution after the filling station was well established. Once refiners recognized that specialized outlets could be used for this purpose, they began to develop elaborate programs to create uniform outlets. The franchise contract proved to be extremely well suited to this goal.

The Business Environment

As one oilman noted in 1926, the "filling station business is the child of the automobile industry." In 1907, when the first known drive-in filling station made its appearance, the 143,000 motor vehicles registered in the United States accounted for a little less than one-quarter of the approximately 32 million gallons of gasoline sold that year. By 1919 the number of automobiles had increased to over 7.5 million, gasoline consumption had risen to more than 280 million gallons, and, in terms of gallons sold, the filling station had become the dominant method of distribution.[1]

The modern economy was in place when the demand for automotive gasoline started to outgrow existing channels of distribution and refiners designed their franchise systems specifically to meet the problems and opportunities of the modern economy. By 1919 the demand for gasoline was national, a few large, well-known firms with the resources to move forcefully into distribution dominated the oil industry, and nearly one-half of all gasoline in the nation was sold through filling stations. As happened in many mass-production industries, refiners found that their great size made them far better equipped to utilize the new institutions established to accommodate conditions in the modern economy than were the retailers who sold their products. One of the more important new institutions was professional advertising.[2]

Advertising had, of course, existed before industrialization, but the emergence of the modern economy changed it in several ways. Most importantly, the expansion of mass production and large-scale business into the making and selling of consumer goods in the last part of the nineteenth century encouraged the creation of brand identification for goods that previously had been nondifferentiated or differentiated by grade rather than producer. In retrospect, given the development of big businesses in the consumer goods industries at the start of the twentieth century, it seems inevitable that this time would be called "the golden age of trademarks." The concentration of production of many generic goods in the hands of a few large-scale manufacturers made it logical for consumers to differentiate goods by producer. In addition, the success of the first branded generic consumer goods such as Uneeda crackers, Welch's grape juice, and Arrow shirts was great enough to convince the most skeptical business person of the very real advantages of creating a strong identity for previously undifferentiated goods. This lesson had been learned so well that by 1920 many business leaders were convinced that, in the modern economy, branded products and sustained advertising were necessities rather than mere sales aids. As the advertising manager of Texaco noted in 1914, the high-volume production of consumer goods had created a new environment that required manufacturers to teach consumers "to discriminate between different sellers" if they wished to be successful.[3]

Much of the early history of gasoline marketing can be summed up as a search, first, for a workable type of retail outlet, and second, for a way to allow manufacturers to teach consumers to discriminate between different sellers. Originally, refiners attempted to move gasoline into the market through existing channels. Refiners typically marketed gasoline directly to large users, such as municipal governments, and disposed of the remainder to retailers through their existing marketing organizations or independent wholesalers of other petroleum products such as kerosene. Wholesalers, including the refiner, generally sold gasoline to hardware stores, garages, automobile dealers, bicycle shops, and the like, which incorporated it into their existing product lines. Physically, gasoline usually arrived at the retailers' outlet in barrels, where it was stored until the time of sale; it was transferred by can and funnel to customers' automobiles. Until 1907 or so, the market for gasoline was still so small that most refiners viewed it as a by-product of their other petroleum businesses. Consequently, they made little attempt to differentiate the product in the eyes of consumers, develop more efficient channels of distribution, or move directly into retailing.[4]

The introduction of the specially designed gasoline pump in 1910 revolutionized the industry by allowing sellers to fuel motorists' cars directly. The pump also made it possible to put tanks below ground, which greatly increased the storage capacity while reducing losses through evaporation and the danger of fire. Because of the high cost of storage and pumping equipment and the bother involved with its installation and operation, most small retailers were reluctant to handle gasoline as a sideline to their main business without assistance. Thus, the connection between refiners and retailers was born. While the need for specialized equipment explains the creation of a close relationship between retailers and refiners, it was the refiners' need to develop a strong identity for their product that caused this relationship to blossom fully. The mobility of the automobile and the necessity of repeat business meant that to be successful, retailers had to provide the type of fast and convenient service that could be offered only through specialized outlets. Refiners were quick to realize that, as the main contact point with customers, these outlets were crucial in building a distinct identity for their products.[5]

As the importance of the filling station steadily increased, rising from less than 10 percent of total gallons sold in 1909 to more than 90 percent in 1929, refiners continued to seek ways to establish a distinct identity for their gasoline in the minds of the public. By 1919 most large oil companies had come to realize that the newness of their product, its lack of any physical characteristics to distinguish it from competitors' gasolines, and the ease with which consumers could purchase it elsewhere made strong brand recognition and loyalty particularly important. Early on, most refiners saw the specialized retail outlet as the most tangible sign of their particular brand. Refiners were also aware that the structure of their industry, where a few large, well-established firms dominated production and a large number of small retailers engaged in distribution, meant that refiners rather than retailers were in the best position to build brand recognition.[6]

The Oil Industry

Oil quickly became an essential component of America's modern economy. Within ten years of the success of Edwin Drake's famous well in 1859, oil production in America had expanded to an annual output of over 4 million barrels. By 1909 the total reached nearly 2 billion barrels. Large supplies of domestic crude and a nearly insatiable demand for petroleum products made oil a major new industry. Because oil refining and transportation were well suited to economies of scale and continuous process production, big businesses also appeared quickly. Until about 1900 refiners concentrated on producing illuminating oils, primarily kerosene. When the demand for oil as a source of light began to taper off as a result of competition from natural gas and the electric light, petroleum refiners were fortunate in that they could easily shift to producing a source of power and lubrication for the country's growing industrial base. Industrial-grade crude oil replaced kerosene as the major oil product in terms of bulk, but the rapid expansion of automobile ownership in the early twentieth century catapulted gasoline to the forefront as America's most valuable refined product as early as 1912.[7]

In gasoline retailing, structure determined strategy. That is, the existing structure of a firm was the most important factor in determining if, how, and where it marketed gasoline. The oil industry was already well established when the demand for gasoline began to grow in the early twentieth century. A number of firms had long experience in the production and marketing of a variety of petroleum products, and it was only logical that they would first try to work gasoline into their existing organizations. Even after it became apparent that gasoline required an entirely new distribution system, a firm's size and structure played a major role in deciding such strategic questions as whether to market gasoline as a branded or unbranded product or whether to use company-owned outlets, dealers, or independent jobbers.[8]

Gasoline was just one of many distillates produced by refiners that typically had already made substantial investments in production and transportation equipment. This meant that their marketing strategies were perhaps more bound to the existing structure of their firms than those of other manufacturers. In any case, in gasoline retailing a firm's existing organization and resources determined its approach to marketing. The major producers, which already had established reputations and greater producing capacity, led in the development of brand identification for gasoline, while smaller refiners, lacking sales organizations that would permit them to reach more than a regional market, tended to market through independent jobbers. During the 1920s it was again the major producers, such as Standard of Indiana, that relied most heavily on company-owned outlets, while smaller firms tended to depend on dealers.[9]

The Sun Oil Company

Sun's origins go back to the early days of the oil industry, and in many ways its history reflects the changes in the industry and in the economy that oil helped to create. Like the industry, Sun was once a supplier of light but moved to power, and, like the industrial economy, Sun shifted from local to national to global markets. In the process, the company grew from a small business to a multinational enterprise. Sun was somewhat unusual in that for most of its first one hundred years, it was a family-owned and operated business. From 1876, when Joseph N. Pew began a series of business ventures that culminated in the creation of the Sun Oil Company in 1901, to 1968, when the last of Pew's descendants retired from active management of the company, Sun remained largely under family control. In the early years, this tradition of family ownership and control gave Sun flexibility to adapt to rapidly changing conditions and thus contributed to its success.[10]

Joseph N. Pew was born in western Pennsylvania in 1848. Twenty years later, after a brief career as a teacher, he set up a real estate, insurance, and loan business. In 1870 he began to speculate in oil as a sideline to his already complex affairs. For the next several years he dabbled in pipeline certificates, a type of warehouse receipt developed in the late 1860s as a way to stabilize the price and to regularize the physical movement of crude from independent producers to refiners. These certificates were very volatile investments, and in 1875, when new discoveries drove down the price of oil, Pew lost $20,000 in cash and was left with a debt of nearly

equal size. The loss from his pipeline investments, coupled with the growing dominance of the Standard Oil Company, led him to shift to seemingly
more promising ventures in natural gas. This move was the first of several
Pew and his descendants would make to avoid being caught in a business
where the potential for expansion was limited either by the nature of the
business itself or by competition from larger competitors like Standard.[11]

Pew's career in the natural gas business began in August 1876, when he
and a partner, Edward Emerson, also a veteran of oil speculation, formed
a company to supply gas to power-drilling equipment in the Bradford
oil field of west-central Pennsylvania. The Bradford site was a particularly astute choice. Nearby supplies of natural gas kept the problems of
supply and cost of transportation to a minimum, and the potential market expanded rapidly. Drillers had been active in the Bradford area since
the 1860s, but production did not begin to boom until 1875. Output continued to expand, and by the early 1880s the Bradford field produced 83
percent of the world's petroleum. Pew and Emerson had concentrated on
supplying drillers during the boom, but in 1881, when production peaked
at Bradford, the partners decided to expand their operations. That year
they established the Keystone Gas Company to provide commercial and
residential gas service to the citizens of Bradford and the city of Olean,
New York, about thirty miles to the northeast.[12]

Although the new firm was profitable, the size of Keystone's market
limited the partners' opportunities for expansion, so Pew and Emerson
again shifted their base of operations. In 1882 they incorporated the Penn
Fuel Company to provide natural gas to Pittsburgh. Unlike their first
two efforts, this move required more capital than the partners could provide, forcing them to sell a majority interest in the company to a group
of wealthy Pittsburgh investors. After gaining control of gas wells in the
Pittsburgh area, the company began laying pipe to the city, and in January 1883 it became the first firm to supply natural gas for residential use
to a major American city. Because of his previous experience Pew was
the managing director, and in this capacity he soon had conflicts with his
Pittsburgh partners. Events came to a head when Pew refused to honor a
request for a bribe to speed up the application process for rights-of-way
and construction permits from the municipal government. This led to his
ouster by his less scrupulous partners.[13]

Although the Pittsburgh gas market had become more competitive in the short time Pew was associated with Penn Fuel, Pew and Emerson, who left with Pew, reentered the business in September 1884 as the principal owners of the Peoples Natural Gas Company. Having learned a lesson from their unfortunate experiences at Penn, the partners deliberately chose to limit the size of Peoples in order to preserve their freedom as individual owner-managers. This choice exacted a price in the form of a relatively low capitalization. As a result, Pew and Emerson found themselves restricted to a small part of the Pittsburgh market with only a limited potential for growth.[14]

While Pew and Emerson were trying to develop a new foothold in the Pittsburgh market, they also reentered the now-more-promising oil business. The discovery of new oil fields in the Lima-Findlay, Ohio, region in late 1885 attracted their interest, and in early 1886 they sent Pew's nephew, Robert C. Pew, to investigate. Based on the younger Pew's recommendation, the partners purchased two drilling leases in Findlay township. While Peoples stagnated, the "Ohio business" grew rapidly. The Findlay leases produced well, and from their base as small producers, Pew and Emerson, following the same strategy they had used in the gas business, integrated forward steadily. In 1888 they established the Sun Oil Line Company of Ohio to provide storage and transportation facilities under their direct control. In 1890 they moved to consolidate their existing oil holdings and establish an administrative base by setting up the Sun Oil Company of Ohio (Sun Ohio) with the intention of eventually moving into refining and marketing.[15]

From their few leases in the Findlay area, the partners quickly expanded drilling operations; eventually, they owned more than 2,500 wells in western Ohio and north-central Indiana. To carry their crude, the Sun Oil Line operated over 175 tank cars. In 1894 Pew and Emerson became half owners of the Diamond Oil Company, which was organized to take over the operations of a small refinery in Toledo. Following the bankruptcy of their partners in 1895, the pair gained complete control of the refinery, thus making Sun Ohio fully integrated from wellhead to retailer.[16]

One of the reasons Sun could expand so quickly was that Ohio oil had a high sulfur content. Until Standard found a way to remove the unpleasant smell that tainted kerosene produced from Ohio oil in 1893, it was a relatively cheap investment. Pew had little interest in the kerosene market, however, and the cheap Ohio oil was well suited for the production of manufactured natural gas. As local supplies of natural gas declined in the East, Pew returned to a market where he had first-hand experience and good connections.[17]

Just as Pew's earlier experience in oil influenced his decision to move into the gas industry, his exposure to gas had a major impact on Sun Oil's development. Pew's long involvement as a relatively minor player in areas dominated by larger competitors had taught him the advantages of vertical integration, and his experience and connections in the gas industry in large part determined Sun's products and markets. One of these connections, the United Gas Improvement Company (UGI), a major supplier of manufactured gas to Philadelphia and other East Coast cities, quickly became Sun's main customer. Pew, who had bought out Emerson's interest in the partners' oil investments in 1899, entered into a partnership with UGI almost immediately as a way to cement relations with his most important customer and acquire the capital needed to expand sufficiently to meet UGI's manufactured gas needs. In 1901 Pew and UGI became major partners in the Sun Oil Company of New Jersey. In October of that year they began construction of a new refinery at Marcus Hook, Pennsylvania, in an effort to cut the cost of transporting crude from Sun's new Spindletop, Texas, wells and manufactured gas to UGI's Philadelphia gas plants.[18]

Pew's connection with UGI had one other major impact on Sun's choice of products. Unlike most other refiners of Ohio and Texas crude, Sun concentrated on the production of artificial gas rather than fuel oil, which many refiners turned to as kerosene production declined. The higher proportion of heavier petroleum factions left by gas gave Pew more incentive than most of his competitors to diversify into lubricating oils, which could be made from these by-products. In 1903, after two years of research, a team that included J. Howard Pew, who would run the company on the death of his father in 1912, devised a commercially feasible industrial lubricating oil. The Pews quickly expanded in order to manufacture a variety of lubricants and related products for both commercial and personal use. It was in this field that the "Sunoco" trademark first appeared and where Sun achieved its earliest public recognition. Thus, when its directors decided to enter the automobile market in 1919, the primary focus of their operations was not gasoline, as might be expected, but the sale of motor oils, where profits were high and the demand was great. (Ford, for example, recommended that Model T owners change their oil every 750 miles.)[19]

Sun's Early Marketing Efforts, 1919–1927

Two factors accounted for J. Howard Pew's decision to move further into the production of motor products, as Sun called its oil and gasoline business, in 1919. First, the dissolution of his partnership with UGI in 1918 freed up much of Sun's refining capacity, enabling the company to enter the larger and potentially more profitable business of serving the automobile market. And second, by 1919 Sun had found it difficult to sell motor oils through filling stations because many refiners required dealers who sold their gasoline to also carry their motor oils exclusively. Pew realized, as he later recalled, that "gasoline was destined to be our most important product, with a new type of lubricant, adapted to motorcars, taking second place." It was not until after production problems were solved in 1927, however, that Sun decided to "go in strong for gasoline."[20]

Once the decision was made to enter the market for motor products, the company moved aggressively. In just ten years, Sun grew from a small-time producer with no retailing system to speak of to the ninth largest gasoline distributor in the United States. Pew's desire to maintain as much control over his operations as possible somewhat slowed Sun's entry into gasoline production. His distaste for the "patent club," which commanded the rights to thermal cracking technology, and his refusal to "pay tribute" to the ethyl corporation for the use of octane-boosting tetraethyl lead meant that Sun had to develop its own refining methods. This took time, but after 1926, when Sun licensed the rights to the technology that produced high-octane gasoline without tetraethyl lead, Sun was in a position to rapidly expand its output. Ultimately, Pew's insistence on avoiding tetraethyl lead made Sun the only major producer of a high-octane, unleaded gasoline. This proved to be a major advantage in building a distinct public image for Sun products.[21]

Much of Sun's early success in motor products was a result of timing. As a relative latecomer to the business, the company could take advantage of the experience of earlier entrants by, as the first head of retail marketing explained, entering the market "after most other companies had made just about all the mistakes possible." By 1919 the filling station was generally recognized as the most effective type of retail outlet, and by 1927, when Sun began its major expansion, the need for close relations between producers and distributors was commonly accepted and effective methods of control were widely known. Sun also had the advantage of entering the market at the beginning of a great expansion. Between 1920 and 1930, gasoline consumption increased almost fourfold, while the number of filling stations, which stood at approximately 15,000 in 1920, increased by approximately 100,000. Sun entered the field just as gasoline moved out of its adolescence—in terms of demand and distribution methods—but before consumers had time to develop any strong brand loyalties.[22]

By the end of the 1920s, Sun, like most of its competitors, had built its retail organization around three general channels of distribution. Two of these, company-owned stations and equipment loans to dealers, had existed from the birth of the filling station. The third method, "lease and license," came into widespread use in the mid-1920s in an attempt to combine the benefits of the earlier methods. Of the three, company-owned stations were the least common. In the very early days of the industry, when the demand for outlets was high but before independent operators had become convinced that filling stations would be profitable, refiners pioneered in station building out of necessity. Because of the great expense involved in constructing and operating a large number of service stations, company-owned units never dominated distribution and became proportionately less important. By the end of the 1920s they constituted only about 15 percent of all stations.[23]

Refiners realized that they would never be able to serve their market areas completely using company-owned and operated stations, but they still found them useful. Early gasoline stations were usually poorly constructed and unattractive; frequently the public regarded them as dangerous eyesores. In much the same way as Isaac Singer and his competitors had used a few company-owned stores to enhance the reputations of their sewing machines during the nineteenth century, some refiners used company-owned stations to build the reputations of their gasoline in the early twentieth century. A few of these marketers went to great lengths to impress their customers through the use of such devices as classical Greek styling complete with statuary and maids to bring customers ice water as they waited to have their tanks filled. But this "gasoline palace" phase passed quickly and had largely died out by the time Sun entered the market in 1919.[24]

The actions of companies like Standard of Indiana, although not as dramatic, reflected better the shape of things to come in the industry. Beginning in 1917, Standard introduced a tasteful and inexpensive design for all of its company-owned outlets in an effort to reduce construction costs and to promote consumer identification with its gasoline. Standard officials also found that company-owned stations had a positive effect on the appearance of dealer stations by giving dealers a reasonable standard to aim for and increasing consumer expectations. And, finally, by the 1930s refiners found company-owned stations useful as a yardstick to measure dealer performance, as a testing ground for new products, and as a training facility for dealers.[25]

Sun's experience with company-owned outlets was fairly typical for a refiner of its size. Sun initiated its move into retailing by opening a company-owned station in 1920. Located in the Philadelphia suburb of Ardmore and built at a cost of $20,000, the station was attractive but not opulent. And, like most company-owned stations, the entire building was designed to promote a distinct image for Sun products and to provide a model for later stations. The company used a distinctive "eyebrow" roofline, which curved up near the main entrance, and its yellow diamond and red arrow trademark to set itself apart from its competitors. Unlike most competitors of its size, however, Sun expended few resources on station building but instead concentrated on developing its dealer network. By 1926 Sun had only twenty-six company-owned outlets in its seventeen-state marketing area. Although no statistics exist on the number of dealer outlets, they clearly must have outnumbered company-owned stations by a sizable number.[26]

In their scramble to establish themselves in the rapidly growing automotive gasoline market of the 1920s, refiners, including Sun, turned to the independent dealer to fill the large gaps left in their marketing areas by the lack of resources. At a total cost of $350 to $550 per retail pump, dealer stations were a far more economical method of reaching the market than the $8,000 to $20,000 per station that Sun spent on company outlets during the mid-1920s. Equipment loans were particularly common in the first half of the 1920s, when excess supplies of crude and a relative shortage of dealers led many refiners to follow a policy of, as one critic put it, "giving away or renting tanks and pumps to every Tom, Dick, and retired scissors grinder" who wished to open a filling station. After 1926 or so, when refiners and dealers had both gained more experience in marketing gasoline and the competition between dealers began to increase, refiners gave less attention to expanding their dealer force and more to developing ways of holding existing dealers and increasing their gallonage.[27]

Unlike their more expansion-minded competitors, Sun's managers took great care never to loan equipment when they did not believe that the expected volume of business would justify the expense. In their quest for outlets, they stressed both commercial accounts and retail dealers. In fact, during the mid-1920s Sun emphasized commercial accounts more than most of its rivals, probably because they were a good market for motor oils and were cheaper to establish because Sun did not pay the cost of installing tanks and equipment (in 1923, about $200 for a 280-gallon underground tank with a single pump). Finally, commercial accounts fit well into Sun's view of its role in distribution. Until the late 1920s Sun acted primarily as a wholesaler; its interest in the product after delivery was confined to making certain that it reached the public in an unadulterated form through pumps carrying the company's trademark.[28]

Until the introduction of "Blue Sunoco" in 1927, Sun recruited its gasoline dealers in much the same way as it enlisted dealers for its commercial and oil accounts. The same company salesmen who solicited orders from existing customers also recruited new accounts as part of their regular duties. In general, salesmen concentrated on existing dealers who, in the early 1920s, frequently handled more than one brand of gasoline. As a result, a high percentage of Sun's sales in the early years was made through multibrand outlets. The company preferred exclusive dealers because of their higher volume and lower equipment costs, but it was willing to accept any dealer with good credit who it believed could average over 2,000 gallons of gasoline per pump per month and offer Sun "a satisfactory volume of his motor oil business."[29]

Legally, the only connection between Sun and its dealers was a one-page lease that obligated Sun to install and lease equipment to the dealer in exchange for a nominal payment, usually one dollar per year for the pump or five dollars a year for the entire system. In exchange, the dealer agreed to purchase a set amount of gasoline each month and not to install or operate any equipment of a competitor without Sun's written permission. The dealer also agreed to purchase gasoline at Sun's regularly posted price at the time it was ordered and to sell it at retail prices established by the company. Because Sun paid for equipment installation, which represented the largest cost of these agreements, leases usually ran from three to five years. However, Sun reserved the right of immediate cancellation if the dealer's financial condition became unacceptable to the company or if the dealer failed to carry out all the provisions of the lease. In cases where Sun canceled the lease with cause before the end of its term, the dealer agreed to pay the cost of installing and removing Sun's equipment. After the initial expiration, the lease automatically renewed itself on a yearly basis until either party gave written notice of termination. In the latter case, the contract lapsed in thirty days.[30]

Although Sun recognized that "purchasers of gasoline insist on service of the first class," it made no attempt to see that their dealers provided it. Instead, the company was content to merely seek out dealers who could sell enough gasoline to make it worthwhile to install storage and pumping equipment. Sun made no attempt to tie its more profitable dealers closer to the company, use their outlets to promote a full range of Sun products, or regulate dealers' operations in any special way. Contracts contained no provisions regarding the appearance of outlets, hours of operation, or advertising. Overall, Sun confined its interference or assistance in dealer operations to equipment loans and a limited amount of advertising materials supplied at no cost or for a nominal fee.[31]

Because Sun was still "primarily . . . interested in the sale of Sunoco Motor Oils," it was slow to realize that the nature of the gasoline market changed during the 1920s. At the start of the decade most refiners, like Sun, were largely content to establish the identity of their product at the pump and then promote it through their own advertising campaigns. And, while aware of the advertising value of single-brand stations, most were satisfied to market the bulk of their output through stations carrying a variety of brands of gasoline as a way to make their products more available. By the mid-1920s, however, refiners began showing a marked preference for single-brand outlets, and by the end of the decade such outlets dominated distribution.[32]

Refiners first turned to exclusive dealers as an inexpensive way to block competitors, but once the system was established, other benefits became apparent. Refiners found that exclusive outlets were usually cheaper to supply than multibrand stations. And because exclusive outlets had a larger storage capacity, they needed less frequent deliveries, thus cutting transportation costs. With the introduction of second- and even third-grade gasolines in the mid-1920s, this concern became even more important, because each grade of gasoline required separate storage and pumping facilities, but the number of tanks the average station could realistically accommodate was limited.[33]

Concurrent with the spread of the one-brand station was a growing brand consciousness among purchasers. Once this developed, gasoline was, at least in the minds of many consumers, no longer a generic good. By the late 1920s, it was primarily the advertising value of exclusive stations that led refiners to prefer them to split accounts. With exclusive contracts, refiners could use the entire outlet to catch the eye of passing motorists through the use of distinctive building designs or paint schemes and large signs. This development also had potential dangers, however. Once the public was "prone to think of the station as representing the supplier, whatever the legal relationship between supplier and distributor may be," it became vital to ensure that a station's appearance and level of service reflected well on the refiner. As a result of exclusive outlets and brand identification, the relationship between refiners and retailers changed from one of producer and distributor to franchiser and franchisee.[34]

This new relationship required new, more effective methods of control. One of the more popular ones was the "lease and license" agreement. Lease and license began during the mid-1920s, when refiners combined the restrictions of two well-established types of contractual arrangements to create a bond stronger than either could produce separately. Texaco was using them as early as 1924, and by 1927 they had spread to virtually all major refiners. Although the form varied from company to company, generally a refiner would lease a favorable site—often from a dealer that already operated a station on the location—and then re-lease the station back to a dealer. The lease to the refiner typically ran from three to ten years, whereas the dealer's lease usually was from three to five years, with an automatic renewal on a yearly basis after the expiration of the original agreement. At the same time that dealers signed a lease, they also usually signed a license to sell the products of the refiner holding the lease. Some refiners, such as Standard of Indiana, allowed operators to sell competing oils, and most allowed dealers to sell products not produced by them. But all provided for immediate or short-term cancellation of both lease and license for handling competing gasolines.[35]

This rather roundabout method of control became popular because it met the needs of both refiners and retailers. Dealers received what amounted to a rebate, as the rent they paid the company was typically one cent per gallon lower than the rent the company paid them. In cases where someone other than the dealer owned the land, refiners were willing to rent at a lower price. Additionally, the refiner provided routine maintenance such as painting and site improvements such as paving and remodeling at little or no expense to the dealer. Refiners gained control of the entire outlet at a cost far less than if they had purchased the site. In short, this system provided stability for the dealer through a longer-term contract and closer affiliation with a larger, well-financed supplier. At the same time, it gave the refiner adequate control over the distribution of its goods and the flexibility necessary to alter its distribution system without being concerned about disposing of unprofitable sites or changing property values and land-use ordinances.[36]

Perhaps the best indication of the changed nature of the relationship between refiners and retailers brought about by lease and license was the amount of attention it attracted from Washington. Because of the oil industry's importance to the economy and the legacy of the Standard Oil Trust, which symbolized the evils of monopoly to a generation of Americans, the federal government was predisposed to take a lively interest in the actions of the oil industry. The new relationship between refiners and retailers quickly caught its attention. As early as 1919, the Federal Trade Commission (FTC) had attempted to prevent refiners from loaning equipment to dealers on the condition that the equipment be used to handle the refiners' products exclusively, believing that such an arrangement limited competition by excluding dealers from handling competing products. However, the federal circuit courts and the U.S. Supreme Court found the use of equipment loans to be legal and beneficial to all parties, as it did not obligate dealers to handle the goods of a single refiner exclusively. Lease and license was another matter entirely.[37]

Lease and license made dealers more subservient to the wishes of refiners and thus drew criticism from the Federal Trade Commission in 1927 and again in 1933; if antichain taxes had not made it unprofitable for re-

The pump with arms. (Photo courtesy of the Sun Company)

finers to continue the practice, it undoubtedly would have done so again. In both cases, investigators expressed concern that by denying independent refiners and retailers access to markets, this system contributed to the growth of monopoly. The commission never was able to outlaw lease and license because of the difficulty in distinguishing between cases in which the refiners acted simply as landlords and those in which the lease was used to control the dealer rather than the site. Nevertheless, the FTC's censure did lessen the likelihood that refiners would use the threat of cancellation to interfere in the day-to-day operation of a dealer's business. Ultimately, the antichain store taxes passed during the 1930s ensured the independence of retailers operating out of leased stations. But refiners such as Sun eventually revived and legitimized what would become a standard practice in the franchise industry: the leasing of store locations by the parent company as a part of the franchise package. Because of their greater resources, expertise, and knowledge of their particular operating system, franchisers were in the best position to locate, develop, and coordinate the placement of outlets. This could be done most effectively through ownership of the individual sites.[38]

Blue Sunoco: Sun Catches Up

As a result of Sun's original background in lubricating oils and J. H. Pew's reluctance to become dependent on any gasoline production technology that Sun did not control, the company lagged behind its competitors in gasoline sales throughout most of the 1920s. That changed in 1927, when Sun engineers hit upon an economical process for producing a high-octane gasoline without tetraethyl lead. As soon as Sun had its own process, it was finally able to concentrate its production and marketing efforts on the larger and potentially more lucrative gasoline business. The shift in emphasis from oil to gasoline produced a corresponding change in the company's marketing strategy and organization. As in 1919, when it entered the motor products field, Sun once again borrowed heavily from its more innovative competitors. The keys to its new marketing strategy were extensive advertising, the expansion of both exclusive dealer and company-controlled outlets, and a new interest in maintaining uniform standards of appearance and service at the retail level.[39]

The results were dramatic. Between 1927 and 1929, Sun's gasoline sales increased by 135 percent, the number of Sunoco dealers swelled from under 2,300 in 1928 to over 9,000 in 1930, and company-controlled stations grew from just over 100 in 1927 to roughly 500 in 1930.[40]

Like other gasoline marketers, Sun designed its advertising program to create a distinct identity for its products, and in this respect Sun surpassed the competition. Beginning in 1927, the company started a three-pronged advertising campaign based on altering the physical appearance of its gasoline, promoting it aggressively in the national and local media, and establishing greater control over the appearance and operation of stations selling Sun products. As a first step, the firm dyed its gasoline blue to distinguish it from competitors' products. Since 1925 management had been toying with the idea of coloring Sun gasoline to facilitate brand recognition and reduce the threat of substitution. In 1927, after production problems had been ironed out, the company decided to move ahead with the plan. While this may seem unimportant today, when most gasoline pumps are "blind" (the customer cannot see the gas as it is dispensed), it was a major selling point in the 1920s and 1930s. Until after World War II, the majority of pumps had glass globes or windows to assure customers that they were actually receiving a full measure of gasoline when the attendant filled their tank.[41]

Sun had been advertising its motor oils in the national press since 1919, but not until 1927 did the company begin to advertise its gasoline in a similar fashion. As might be expected, the first national advertising campaign announced the introduction of Blue Sunoco, "the same knock less, non-poisonous motor fuel as the colorless Sunoco which carried you over high hills, shot you out in front at the traffic signal, and gave you the most miles for your dollar." In addition to stressing the visual difference between Blue Sunoco and competing brands, Sun strove to create an image of exceptional quality and value. To do this, top management chose to produce only one grade of gasoline. From 1927 until the mid-1950s, Sun promoted Blue Sunoco as "the premium gas at the regular price."[42]

To further highlight the distinctiveness of its gasoline, Sun emphasized that its refining process allowed the production of a premium-quality, "natural" nonleaded, and, therefore, "non-poisonous" high-octane gasoline. The company particularly stressed this last difference through the mid-1930s because of lingering public fear of the highly poisonous tetraethyl lead, which caused the death of several station attendants when it was introduced in the early 1920s. Overall, it is difficult to judge advertising's contribution to the considerable success of Blue Sunoco, but the sevenfold increase in advertising expenditures between 1926 and 1930 clearly shows Sun's new commitment to the gasoline business and its recognition of the importance of establishing a strong identity for its product.

Stationmen in winter uniform. By the early 1930s Sun's desire for station uniformity led the company to provide dealers with assistance in advertising, uniforms, and training and gave them real advantages over their unaffiliated counterparts. (Photo courtesy of the Sun Company)

Its new emphasis on gasoline sales and advertising also brought Sun more in line with industry practices regarding dealer outlets. Since the mid-1920s refiners had understood that dealer outlets were excellent advertising tools and took more interest in the operation of the places that sold their products. In 1927 Sun joined their ranks. One of the first manifestations of this change was the company's new policy of recruiting only exclusive dealers and seeing that they kept their stations "in a manner equal with our [Sun] standards." Unlike many of its competitors, Sun was slow to make extensive use of lease and license agreements to force dealers to maintain company standards of operation. Instead, until the late 1930s, it continued to rely on dealers' agreements and equipment loans, along with the threat of cancellation, to control dealers. Sun used lease and license primarily as a cheap way to secure long-term control over especially desirable locations.[43]

Like earlier contracts, those after 1927 required dealers to buy a minimum amount of gas each month, stipulated that Sun products be sold at prices established by the company, and provided dealers with storage and pumping equipment. In addition, for the first time Sun formalized the condition that dealers also purchase at least a major part of their oil and grease requirements from the company. As an enticement for dealers to handle Sun products exclusively, the company adopted the standard industry practice of creating a one-half-cent-per-gallon price differential between exclusive and nonexclusive accounts. Other than this and the inclusion of a list of the types of advertising signs provided by the company, the contracts remained much as they had during the mid-1920s.[44]

If contracts did not adequately reflect the importance of maintaining uniform standards of service and appearance, the directives of the marketing department did. One of the best indications of the new concern about the image projected by outlets handling its products was the company's first operations manual, written for service station personnel in 1930. This manual not only described the responsibilities of station managers and employees but also stated clearly that stations selling Sun products should provide a standard appearance and a high level of service. As noted in the first paragraph, "The design, colors, signs and equipment of the hundreds of Sunoco Stations have been made and are being made as nearly uniform as possible so that they may have a uniformity of their own. This is important because this sameness of appearance makes it easy for the motorist to recognize the station as he approaches; he knows he is nearing a place where he can fill up with Sunoco products and secure the same service with which he is familiar at other Sun Oil Company Stations." The remainder of the manual covered in great detail the variety of ways that the stationman could maintain this uniformity, ranging from the display and operation of all station equipment to the proper angle of his uniform cap.[45]

The operations manual was originally intended only for the use of employees at company-owned stations. However, the same standards applied to the company's exclusive outlets, and, as in the case of Ford, the logic of providing dealers with copies of the manual soon prevailed. By the mid-1930s Sun provided all exclusive dealers with a copy, and after 1934 the ideas expressed in the manual were also echoed in the *Sunoco Diamond*, a house organ established to provide "a monthly meeting place for every dealer—large or small—in the Sunoco distribution organization." In its articles, advertisements, and editorials, the *Diamond* stressed the importance of the community of interest that existed between the company and its dealers and the importance of maintaining uniform standards of service and appearance.[46]

Like the service station, Sun's marketing organization reached maturity during the 1920s and early 1930s. As late as 1926 Sun was still a relatively minor company in the gasoline business. But just three years later, it was selling more gasoline than Standard of Ohio or Union Oil of California. While much of its success was due to the company's development of a technology to produce a high-quality gasoline cheaply, changes in marketing policies also deserve a good deal of the credit. After the introduction of Blue Sunoco in 1927, management came to realize that the relationship between the company and its dealers was more than simply one of wholesaler to retailer. Due in large part to refiners' efforts to create a distinct identity for their products and a growing preference for exclusive outlets, dealers came to be identified with the company whose products they sold. This, in turn, required refiners to ensure that the operations of their dealers would reflect well on them.[47]

The "Iowa Plan" and the Birth of Modern Franchising

The modern filling station franchise, with dealer control and outlet uniformity based more on refiners making it advantageous for dealers to conform to their standards and less on contractual obligation, was forged out of the conflicting needs of refiner control and dealer independence. The public's preference for nationally branded gasoline sold from exclusive dealer stations established the need for close connections between refiners and dealers. The passage of anti–chain store legislation in the early 1930s created the need for greater dealer independence. It did so by requiring refiners to pay a steeply graduated tax based on the number of outlets they controlled. Despite dire warnings by refiners, the large-scale conversion of company-owned and tightly controlled dealer stations to a new, less restrictive type of lease and license agreement did not lead to anarchy in retailing. Instead, because both parties had a strong interest in maintaining fairly uniform standards, refiners were able to find equally effective but less direct methods of controlling dealers that outlived the antichain taxes of the 1930s.[48]

The influence of antichain taxes on the relationship between refiners and retailers has been consistently misunderstood since the issue came into the spotlight with the passage of West Virginia's chain tax in 1932. At the time, refiners typically viewed antichain laws as illegal and misguided legislation that would bring chaos to an already volatile market by removing the stabilizing influence of refiners on prices and levels of service. More recently, historians have tended to discount the importance of antichain laws in gasoline retailing, citing the trend away from company-owned stations in favor of lease and license agreements during the last part of the 1920s as proof that chain taxes only sped up an inevitable development. Both views are too extreme. In fact, as even some refiners came to admit, dealer turnover, crossover to new suppliers, or price fluctuations did not increase noticeably after antichain taxes forced refiners to abandon their direct control over retailers. On the other issue, it is true that lease and license agreements had been a major trend in the industry since the mid-1920s, but their structure and intent changed greatly after anti–chain store taxes led to the removal of their restrictive provision governing things such as prices and hours of operation.[49]

Antichain legislation was designed to protect the livelihood of independent grocers and druggists who were threatened by the expansion of chains during the early 1920s. The bulk purchasing and lower distribution costs of chain stores left most independents unable to compete in terms of either price or variety. As these traditional strongholds of small business came under increasing competitive pressure from larger, more efficient chain operations, the independents turned to state and local governments for relief. Basing their arguments on the social benefits of a small, locally owned business, independents by 1927 had lobbied for legislation that would offset the competitive advantage of the chains through discriminatory taxes in fifteen states. Three states passed antichain laws only to have them declared unconstitutional almost immediately.[50]

The Great Depression rekindled the antichain movement, which gained considerable momentum beginning in 1932. By 1935, the year the "Iowa Plan" went into effect, eleven states had enforceable chain store tax laws on the books. These laws varied from state to state, but all were designed to limit or destroy retail chain stores by taxing them at a higher rate than single- or double-unit retailers. Typically, legislatures did this through a graduated tax that increased sharply as the number of "controlled" outlets rose. Iowa's tax was fairly typical in the penalties it imposed. It placed no tax on the first unit, $5 on the second through tenth units, $15 on units eleven through twenty, and so on; all units above fifty were taxed at a rate of $155 each.[51]

Because of the large number of service stations needed to market gasoline effectively and the relatively low profits per station, refiners were particularly hard hit by antichain laws. After a few unsuccessful attempts to fight the constitutionality of chain taxes, most refiners chose to abandon the widespread use of company-controlled outlets. The movement away from company stations started in 1932, when Standard of New Jersey lost its fight to have West Virginia's chain tax struck down as unconstitutional, and continued erratically until the passage of Iowa's chain tax and Standard of Indiana's dramatic announcement that it would lease over 8,000 stations that it operated before the law took effect.[52]

The basis of the Iowa Plan, as the refiners' attempt to avoid antichain laws came to be called, was not the leasing of the stations. That in itself would not have been enough to escape the tax, as most states based their definition of a chain on control rather than ownership. Instead, what Standard of Indiana and most other refiners stressed was that their dealers were now truly free agents. They set their own prices and hours and sold as many brands of gasoline as they wished, along with whatever other products they cared to stock. Contracts, where they still existed, usually allowed either party to cancel with thirty days' notice.

What most refiners feared about the Iowa Plan was a return to the earliest days of the filling station, when brand identity was established at the pump. In theory, this should have been the result, for refiners no longer had the right to control any part of the station but the pump. In practice, things worked out quite differently. Because both refiners and dealers had a direct interest in preserving outlet uniformity, on the surface at least things continued as before. The chaos of widely fluctuating prices, illegal substitution of brands, and dealers switching refiners—all of which analysts had predicted—failed to happen. In fact, instead of chaos and lost sales, refiners discovered that independent outlets generally experienced an increase in sales after their conversion. As independents, their new operators had a greater incentive to keep longer hours and work harder to develop new business. Thus, much to their surprise, refiners found that, under the Iowa Plan, their gasoline sales increased and their administrative costs decreased. For this reason, refiners' public outrage over antichain taxes lessened markedly after about 1936.[53] Like its competitors, Sun took various steps to shield itself from chain taxes. In 1936, when roughly 9,500 stations handled Sun products, the company altered its contracts to remove the requirement that its over 6,500 formerly exclusive dealers purchase all their motor products from Sun. The new contracts stipulated that if during any given month the dealers did not purchase exclusively from Sun, they had to pay the divided station price of one-half cent more per gallon charged to multibrand dealers. For a few years the company also removed its thirty-day cancellation clause and retained, but did not use, the minimum monthly purchase requirements clause for gasoline and oil. From 1936 until 1939, Sun also leased nearly all of its approximately 500 company-owned outlets, retaining only a handful for training purposes, and eliminated all stipulations that their lessee dealers handle Sun products exclusively. To further separate itself from its dealers, Sun increased its immediate-termination-for-cause notice by thirty days and replaced routine supervision with periodic maintenance/inspection visits and three forty-minute visits per week by company salesmen.[54]

For Sun, as for its competitors, antichain legislation forced the company to "provide a contract which does not give the company any control over the operation of the dealer's business or the dealer's operation of that business." But, because successful gasoline retailing still required close connections with retailers to promote brand identity, refiners were forced to develop new methods of ensuring dealer uniformity. At Sun, and throughout the industry, the most common solution was to offer enticements that would both help the dealer and promote a uniform image for the company. Sun's inducements ranged from company assistance in station renovation, including company-designed station plans, to discounts on company-supplied building materials and accessories, advertising aids, uniform discounts, and management tools such as accounting systems. Thus, Sun kept its marketing system intact by making the company way the easiest and cheapest way for dealers to operate their businesses and by emphasizing the advantages of uniformity.[55]

Maturity

At Sun, antichain legislation was followed closely by, but not directly related to, a major drive to consolidate and upgrade the company's retail organization. This program formed the core of Sun's marketing strategy from 1939 through the 1960s. Termed the "objective development plan," it was designed to give the company control over the retailing of its products by controlling the dealers' environment. To carry out this plan, Sun sought to acquire prime station locations through either purchase or long-term lease, to establish a more uniform outlet appearance, to expand and standardize the products and services available at Sun stations, and, finally, to staff these stations with "carefully trained operators" schooled at company-owned training stations. To see that these plans were implemented, the marketing department required its salesmen to act as informal inspectors and advisers and to sell dealers on the benefits of the Sun system.[56]

The immediate reason for the objective development plan was the conviction of management that the nature of the gasoline market had changed during the 1930s; stations offering "only gasoline facilities or very poor service facilities . . . [would] ultimately pass out of the business." The number of service stations actually increased during the Great Depression, whereas consumption remained fairly steady. As a result, dealers were forced to lower their margin from about four cents per gallon to two or three cents, depending on conditions. Moreover, according to a 1937 company survey, many Sun dealers had inferior facilities and "were selling approximately 2,000 less gallons of gasoline per month than the 14,000 gallon average of competitive stations and they were distinctly behind in the handling of TBA [tires, batteries, and accessories]."[57]

Management was particularly distressed by the poor performance of many Sun stations owing to the company's long-standing strategy of using fewer but higher-gallonage stations than their competitors as a way to cut transportation costs. Research for the objective development plan indicated that Sun should extend this strategy and further trim its dealer force, while upgrading the appearance and service of its remaining outlets. The company's first step in this direction was to reduce the number of multibrand dealers carrying Sun products. Although Sun's policy of accepting only single-brand outlets had been in effect for ten years, old

The Sun Oil Company

A typical Sun station of the 1920s and 1930s. Note the outdoor bay for oil changes on the left side of the building. (Photo courtesy of the Sun Company)

multibrand dealers remained and numerous exceptions had been made for the sake of market coverage. In 1936 nearly one-third of all Sun outlets were still split accounts. Beginning in 1937 these stations were systematically converted or dropped, and by the end of World War II only about 5 percent of Sun stations carried more than one brand of gasoline.[58]

In the late 1930s, Sun made steady progress in its drive to eliminate marginal outlets and upgrade remaining facilities. In 1937 it began to issue credit cards that were honored at all stations selling Sun products exclusively. The next year the company introduced its "A to Z" lubrication service as a separate franchise to all exclusive dealers who agreed to install the necessary facilities and handle only Sun oils and lubricants. In 1939, when the objective development plan was formally implemented, the company instituted its first comprehensive dealer training program. The first two programs met Sun's immediate needs by offering dealers a free or low-cost means of improving their stations and broadening their services, but only if they were willing to handle Sun products exclusively and adhere to company standards. The latter program, which was futuristic, seems to have been based on the assumption that Sun-trained dealers would follow company procedures more diligently than those who received their training elsewhere.[59]

America's entry into World War II temporarily halted further implementation of these programs, but the war actually accelerated one of the most important goals of the objective development plan: the buying or leasing of choice station sites. In 1936 Sun controlled slightly less than 6 percent of more than 9,000 dealer locations. By 1941 the number of Sun dealers had been reduced to about 7,200, of which 1,546 or 21 percent operated out of stations controlled by the company. By 1949 approximately 28 percent of Sun's 6,562 dealers operated out of company-controlled sites.[60]

With the coming of peace in 1945, the company moved vigorously to revitalize its dealer network. As a major supplier of petroleum and ships during the war, Sun had prospered while natural attrition, caused by restricted supplies of gasoline and TBA, thinned the least profitable outlets from its retailing organization. Thus, the war left Sun with the opportunity to rebuild its dealer network in a coherent way and with the resources to carry out the job. Starting in 1944, management began to plan an ambitious campaign to refurbish its stations and train its dealers so that when peace came, the company would be ready to act. Less than three months after the war ended, in a move timed to coincide with the introduction of Sun's new higher-octane "Dynafuel," the company announced plans for the construction of 400 new stations to be staffed primarily by veterans.[61]

Even with its smaller, more profitable dealer system, management realized that it was not practical to own all the stations selling Sunoco products. Sun executives continued to grapple with the often-opposing requirements of dealer independence and station uniformity. In the postwar era, Sun stressed uniformity even more than it had in the 1930s, but the method was roughly the same one outlined in the objective development plan of the 1930s. Because the company could not control its dealers, it sought to control their environment. In the case of choice locations, this meant ownership of the station. At less desirable sites, uniformity was achieved through offers of assistance in everything from renovations, where the company provided free plans and discounts on special materials, to low-cost dealer uniforms. In other words, Sun took care that its comprehensive program offered dealers the path of least resistance in organizing their businesses.[62] While management proceeded with its plans to tie dealers more closely to the company, the legal climate was moving in the opposite direction. In the postwar era, the courts began to require that contracts give dealers greater independence. The most serious threat came from a 1949 decision that effectively banned exclusive dealing contracts. Antichain laws had shown refiners that the contract, combined with the threat of cancellation, was not the only way to achieve uniformity. Nevertheless, to build the image of their products, they still needed stations that sold only one brand of gasoline. To ensure control, most refiners favored one-brand stations. In a series of cases from the late 1940s through the mid-1950s, the courts acted to equalize the legal relationship between refiners and dealers by curtailing the use of exclusive dealing contracts for the sale of gasoline and basing contracts on the sale of TBA items. The assumption was that exclusive dealing contracts put dealers under the power of refiners by making dealers synonymous with the refiner whose gasoline they sold. To an extent this was true, but as events would show, most dealers willingly gave up some measure of independence in exchange for the substantial economic benefits they received from their affiliation with a single supplier.[63]

The best known exclusive dealing decisions came out of the "Standard Stations" case of 1949. In June of that year, a ruling of the Supreme Court showed that the majority of justices recognized, but did not fully comprehend, the reasons for the close relations between refiners and dealers. The case revolved around Standard of California's use of exclusive dealing contracts. Justice Felix Frankfurter wrote the majority opinion, which found Standard guilty of antitrust violations on the grounds that their contracts tended to reduce competition. Because most refiners used contracts similar to those of Standard of California, this decision could have had an even greater impact than that predicted for antichain legislation in the 1930s. The fact that it did not illustrates the importance of the economic ties that bound dealers to refiners. As Justice Frankfurter himself noted in the decision, "If in fact it is economically desirable for service stations to confine themselves to the sale of the petroleum products of a single supplier, they will continue to do so though not bound by contract." Nearly all of them continued to do so. Thus, despite the legal fiction that dealers were independent retailers whose every purchase was made on the open market and who sold their goods entirely through their own efforts, dealers remained closely allied to the refiners whose products they sold.[64]

In a similar case begun in 1950, the U.S. attorney general charged that the Sun Oil Company restricted competition through two practices: (1) the use of exclusive dealing contracts that forbade dealers to sell any gasoline but Sun's, and (2) the use of tying contracts that required dealers who sold Sun gasoline exclusively to also sell Sun's motor oils and other products. Nine years later the company was found guilty on both counts. Consequently, Sun was required to remove from its contracts the stated maximum and minimum amounts of petroleum products that dealers could be required to buy in a given month, and it could no longer charge dealers who did not handle Sun products exclusively a half cent per gallon more for gasoline. But, as in the Standard Stations case a decade earlier, Sun's defeat in 1959 did not alter the basic nature of the relationship between the company and its dealers. Sun continued to control its dealers by creating an environment where it was in the dealer's best interests to do what the company wanted.[65]

Perhaps the importance of the connection between refiners and dealers was best illustrated after passage of the Petroleum Marketing Practices Act of 1978 (PMPA). The 1970s were uneasy years for most gasoline dealers. The oil shock of 1973 set off a wave of price increases, temporary shortages, and realignments that had forced the closure of nearly 25 percent of all gasoline stations by mid-1978. To protect the owners of the roughly 170,000 stations that remained open, Congress passed the PMPA in June 1978. Much like the Federal Automobile Dealers Franchise Act, the PMPA prohibited the termination or nonrenewal of dealers without just cause. Also like the automobile dealer day-in-court law, the PMPA did not significantly alter existing relationships. Rather, this legislation recognized the special nature of the franchise relationship and, as was the case with auto dealers, sought to make it fair rather than equal.[66]

The Sun Oil Company

Conclusion

As Congress recognized in 1978, most gasoline dealers do not operate freely in an open market. Since the 1920s they have been tied closely to one of several major refiners. Part of the confusion about the status of service station operators relates to the nature of the products they sell. In the case of automobiles, farm equipment, or most other goods sold through a product franchise, the need for close ties between manufacturers and marketers is readily apparent and, as a result, has been largely unquestioned. With generic goods such as gasoline, the usefulness of such close ties is less obvious although they are equally desirable.

Unlike the close relationship between the producers of complex goods and those who sell them, the ties between refiners and retailers have been required more by the structure of the industry, the public's preference for branded goods, and the utilization of the outlet as a tool for building brand identification and loyalty. When the demand for automotive gasoline rapidly increased in the early twentieth century, a handful of firms already dominated the industry. With their great size and tremendous resources, it was logical that they would take the lead in coordinating the distribution and promotion of their products, for no other group had the ability or incentive to do so. Originally, refiners showed little concern for how retailers, who stood at the end of their distribution systems, conducted their businesses, but once it became clear that specialized outlets carrying the gasoline of a single refiner were going to dominate the industry, refiners turned their attention to obtaining greater control over dealer operations.

Refiners needed this control primarily because the filling station was the most important link between themselves and consumers. Unlike other branded generic products such as breakfast cereals, competing brands of gasoline were not usually sold in the same outlet where consumers could make their selections after they arrived. By 1930 the choice of the outlet and the brand of gasoline that consumers purchased were one and the same. Regardless of whether consumers chose the outlet because of the brand or the brand because of the outlet, the fortunes of refiners and their dealers were inexorably linked.

Refiners tried several methods to tie dealers more closely to their companies. Until anti–chain store taxes made direct control prohibitively expensive, refiners relied on a carrot-and-stick approach that combined dealer assistance with legally enforceable controls over prices and hours of operation. Starting in the 1930s refiners placed more emphasis on the community of interest between refiners and dealers, providing services that made it advantageous for the dealer to voluntarily follow company guidelines on appearance, levels of service, and other areas where uniformity was important.

Companies like Sun have been successful in replacing legal control with control based on economic self-interest because of the very real benefits accruing to dealers. "Bob's Sunoco," for example, stands a better chance of prospering than "Bob's Gas" due to the advantages—ranging from strong brand loyalty and extensive consumer credit to free paint and advice— that only affiliation with a major refiner can supply. As most dealers have doubtless realized, however, these services come at a price. Like all franchise relationships, the one between refiners and dealers is symbiotic but unequal. By tying themselves so closely to a single supplier, dealers enjoy advantages that complete independence can never provide. On the other hand, if a refiner chooses to consolidate its market area, as some did after the oil shocks of the 1970s, or if they become the targets of boycotts, then dealers can be seriously damaged regardless of how well they run their businesses.

4

The Franchise Industry
and Domino's Pizza

Once franchising became a desirable tool for building a brand identity for generic goods, the stage was set for the expansion of business-format franchising. The owner of a business-format franchise bought not only the right to sell a manufacturer's product but also a complete package of services that typically included a fully equipped outlet, training, continued advice, and regular assistance in virtually all areas of operation. This, in turn, led to the situation where the franchise became a product in its own right and ultimately to the creation of a franchise industry where the franchise holder was the customer and the opportunity for business success was the product.

This chapter considers the development of business-format franchising and its evolution into a distinct industry. The first part focuses on the new type of franchiser who has appeared since the 1920s. Specifically, it focuses on retailers who provided a service rather than produced a product. The second part of the chapter examines the development of Domino's Pizza to provide a detailed look at how a typical franchise industry firm evolved from a traditional small business into a large-scale franchise industry firm. In particular, it considers the services that franchise industry firms offer and the internal infrastructure required to produce these services in volume.

Spreading the System

In much the same way that the birth of the modern economy made product franchising possible, its maturation led to the creation of business-format franchising. As the previous chapters have shown, the rise of big business in the last half of the nineteenth century drastically altered the U.S. economy. Throughout most of the twentieth century, the focus of American economic development has been on adjusting to big business. A major part of that adjustment has been the attempt to determine which sectors of the economy are amenable to the efficiencies of the large-scale enterprise.

Like any significant institution, big business adapted to its environment but also shaped it. In doing so, it set the stage for the creation of the franchise industry. By the 1920s, the professionalization and specialization introduced by big business had reached the point where large firms had access to a host of managerial tools and professional services specifically designed to make their operations more efficient. Because smaller firms could not afford most of these services, a vast market remained largely untapped until after World War II. In the postwar era, perceptive entrepreneurs discovered a way to bring big business into the production of small business by bundling many of these specialized services together as a comprehensive and uniform package that could be produced in high volume at a relatively low cost.

Social changes resulting from the dominance of big business were at least as important in creating the franchise industry. The public preference for nationally branded goods and services was as much a social as an economic occurrence. Once the public came to prefer branded goods to their generic counterparts, it was possible to use the franchise system to sell a nearly unlimited range of goods and services. Most importantly though, the public's acceptance of the economic efficiency of big business and its faith in the abilities of large bureaucratic institutions in general led people to accept the apparent contradiction of seeking the advantages of small business ownership through affiliation with a large-scale enterprise

The Franchise Industry and Domino's Pizza

The new American economy and society combined to create an environment that made franchising more attractive than independent ownership by developing a clientele that accepted, without question, the economic efficiency of big business even as it sought the independence of small business ownership.

After the public developed a preference for branded generic goods and oil refiners proved that the franchise system could be adapted to the sale of services and transitory goods, it was likely that others would adopt the system. Many of these new franchisers, such as A & W Root Beer, which began franchise operations in 1925, and Howard Johnson's, which opened its first outlet in 1935, came from the service sector and consequently had different needs and a different perspective than earlier franchisers. Most were small retailers whose products were produced and/or consumed where they were sold. This made the outlet a part of the product in a very real way, and as such the need for stringent control and outlet uniformity was even more important than it had been for refiners. For service industries to succeed, they needed to reproduce the entire outlet, since it was really the product they hoped to sell. In doing so, these new "system franchisers," as they were called, served as forerunners to the franchise industry.

In the early years, however, the organization and operation of system franchisers differed little from those of the more traditional users of the system. A & W, Howard Johnson's, and the rest were still drawn to franchising as a cheap and effective way to expand distribution. The main difference was their awareness that the nature of their business demanded that they focus on the entire outlet and not just the goods sold through it. As the case of Howard Johnson's restaurants illustrates, although successful system franchisers sold a complete business, they were still more interested in selling to the general public than the franchisees who operated their outlets.

Howard Johnson began the company that bears his name in 1925, when he took over a floundering soda fountain/drugstore in Wollaston, Massachusetts. Sales grew quickly once Johnson decided to concentrate on the soda fountain. Because he could not find a suitable ice cream from local suppliers, Johnson began to make his own in the store, and by the end of the summer it was apparent that his product had broad public appeal. His "homemade" ice cream was such a hit that he decided to set up a small ice cream stand on the beach at a nearby resort to catch more of the summer business. This crude wooden stand, which sold only ice cream and soda, was so popular that on the day it opened, it was reported that it took twelve policemen to control the crowds that gathered for the sodas and nickel cones. The success of these operations convinced Johnson that his fortune lay in the food-service industry, and in 1929 he expanded again, this time adding meals to complement his dessert menu. Johnson opened his first restaurant in suburban Boston. After a rough start due to poor cost control, it too began to thrive and Johnson developed plans for further expansion.[1]

His main problem was financing. The depression, combined with bankers' traditional reluctance to lend money to restaurateurs because of their high failure rate, made it difficult to acquire the funds with which to grow. To make matters worse, Johnson proposed that his new restaurants have the same distinctive appearance and specialized layout as the first one. This gave these structures little application for anything other than a Howard Johnson's eatery and thus reduced their value as security. Johnson was a frustrated man. He had a successful business but was unable to tap the normal sources of capital for expansion. He found the solution to his problem in franchising.[2]

Johnson gave his first franchise to Reginald Sprague, an old friend, in 1935. Sprague had approached Johnson about building an ice cream store on some land that his father owned. Johnson was willing but because the banks would not supply the necessary credit, he proposed that Sprague build and operate a Howard Johnson's ice cream shop under license. In return for the right to use the Johnson name and assistance in designing, furnishing, and managing the business, Sprague agreed to purchase all his supplies from Johnson and to operate the shop according to standards set by the parent company.[3]

The immediate success of Sprague's restaurant persuaded Johnson that franchising could give him the capital he needed to expand his own operations, and he began to franchise in earnest. With the profits from increased supply sales fueling company growth and the franchisees bearing the cost of establishing their own outlets, the Johnson restaurants expanded rapidly. In 1936 Johnson began to convert his 13 ice cream stands into full-service restaurants, financed in part through profits from the 39 new franchised outlets opened that year. Four years later, Johnson had 132 restaurants: 40 company-owned outlets and 92 franchisees scattered along the main highways linking the East Coast of the United States.[4] By 1940 Johnson had come a long way in building his franchise operations. Of the $207 million his business earned that year, over one-half—$132 million—came from his supply company, which dealt primarily with the franchised stores. Additionally, Johnson, like many of the new franchisers, revived the practice of charging a fee for the right to market his product. Unlike earlier franchisers, such as Isaac Singer during the 1850s, Johnson's $1,000 fee was not intended to be a quick and easy way to obtain revenue. Rather, this money paid for the multitude of services that the company provided its franchisees before their outlets earned the parent company a profit from supply sales. In 1940 Johnson had a staff of twenty-seven architects to design outlets that tailored Johnson's characteristic Georgian style to the individual wishes of the franchise owner and the peculiarities of the location. Additionally, he employed an extensive staff to offer advice and supervise the equipping, furnishing, and managing of the outlet and then to inspect its operations.[5]

Much of Johnson's success can be attributed to the care he took to give the public a uniform product and his strong support and supervision of franchisees. Unlike some of his less perceptive competitors, such as Dairy Queen, which failed to establish uniform levels of service and cleanliness and suffered for it, Johnson understood that the reputation of his business depended on the entire operation of the unit and not just on the quality of the products it sold.

Howard Johnson used three major methods to control his franchisees. First, the franchise contract itself gave the parent company the right "to inspect the merchandise and methods of operating the [franchisee's] business in all its divisions or departments for the purpose of determining whether said business is being conducted according to HOWARD JOHNSON'S standards." To carry out these inspections, Johnson employed "special investigators"; their identities were known only to the owner and manager of the outlet. These inspectors provided regular, detailed reports on the hours of operation, the quality of the service and food, and the general operation of the unit. As an additional check, the company also fielded a force of traveling inspectors called "shoppers," who regularly made anonymous visits to the stores to see that Johnson's standards were enforced in all aspects of their operation—from the politeness of the servers to the size of the portions served.[6]

Second, by requiring his outlets to buy virtually all their supplies from him, including such nonfood items as matches, Johnson kept a constant watch on the quality of the products sold under his name. Although he required the franchisees to purchase materials primarily because of the captive market they provided, the benefits of standardization became increasingly important as the number of franchisees increased. By monitoring retail sales and checking them against supply purchases, Johnson also had an added, if somewhat crude, indicator of portion size, waste, or theft; this proved useful to both parties. Although some franchisees complained that the rates charged by the company were too high, overall prices were competitive with independent suppliers.

Finally, Johnson maintained control over his franchisees by partially incorporating them into the management of the company. During the 1930s he established an executive council of agents composed of franchisees and members of the parent company. The council had no power to set standards or settle disputes, but it did serve as a forum where issues could be debated and allowed franchisees some input into the establishment of company policy.

Johnson was also typical of the new franchisers in that he built his business along the nation's expanding highway system. There are several reasons why franchise industry firms tended to show up first and continue to appear most often along transportation arteries. The edge of the highway gave a firm like Johnson's an environment that had much to offer prospective franchisees. One of the chief attractions of the Johnson name was the promise of a uniformly high-quality meal in familiar surroundings. Local restaurants serving a local clientele could, over time, build such a reputation. Small roadside restaurants could not. Johnson designed and located his restaurants specifically to cater to the transient customer who had no knowledge of local eateries. Just as travelers of the 1920s tended to prefer familiar brands and food products to unfamiliar local fare when they stopped at the food stands, tearooms, and small restaurants that dotted the roadside, travelers of the 1930s soon preferred the familiarity of the products, prices, and atmosphere of chain restaurants. Because franchising enabled a firm to expand much more rapidly than company ownership, restaurateurs—like Johnson—who served the roadside market increasingly turned to it as the quickest way to maximize the advantages of comprehensive market coverage.[7]

The development of franchising at Howard Johnson's illustrates the increasingly different focus that the new service franchisers brought to the system. In the first place, Johnson was far more interested in establishing uniform standards and close connections with his franchisees than earlier product franchisers. The makers of complex and expensive goods were always concerned that dealers sold their products at uniform prices and gave good service. But beyond that, product franchisers generally confined their standardization efforts to accounting techniques and similar changes that made it easier to coordinate distribution and administer the system. Because the outlet was not a part of the product in the sale of complex goods (although price and service were), franchisers of items such as farm implements and automobiles never felt much pressure to achieve the levels of control required by the newer franchisers. Even in the case of gasoline service stations, where the outlet was a significant part of the product, refiners were somewhat slower than service franchisers to recognize the importance of the outlet in establishing a reputation for their products.

Once franchising moved into the service sector, its potential for expansion became far less limited and its transformation into a product far more likely. Because the franchise holder purchased a comprehensive package that usually included the outlet and always included expert assistance, the product actually sold through the outlet was less important than the package it came with. In contrast, product franchisers had little incentive to make the outlet a major part of their product and little to gain by converting the outlet into a product in its own right. They had large investments in production facilities and earned high profits from the sale of their goods. This made them unwilling to move into a new area, the sale of franchised outlets, that might disrupt or conflict with effective distribution in the old.

The Franchise Boom and the Franchise Industry

Like many of the economic changes accompanying the rise of big business, business-format franchising started to bud in the 1920s but did not fully flower until after the Great Depression and World War II. As the economy expanded and matured in the postwar era, the business environment became even more conducive to the evolution of franchising into an industry. The great expansion of the service and retail sectors in particular aided the growth of business-format franchising by increasing the size of its natural habitat, while growth in personal income increased people's ability to buy both franchised goods and franchised businesses.[8]

The social environment of postwar America was even more favorable to the development of the franchise industry. After the war, the country experienced a wave of interest in small business that, to an extent, continues to the present day. The United States has always had a vigorous small business population, but in the postwar period the number of Americans interested in self-employment rose dramatically. Although the reasons why people wish to own their own business are open to debate, most researchers agree that the most common cause is a break in career path. The depression, World War II, and, to a lesser degree, the Korean War all provided such breaks on a national scale. In the first full year of peace after World War II, Americans began or purchased over 1.2 million businesses. This was more than twice the 1940 level. Over one-half of these startups were in the retail and service industries, where the advantages of business-format franchising are greatest.[9]

The wartime experience also had a more lasting influence on the desire for small business ownership and the eventual creation of the franchise industry. During the war, two long-standing and somewhat contradictory attitudes toward small business became more pronounced. Since at least the start of the twentieth century, Americans had been decrying the social consequences of what they perceived to be the passing of the small business owner, while at the same time questioning the economic usefulness of small business. At times it seemed that many people wanted a big business economy in a society made up of small business owners. The war intensified these views. The overwhelming importance of large-scale industry to the nation's ability to become "the arsenal for democracy" was as undeniable s it was well known, and the effectiveness of the U.S. military, another arge-scale enterprise, in projecting America's will on a global basis further reinforced beliefs about the effectiveness of large-scale institutions n modern America.[10] On the other hand, one of the chief aims of the war had been the projection of traditional American values. During and after the war these values were often expressed in terms of the freedom of economic opportunity fostered by the American political and economic system. One of the chief symbols of this opportunity was the small business owner, who continued to be glorified as the embodiment of traditional American values of freedom, independence, and self-reliance in the cold war years.[11]

The small business owner became a more powerful symbol of traditional American values at a time when people were once again beginning to question the social effects of big business. The 1950s is generally depicted as an era of great conformity, but it was also a time of great uncertainty over the homogenizing forces of big business. Popular books such as *The Lonely Crowd* (1950), *White Collar* (1951), *The Man in the Gray Flannel Suit* (1955), and *The Organization Man* (1956) all raised serious questions about the changes in American society produced by the rise of large and impersonal institutions.[12]

These concerns were magnified by the economic realities of the modern era. Starting in the mid-1940s, there was a growing realization at all levels of society that in an industrial economy the chances for upward mobility by those who toiled on the shop floor were limited and likely to remain so. The chance of making the transition from labor to management in a large industrial firm were never great for the average worker, but the growing professionalization of management at all levels, which accelerated after the war, effectively capped the worker's potential for advancement at a much lower level. By formalizing the training required for promotion into even the lower levels of management and shifting it from the factory to the university, business leaders disrupted one of labor's traditional paths of advancement. This increased the attractiveness of small business ownership as an avenue for upward mobility even as people continued to doubt its economic viability.[13]

The renewed interest in small business might well have been expressed along the more traditional lines of completely independent ownership if a basic faith in the economic power of big business were not already well ingrained in the public mind and the success of the franchise system as a path to small business ownership were not already established. As it turned out, postwar franchisers were in the enviable position of being able to offer a solution to all these concerns. They sold franchising as a method that combined the economic efficiency of big business with the personal satisfaction and social advantages of small business ownership. In this way, franchisers helped create the image of a new, more viable, "modern" type of small business that appealed to the large numbers of people who liked the idea of small business ownership but recognized its economic weakness and lacked the experience or courage to make the attempt on their own. To the members of a generation that had been raised on branded goods—mass-produced to uniformly high standards—and that tended to be suspicious of "homemade" or unbranded products, the ability to buy a business in much the same way they could buy a car—by looking for one with a style they liked from a company with a proven reputation—held a tremendous appeal. It is no wonder that when franchisers such as Ray Kroc of McDonald's declared that "Franchising has become an updated version of the American Dream," people were ready to listen.[14]

Conditions were ripe for the expansion of franchising after the war, and for the next fifteen years the industry grew rapidly but quietly. Between 1945 and 1960, franchisers opened an estimated 100,000 outlets selling everything from hot dogs to water softeners. What changed this rapid but steady expansion to a boom was the publicity generated in the late 1950s when both the popular and business press discovered franchising. Articles on "Franchises: Big New Frontier for Small Business" and "The Everlasting Dream—Be Your Own Boss" began to appear regularly in the press and continued to be a common occurrence through the mid-1960s. The tone of these pieces ran from cautious optimism to obvious enthusiasm, but all of them presented franchising as a unique type of business opportunity that separated this new breed of hot dog vendors or water softener salesmen from their nonfranchised counterparts. For the first time, franchising gained wide publicity as an enterprise whose product was a near-guarantee of business success, and large numbers of people who saw franchising in this light were drawn into both sides of the business. As might be expected, this changed the character of the industry. The pioneers of business-format franchising had given a great deal of attention to marketing their outlets, but most still did not think of themselves as being in the franchise business. This was much less often the case for the generation that entered franchising after the late 1950s.[15]

The rapid expansion of business-format franchising in the postwar period also led to the creation of supporting institutions such as trade associations and a host of services—ranging from insurance to consulting—that further reinforced the belief that franchising was a distinct industry. By the late 1950s, the number of franchisers had reached a "critical mass," which made it profitable to provide these services, while the growing realization that franchising was a distinct business in itself contributed to the feeling that franchisers should have the trappings of an industry.[16]

Among the supporting institutions, the International Franchise Association (IFA) best illustrates the consciousness among franchisers that they were members of a distinct industry. The IFA grew out of an informal meeting of franchisers who were attending one of the many small business exhibitions that were common in the late 1950s and early 1960s. Since its formal organization in 1960, the IFA had continually expanded its operations to take on all the normal functions of a trade association. Because of the members' original concern about the number of unscrupulous operators in the boom years of the late 1950s and early 1960s, the IFA began a drive for self-policing within the industry and formulated the first code of ethics for franchisers. More recently, the association, which had over 250 members in 1987, has acted as a clearinghouse for information on the industry through its own monthly publications, sponsorship of seminars on various aspects of franchising, and support to both individuals and institutions interested in franchising, such as the University of Nebraska's International Center for Franchise Studies. In addition, since the early 1960s the IFA has been extremely active as the industry's political representative in matters of franchise law. This role has become increasingly important as franchisers and government officials have each tried to define the boundaries of the relationship between franchisees and the parent company.[17]

The federal government became interested in business-format franchising shortly after the boom began, and in 1963 the Small Business Administration sponsored a pioneering study of franchising. Although it failed to recognize the creation of a distinct franchise industry, the study did speak highly of franchising as a method of increasing the potential for successful small business ownership. Of the problems the study found, the most important was the lack of any clear legal definition of business-format franchising or accompanying legislation defining the rights and obligations of each party, leaving the door open for potential clashes with existing antitrust laws. Two cornerstones of business-format franchising in the 1960s were the use of exclusive dealing contracts that forbade the sale of "outside" or nonsystem products at the unit and tying provisions that required franchisees to buy some or all of their equipment and supplies from the parent company or a select number of authorized suppliers.[18]

In the immediate postwar period antitrust cases such as those against Standard Oil of California in 1949 and the Sun Oil Company in 1959 effectively limited the control all franchisers could legally exert over their dealers. Both the Standard Stations and Sun Oil cases treated refiners and dealers as if both parties were independent firms operating in an open market. While these decisions had little impact on the oil industry, they helped create a climate of uncertainty among the newly developing franchise industry firms, which required far greater control over the outlets that were now their main product.[19]

During the 1960s and 1970s, when the number of cases involving system franchisers began to multiply as a result of the franchise boom, the courts started to show an awareness that this was a new type of franchise system. But this recognition came slowly. Even when the courts realized that they were dealing with a new business arrangement, they were often unsure what its boundaries should be. For example, in 1962, in *Susser v. Carvel Corporation*, one of the first major cases dealing with a system franchiser, the judiciary perceived that the uniqueness of system franchising placed limits on franchise holders, that it made them something less than independent business owners operating in an entirely free market. Moving from the assumption that "the cornerstone of the franchise system must be the trademark or trade name of a product," the court ruled that Carvel, a business-format franchiser whose outlets sold ice cream products, had the right to limit the actions of its franchisees in order to preserve the uniformity of its marketing system, as that uniformity was essential in protecting the integrity of Carvel's trade name. Specifically, the court concluded that Carvel's requirement that its franchisees sell only the company's products did not violate antitrust laws and that Carvel had the right to force franchisees to buy only from company-authorized suppliers of ice cream and related products if it was done for quality control purposes.[20] As is true of any new business relationship, defining the boundaries of legally acceptable behavior within business-format franchising was a complicated and sometimes contradictory process. In a partial reversal of the principles set down in the *Carvel* decision, the courts ruled in 1971, *Seigel v. Chicken Delight, Inc.*, that Chicken Delight, another system franchiser, could not require its franchisees to purchase supplies and equipment from either the company or authorized suppliers as long as products of equal quality could be bought on the open market. By moving from a supplier-based system of quality control to one grounded in performance standards, the Chicken Delight case proved to be devastating to system franchisers that relied extensively on franchisees as a captive market for their products. Chicken Delight itself was one of the first casualties, failing shortly after the decision. In the long run, however, this ruling has probably worked to the benefit of the industry as a whole by removing a serious conflict of interest between the parent company and franchisees.[21]

More recently, the judiciary has recognized business-format franchising as a distinct type of arrangement separate from product franchising and accepted the notion of the business-format franchise as a comprehensive package of goods that need to be sold as a complete unit. In the case of *Principe v. McDonald's Corporation* in 1980, in what can fairly be termed a ringing endorsement of the company's franchise system, the court ruled that McDonald's was within its rights when it tied the use of the McDonald's trade name and system to the execution of a store lease at a site chosen by the company. While recognizing that the lease was not directly necessary to maintain the quality or good name of the product, the court nonetheless allowed McDonald's to require it on the ground that it was McDonald's total franchise "formula that produced system wide success, the formula that promises to make each new McDonald's store successful, [and] that formula is what McDonald's sells its franchisees."[22]

At the same time the judicial branch was trying to fit business-format franchising into existing law, the legislative and executive branches were beginning their own attempts to define and regulate it. The concerns addressed by new legislation fell into two broad groups: (1) full and accurate presale disclosure to prospective franchisees of information about the company and its contract, and (2) the fairness of the contract itself. California passed the first franchise disclosure law in 1970, with several other states following shortly afterward. In 1971 the Federal Trade Commission also chose the disclosure approach with the publication of a draft Trade Regulation Rule governing the sale of franchises that largely mirrored the California law. A revised version of the rule became effective in 1979 and since then has largely governed the initial contact between franchiser and franchisees.[23]

Legislation such as the FTC rule marked a major step forward in the recognition that franchise industry firms were really in the business of supplying their clients with a service that made business ownership easier. These laws, which were modeled after those governing the sale of securities, explicitly accepted the idea that system franchises were in fact business opportunities and attempted to correct perceived imbalances in the system by ensuring that potential franchisees received a full and fair statement of the services provided by the parent company as well as a complete explanation of their obligations under the contract. Under the guidelines established by the FTC rule, franchisers are required to supply potential customers with all relevant information about the company—including the number of years in business, the number of unit failures, and lawsuits in which it is currently involved—as well as the information to support any claims made by the company or its franchise brokers.[24]

Disclosure laws have achieved wide support from all concerned parties. On the other hand, legislation dealing with the contents of franchise contracts has been controversial. Here, legislation is confined to the states and little uniformity exists other than a concern for fairness, particularly as it relates to questions of contract renewal, termination, and sale to a third party. Fewer than twenty states currently have such laws, and all of them are designed to limit the power of franchisers over their clients. Although the lack of legislation in this area came to be attributed in part to the efforts of groups such as the IFA, legislators' traditional reluctance to tamper with the freedom of contract between informed parties, the complexity of the issues involved, and a general satisfaction with current practices have also played a major role. Of the laws that do exist, none of the provisions weigh heavily on franchisers. Typically, states that regulate franchise contracts forbid nonrenewal without just cause and require that in cases where renewal is denied, the company repurchase the outlet or find another buyer who is willing to pay the fair market value; if franchisees wish to sell before the expiration of their contracts, they may do so provided that the purchaser is agreeable to the parent company.[25]

As the case of Domino's Pizza will show, governmental regulation has not fundamentally altered the franchise industry's course of development. In general, legislation has legitimized rather than redefined the core relationship between the parent company and its clients, hardened existing paths of development, and changed only a few provisions of the contract. As is often the case in the creation of new methods of conducting business, the franchise industry was not regulated until after generally accepted standards already existed. At most, governmental regulation has tended to drive the less scrupulous operators out of the system through disclosure laws and to bring greater uniformity to the industry through the guarantee of certain basic rights to both the franchiser and the franchisee. As with product franchising, the connections between parties are typically closer than a reading of the franchise laws would suggest because of mutual self-interest and the tendency of both the parent company and franchisees to internalize conflicts through the use of joint advisory committees and arbitration boards.

Domino's Pizza

In most ways, Domino's Pizza is a typical franchise industry firm. The company came into being at the start of franchising's transition from a method of distribution to a separate industry and over the next twenty-five years followed a pattern common to successful franchisers. In the beginning Domino's was a traditional small business; it became a franchiser only after its product and the system for its production were well developed. Tom Monaghan, one of Domino's founders, turned to franchising in 1967 because of the success of McDonald's. But as often happens with new franchisers, Monaghan did not fully realize that he had entered a new business and so failed to develop adequate training programs for franchisees and other services that now made up his main product. As a result, the company underwent a crisis that lasted until Domino's had built the infrastructure and developed the techniques required for its new market. Once the company possessed a system to produce franchises with the same efficiency it had earlier used to manufacture pizzas, it was able to begin the rapid expansion characteristic of a successful franchise industry firm. By the late 1970s Domino's was opening more than three new outlets a week.[26]

Finding the Product, 1960–1967

Tom and Jim Monaghan founded Domino's in December 1960, when they purchased a small pizza shop in Ypsilanti, Michigan, for $500 cash and agreed to assume the store's $8,000 debt. Neither of the brothers planned to work in the business full-time. Jim, who had convinced his older brother to invest in the shop, viewed it primarily as a potentially profitable hobby. Tom saw Dominick's, as the business was called then, as a part-time venture to help cover the cost of his studies at the University of Michigan. The brothers bought the shop from Dominick DeVarti, a friend of Jim's and a restaurateur from the nearby city of Ann Arbor. DeVarti had found that he could not give the store the attention it needed to be profitable so he was willing to sell it cheaply. Jim believed that he and his brother had found a bargain. At first it seemed that he might be right. Sales increased quickly under the Monaghans' constant supervision; by June the store was earning about $400 a week in profits, but then sales quickly fell off when most of the students, who were the main customers, went home for the summer. Faced with the prospect of a lean period, Jim, who had never given up his job at the post office, finally tired of the long hours and sold Tom his half of the business in 1961 for full ownership of the firm's delivery car, a 1959 Volkswagen Beetle.[27]

After his brother's abrupt departure, Tom found that increasingly the shop required more effort and produced less money than expected. Jim's departure forced a choice that Monaghan had been considering for some time, and the same year he decided to quit school so he could devote more energy to the business. Had the store been more profitable, Monaghan might not have been tempted either to improve its operation or open additional outlets, but as it was, he felt compelled to do both and in the process developed Domino's franchising system.[28]

The profits and appearance of the original store were unimpressive, but in a rough way it already contained the key elements of Domino's future format. Its location next to the Eastern Michigan University campus proved to be well suited to Domino's products, and to this day the company continues to concentrate on reaching the student market. Like modern

Domino's outlets, the original store was small, had a limited menu, and relied on takeout and free delivery for the bulk of its business. Although Monaghan experimented with other formats and other locations for the next five or six years, he directed most of his efforts toward perfecting the shop and format he had purchased from DeVarti.[29] The process of refining Domino's system for making pizza proceeded in a piecemeal fashion and by the mid-1960s had come to include almost every aspect of the business. As part of the original purchase arrangement, DeVarti had given the Monaghans recipes and lessons in pizza making, but these brief sessions left the brothers unprepared for the complexities of operating and managing even their single outlet. Painfully aware of his lack of experience, Tom spent much of his time visiting pizzerias in other cities to get advice on recipes and operations. Among the first fruits of these visits, which by 1969 had taken him to over three hundred stores, was a new sauce recipe from an operator in nearby Lansing. Other changes included the installation of a "ferris wheel" type of revolving oven, which could accommodate more pies in less space than conventional ovens, and the practice of placing pizzas on rigid screens rather than directly on the oven shelves, which allowed for faster, easier handling and reduced the losses from misshaped pies.[30]

Monaghan's own experiences in the shop led to further refinements. Before the end of the first year, he restructured the interior of the store and rearranged counters, coolers, and work areas to improve the flow of work in all phases of the operation from order taking to delivery. When completed, Monaghan's system was reminiscent of those developed by the managers of White Castle Hamburgers in the 1920s, the McDonald brothers in the 1940s, and other fast-food pioneers. In each case, success depended on adapting the techniques of mass production to the restaurant business. In taking this approach, Monaghan, like the others, viewed the production process as a unified whole, requiring the standardization of materials, thoughtful placement of equipment, and detailed division of labor—all geared to achieve continuous production of a limited product line. And as in the case of other fast-food pioneers, Monaghan's marketing strategy of speedy service and uniform quality led him to a mass-production system. He found that during peak times, the only way to ensure fast delivery was to create a comprehensive and coordinated system of production that covered every step in the pizza-making process.

Domino's entered the franchise industry in 1967 with a significant advantage, its production system was standardized and therefore more easily reproducible.[31]

Franchising was still a long way off in August 1961, when Monaghan's brother left the shop. After school ended for the summer, sales fell to almost nothing and Tom was unsure how to revive his now-dormant business. Recognizing that part of his problem was ignorance, Monaghan took in a partner later that year in hopes of getting the experience he believed the business needed. On the surface, his choice of James Gilmore seemed perfect. In his fifties at the time, Gilmore had long familiarity with the formal dining, institutional, and casual sides of the restaurant business. In fact, Gilmore had worked in just about every area of the business except the fast-food sector, where Monaghan was struggling to find his niche. Overall, Monaghan's four-year partnership with Gilmore was a disappointment because it slowed development by pulling the company into more conventional, and for Domino's, unprofitable, restaurants. Monaghan, whose interests lay in the fast-food sector, discovered that conventional restaurant practices, which emphasized broad menus, individualized sit-down service, and high overhead, did not blend well with his strategy of high-volume and low-profit margins.[32]

In 1965 he severed his partnership with Gilmore and returned the company to its original base in pizza. At the same time he was also beginning to consider the possibilities of franchising. Ray Kroc's well-publicized success in moving McDonald's into an area where the potential for growth and profits was much higher first put the idea into his mind. Monaghan knew that the pizza business alone would never give him more than a moderate income. As the owner of three stores by 1965, he was coming to realize than his potential for expansion using company ownership was limited but that his format and past experience were amenable to expansion through franchising.[33]

Monaghan also had first-hand experience with the problems of establishing a small business, a perspective that undoubtedly gave him additional faith in the value of franchising. In its early years, Domino's had lurched from crisis to crisis, most of which were brought about by the Monaghans' inexperience. One of its first trials occurred before the store even opened. Prior to selling the shop, DeVarti contracted for a quarter-page advertisement in the yellow pages costing nearly $70 a month, a sizable amount considering that the shop's monthly rent was only $100. Neither brother had thought to ask about any agreements that might be binding on them in their new business, so they were taken by surprise when the telephone company refused to connect their phones until they agreed to pay for the advertisement. The Monaghans resisted on the grounds that they had not requested and could not afford the ad. The telephone company stood firm. Thus, for its first month Domino's had no telephone. For a business that specialized in take-out and delivery services, the lack of a phone was catastrophic, so in the end the brothers were forced to pay for an ad they did not want.[34]

Tom Monaghan's lack of experience showed most clearly in the administrative side of the business. For months he kept the accounts in a spiral-ring notebook with "income" listed on one half of the page and "outgo" on the other. During their first four months of operation, the Monaghans were unaware that they were required to charge a state sales tax. It was only Tom's chance conversation with a bookkeeper that saved them from a potentially crippling tax liability. Inexperience also made ordering supplies a problem, and in the first year Monaghan often had to run to nearby groceries to purchase toppings.[35]

The reorientation of the company after Gilmore's departure, finalizing the name change to Domino's, and the addition of another corporate store delayed the move to franchising until 1967, when Monaghan sold his first three franchises. By then Domino's was well placed to begin franchising. Its emphasis on uniform quality and rapid delivery had given it a unique and complete system for operating a pizza shop. The company had a clear, well-established local identity, and its management was experienced, if not yet professional, in the tasks supporting store openings, such as site selection and lease negotiation. It also had the beginnings of a supply and administrative system. To save space and enhance quality control at its company stores, Domino's prepared all raw materials off-site and delivered them to the outlets daily. The accounts of all four stores were likewise centralized, with the home office processing the outlets' financial records. This gave Monaghan's staff at least some experience with collecting and organizing financial data from a number of stores.[36]

During his first two years as a franchiser, Monaghan moved slowly and avoided problems. In his first sale, for example, he sidestepped difficulties with site selection, remodeling, and equipment supply by selling the licensee an existing outlet. This method was clearly unsuitable for any major expansion, however, and in the next sale, he took responsibility for locating, leasing, remodeling, and equipping the outlet and training the franchisee. Once the outlet opened, Domino's was committed to furnish the owner with all supplies needed to produce and package the pizza, to provide advertising, and to keep all financial records. In exchange, Domino's received a franchise fee of $4,475, a royalty of 2½ percent on gross to be paid monthly, a 2 percent advertising fee to be used for the general benefit of all members of the Domino's system, a 1 percent bookkeeping fee, and the profits from equipment and supply sales.[37]

Tom Monaghan quickly threw himself into the franchise business with gusto and fell into the overexpansion trap that often destroys new business-format franchisers. His first mistake was to commit his company to providing too many services to his franchisees. His second was his failure to create an infrastructure capable of producing the services he promised. Like many new franchisers, Monaghan did not realize that he was in a new business. After 1969 his main product was pizza shops, not pizza. That demanded new production techniques, which he was slow to develop.

As late as 1969, Monaghan still viewed franchises as products that could be made using what amounted to craft production techniques. The terms of his franchise agreements varied, stores were located without any formal analysis of traffic patterns or neighborhood demographics, and owners were expected to run their stores after only a few weeks of informal instruction. To be successful, a franchise industry firm needs to produce the bundle of services that make up its product in high volume at a relatively low cost. This, in turn, requires an organization capable of providing a uniform product using techniques that approximate economies of scale and scope. Domino's did not develop such a system until a near-failure prompted the company to reorganize its franchise production system.[38]

Monaghan made a few slight adjustments to meet the demands of his new business, but these changes were designed to increase sales, not improve production. For example, during this period, Domino's came up with an innovative method of financing franchise sales. In order to make the $15,000 cost of establishing an outlet more affordable to the company employees who were Domino's main market, Monaghan worked out a system whereby Domino's would find two outside investors who were each willing to purchase a one-quarter interest in a new store, with Domino's purchasing another quarter. The franchisee could then either pay cash and acquire the remaining 25 percent share right away or pay nothing and receive the share after the store cleared $6,000 in profits. Aside from giving the company an added voice in the operation of its stores, this approach provided a way to attract ambitious store managers and interest them in purchasing franchises of their own. In 1969 a Domino's manager could buy 25 percent of a franchise unit for an initial cash payment of $1,250, which, according to Monaghan, would "return $3,000.00 to $5,000.00 the first year."[39]

To help reach the general public, Domino's developed its first promotional literature in 1969. According to this brochure, the company offered a "unique franchise opportunity" with numerous benefits provided by "DOMINO'S STAFF for training, production, and accounting." Before the drive for new franchises was fully underway, however, Domino's flimsy support organization collapsed under the first trickle of what Monaghan had hoped would be a flood of franchisees.[40]

In 1969 Monaghan launched a campaign to make Domino's "the MacDonald's [sic] of the pizza industry," and for a brief time his goal seemed realistic. Between the opening of corporate stores, the sale of single-store franchises, and the efforts of a few area franchisees who had the exclusive right to develop Domino's stores in a given territory, the company was opening one store a week. In June 1969, with twenty-two stores already open, Monaghan confidently predicted that "by the time the Christmas party season arrives we'll have 100 [stores] in operation." Instead, by Christmas Domino's had opened only forty-four stores and faced a nearly crushing $1.5 million debt.[41]

Domino's crash of 1969 came suddenly. Ever the optimist, Tom Monaghan had relied heavily on credit to finance expansion and operating costs and to cover the lavish spending by the home office, which after too many lean years did not always use its newfound wealth wisely. When royalty payments and supply profits from spottily trained and poorly supported franchisees were lower than anticipated and franchise sales lagged, Domino's found itself unable to pay its approximately $1.5 million debt. To make matters worse, the commissary and main offices had been destroyed in a fire in early 1968, disrupting deliveries and forcing the company to reconstruct its records, a task that strained an already-overburdened system.[42]

At the center of the problems leading to the crash was the lack of an organized franchise production system. The company came out with its then-famous "Domino's people are pizza people, period" advertising slogan in 1969, but by that time this statement was no longer true. The home office's primary job was the manufacture and sale of the host of services that made up the Domino's franchise, and the company was only beginning to professionalize its operations in these areas. Without a strong production and control system, quality suffered, and this in turn drew down royalty payments and supply profits. Company sales, for example, rose from $2 million in 1968 to $4 million in 1969, a 100 percent increase. At the same time, however, sales per store dropped about 45 percent. The growing confusion at the home office probably also accounted for some of the slump in franchise sales, as the company recruited most of its franchisees from within and those employees already had first-hand knowledge of Domino's problems.[43]

Recovery from the crash of 1969 came slowly. Creditors' confidence in Monaghan was badly shaken, and in May 1970 the Ypsilanti Savings Bank, which held a large portion of the company's debt, forced him to temporarily turn over control of Domino's to an area businessman who specialized in rescuing troubled companies. The original arrangement was for two years, but the bank's interim manager found the situation so difficult that after ten months he returned Monaghan to the helm. Monaghan's first action was to slash the corporate staff and call a temporary halt to expansion. To pay off the company's most pressing debts, he sold $50,000 worth of his stock and borrowed from franchisees and suppliers. These changes were only stopgap measures, however, and before Monaghan had a chance to go much further he had to deal with a revolt among a small group of franchisees.[44]

Franchisee discontent over inadequate bookkeeping and supply services had existed for some time and finally boiled over shortly after Monaghan's return. In early 1971, thirteen franchisees brought a class-action suit against Domino's, charging that it violated antitrust laws because some early contracts required franchisees to purchase supplies from Domino's or a company-approved supplier. The real issue, however, was the company's inability to provide continuing support and service at a level that franchisees believed justified royalty payments of 5.5 percent of gross sales. During the expansion of 1969, Domino's promised new recruits easy access to its "professional team of experts," which stood ready to assist the franchise holder in "any area" of his or her business. Unfortunately, Domino's made this commitment before it had the ability to keep it, and as the home office cut service and raised supply prices to forestall bankruptcy, franchisee discontent mounted. The suit itself simmered until 1973, when Monaghan bought out several disgruntled franchisees and began to improve his supply and support services.[45]

In an effort to correct the problems that had led to the crash of 1969 and the revolt of 1971, management began to build a system that would make the company into a true franchise industry firm. Over the next eight years, it redesigned and refined its corporate infrastructure until it could provide the services its franchisees had contracted for in high volume at a relatively low cost.

Building the Infrastructure

In 1972, with Monaghan back in control and the company's position fairly stable, management was able to begin the tasks of analyzing the causes of the crash and devising a way to ensure full recovery and future growth. It was clear to Monaghan that the administrative tangle that had prevented the home office from realizing the extent of the company's problems in training, supervision, and cash flow was directly related to the rapid expansion of 1969. The earlier success of the nonfranchised units proved that Domino's had a good product, but, as the crash itself demonstrated, the flaw was in production.[46]

One of the first major changes undertaken by Monaghan was to shift some of the burdens of franchisee recruiting and development to his existing franchisees. Prior to 1969, most of Domino's expansion came through the sale of single-unit franchises, which granted the holder the right to operate a single store. This allowed the company greater control and produced higher per-unit profits, but it also put too great a burden on the firm in training, supply, and service. In the early 1970s Domino's did not have the personnel or the organization to carry out these functions on a large scale. Therefore, as many franchisers do in their early years, Domino's began to push the sale of larger territories. As a general rule, it sold the rights to build and operate stores in an entire city, but in some cases it granted the rights to develop entire states.[47]

From Monaghan's standpoint, the main attraction of the area franchise was not the slightly larger fee that Domino's charged, but rather its potential for rapid expansion. The company could keep its initial fee fairly low ($10,000 in 1973) because area franchisees had to "license, appoint, establish, train, supervise and control all DOMINO Pizza stores" in their particular area. In effect, it formed a series of partnerships with its area franchisees giving them greater profits in exchange for assuming much of the responsibility for managing a given territory according to company standards. Unlike other firms that relied heavily on this method for expansion, Domino's could use area franchisees with a fair amount of confidence because the company had always recruited most of its franchisees from within. In this way, Monaghan had reasonable assurance that area franchises would be more likely to follow the Domino's model in locating, supplying, and operating units.[48]

While Domino's was delegating responsibility for holding the system together to its area franchisees, the home office was revamping its recruitment, training, and support programs to ensure that it would regain control over its operations. Monaghan's goal was to provide franchisees with a level of training that would guarantee their ability to operate their stores in a profitable, professional way and to maintain the uniform product quality that was vital to the success of the parent company.

In looking back at the reasons for the crash of 1969, Monaghan believed that one of the chief causes for the uneven performance of Domino's outlets was the decision to market franchises to people from outside the company. These new franchisees, he thought, had lacked adequate experience and training. Given the sketchy training franchisees actually received, he may have been right. But one of the main reasons people buy a franchise is so training can substitute for experience, at least in the critical first few years when most small businesses fail. Thus, if Domino's wished to become a true franchise industry firm, it had to provide better training.[49]

To correct problems in training, Domino's reverted back to its original policy of selling most franchises internally. It also formalized its training program to make sure that future franchise holders, whether internal or not, received adequate instruction to master Domino's methods. This shift caused growth to slow somewhat, and the company ended 1972 with only thirty-four stores open. Yet sales at these remaining outlets more than doubled between 1969 and 1972. Despite the growth in sales, Monaghan was still interested in expansion, but he realized that, given its relatively small base, it would be impossible for Domino's to expand quickly by relying on franchise sales to former employees. Thus, for all these reasons training became a top priority in Domino's rebirth.[50]

One of Monaghan's most important changes occurred in 1973, when he established the "College of Pizzarology." Modeled after McDonald's famous "Hamburger University," Domino's school combined classroom instruction with in-store training. The curriculum changed somewhat between 1973 and 1978, but generally it consisted of a number of short but intensive courses in management and operations and several weeks of paid apprenticeship, when franchisees observed and performed every task associated with operating a store. By formalizing the initial training and taking it out of the shop, Monaghan not only captured economies of scale and enhanced uniformity but also guaranteed that the focus would be on training because instructors no longer had to divide their attention between training franchisees and serving customers. Once trainees had mastered the basics, the formal apprenticeship in a company-owned outlet was a vital part of the instructional program, giving new franchisees familiarity with the rhythms of the business and an understanding of how Domino's techniques worked in practice.[51]

Throughout the 1970s and into the 1980s, Domino's continued to stress adequate instruction at all levels. Franchisees who wished to extend their month-long initial training program could do so. To guarantee that training filtered down to the shop floor, the company developed a week-long course for franchise holders' employees. To supplement and reinforce worker training, Domino's offered—for a fee—a wide variety of instructional tapes and similar materials that franchisees could use in teaching themselves and their employees Domino's methods.[52]

By the mid-1970s, then, Domino's had begun a formal system of training, and Monaghan again felt ready to try selling franchisees to outsiders. Because Domino's did "not have a staff specifically for this purpose," he turned to one of a host of firms that sprang up to serve the growing franchise industry. In mid-1974 Domino's began negotiations with Seltz Franchise Developments of New York to prepare franchise recruiting materials and find potential customers for the company. Perhaps because

The Domino's system in action. Note the emphasis on uniformity and continuous flow production. (Photo courtesy of Domino's Pizza, Inc.)

Domino's traditionally had recruited franchisees from within the company or possibly because the company was still following a conservative policy of expansion, very little came of this second effort to enter the general franchise market. By the time Monaghan finally initiated his second major franchise campaign in 1978, Domino's already possessed a franchise development program that was capable of recruiting an adequate number of franchisees.[53]

In recruiting franchisees from the ranks of company employees, progress was more rapid. From the start, Monaghan had favored this policy. In part, this was due to his faith in the soundness of his system. He believed that employees, who understood the company, would be more interested in buying into it than outsiders. Moreover, this approach simplified training because franchisees from within were already familiar with most aspects of the business. Finally, Monaghan thought that this policy led to greater employee productivity and loyalty because it offered employees the chance for ownership. Like Domino's training system, internal recruitment became a formal program during the 1970s.[54]

From the earliest days of the business, Monaghan had encouraged corporate store managers to purchase a part interest in the stores they operated, so the move from manager to franchisee was often a short and logical step. During the late 1970s, however, the company made two specific changes to codify this system and increase franchise sales. The first action, taken in 1979, was the establishment of a sponsorship program, whereby the company agreed to pay existing franchisees either $15,000 in one lump sum or a percentage of the royalties produced by any qualified managers during the first five years following their purchase of a Domino's franchise. The rationale for this move was that existing franchisees had already provided Domino's with a service by training the new store owner; if the firm compensated them for the loss of experienced personnel, owners might be more willing to encourage employees to establish outlets of their own.[55]

The second change made in the late 1970s was an attempt to stimulate future franchise sales by creating a new position, the Corporate Area Representative, whose job was to act as an interface between the regional sales office and the outlets and to coordinate local activities, such as special sales promotions, between outlets. This position was unique in that it was "not structured to offer potential as a permanent career." Instead, Domino's managers believed that "going into franchising" was the next logical step.[56]

Overall, the internal recruiting programs were very effective. In the early 1980s Monaghan estimated that 92 percent of Domino's franchise holders were former company employees. Moreover, as the company expanded, so did its pool of potential internal candidates. Despite the preponderance of internal franchisees, Domino's did sell franchises to outsiders and, like so many of the company's operations, this system became more organized in the late 1970s. In 1978 the firm appointed its first full-time director of franchise marketing and began to market franchises to the general public.[57]

One of the most valuable services that Domino's offered its new franchisees was a greatly improved operations manual. Franchisees have been known to refer to their operations manual as "the bible"—and with good reason. Running almost any business is a complicated affair and no matter how thorough their training, most franchisees are likely to need occasional assistance in determining procedures and policies. At these times, the operations manual serves as the final authority. Domino's drew up its first manual in 1972. Designed as a reference work rather than a unified explanation of outlet operations, the manual defies easy summary. By the late 1970s it was roughly two inches thick and described the correct procedure for every aspect of store operations down to the smallest detail, from checking the quality of supplies through the actual delivery of a pizza. Like the courses at the College of Pizzarology, the content of the operations manual evolved throughout the mid-1970s. Thus, by 1979 the company had perfected a formal training program that explained every aspect of outlet operations.[58]

Company officials also exhibited a keen awareness of their true product when they established strict proprietary rights to the contents of the operations manual and training aids. Manuals were loaned to every store owner or manager but they remained the property of the home office. To ensure that managers did not learn their trade at Domino's and then leave to start a competing shop, a clause in their contract prohibited franchisees from owning a competing business for one year (later this was changed to two years) after the expiration of their franchise. Contracts also barred franchisees from ever using trade secrets learned during their association with the company.[59]

Another crucial area where Domino's professionalized its support system was in store identification. Because it catered to the take-out trade, the company had largely ignored store appearance and concentrated on product uniformity and speedy service for most of the ten years following the design of the corporate logo in 1965. Beginning in 1975, however, Domino's extended its search for a coherent image beyond pizza and free delivery and undertook a systematic approach to creating a uniform appearance for its outlets and the company as a whole. In that year, Domino's commissioned Group 243 Design, the firm, run by a former employee, that had been doing most of Domino's site selection and remodeling work, to develop an "identity manual" that would establish a standard image for all of its outlets. Although Domino's had always required franchisees to display uniform signs on buildings and delivery vehicles, the introduction of the identity manual was a major step forward in building a complete and uniform image for the entire Domino's system. The manual eventually covered every aspect of the store, including not only detailed designs for outlets in a variety of styles but also standardized plans and specifications for equipment and fixtures, employee uniforms, stationery, business cards, and so forth.[60]

To safeguard its new image, Domino's followed the standard industry practice of only loaning franchisees the identity manual. It is unclear whether this increased concern about protecting the company's image stemmed from an awareness that success in the franchise industry depended on extending the company's proprietary claims beyond its product or whether it was merely part of the process of professionalization. In either case, the results were the same. By the mid-1970s Domino's sold a franchise that promised—and delivered—its holder a complete business, and, consequently, the company found it necessary to safeguard the integrity of the entire system.[61]

The importance of protecting its trade name was forcefully brought home to management in 1975 when Amstar, the producer of Domino sugar, sued Domino's Pizza for trademark infringement. For the next five years Domino's found itself enmeshed in a legal battle that cost the company millions of dollars and thousands of hours. For Domino's, it was vital to win this suit. As the company itself had come to appreciate only shortly before Amstar's action, one of the key parts of the system a franchisee purchased was the recognition that went with the Domino's name. Although under the terms of the franchise contracts Domino's had the right to alter its trademarks, Amstar's initial victory in the case caused serious concern among franchisees and was used as an excuse by a few dissatisfied ones to temporarily withhold payment of their 5½ percent royalty fee and 3 percent advertising contribution.[62]

Tom Monaghan's actions after his firm won the case on appeal clearly demonstrated his belief in the importance of trade names. After losing in the lower court, Domino's was ordered to remove its name from all stores within eighteen months. Having planned for this contingency, the company's design group had come up with a new name, Pizza Dispatch, and as the trial progressed, several outlets were opened using this designation. Monaghan and Group 243 Design officials were surprised to learn that the new name actually tested better than Domino's in defining the outlet's product. Even after Domino's successful appeal in 1980, some executives argued in favor of keeping the name, Pizza Dispatch. Monaghan agreed that that appellation more accurately described the Domino's system but rejected the change on the ground that the company's franchisees had purchased the right to use the Domino's name and to the consumer acceptance that it had engendered. Domino's did not completely abandon the Pizza Dispatch trade name and continues to operate stores that use it. The image of these new stores, which are essentially identical to Domino's, remains distinct and is marketed as a separate franchise—in much the same way that a product franchiser like Ford grants separate contracts for its Lincoln and Mercury lines.[63]

An additional motive for standardizing the equipment and appearance of outlets seems to have been the desire to recapture some of the lucrative supply business for the company or, at the very least, to increase its level of service and hence the franchisees' reliance on the home office. Like most other franchisers, Domino's offered a full line of equipment and supplies to its dealers; however, since the *Chicken Delight* decision of 1971, it had allowed them to purchase from whatever sources they wished as long as they met the company's standards for quality. Domino's managers believed that with the advantages of bulk purchasing, coupled with the firm's ability to provide its outlets with a full line of equipment and supplies at a competitive price, they would be able to capture most of this lucrative market. After 1978, when Monaghan expanded his commissary system, this did, in fact, happen. By speeding up deliveries, reducing prices, and simplifying ordering, the company increased franchisee use from 63 percent in 1978 to over 90 percent by the early 1980s. And even though some franchisees chose not to use the commissary service, Domino's still gained because simply having it made the franchises more salable. People buy franchises because they offer advantages over independent ownership. Instead of having to shop for equipment and then deal with a multitude of supplies once the outlet was established, franchisees could buy everything they needed from the company and have it delivered on the same truck.[64]

By the late 1970s, then, Monaghan had made great strides in reorienting his business and building a solid system to provide a complete package of services designed to virtually guarantee franchise success. Improvements in training, store design, and outlet supply operations all strengthened the power of the home office by increasing its ability to make a uniform product, the Domino's Pizza shop, in high volume and at a relatively low cost. As typically occurs with mature business-format franchisers, the completion of a corporate infrastructure to provide these services led to a policy restricting the authority of large area franchises. This change reflected the enhanced capabilities of the home office, the desire of its managers to gain economies of scale and scope, and perhaps Monaghan's increased awareness that ultimately Domino's success rested on its ability to provide the public with a uniform product and its franchisees with the means to satisfy this demand. In 1979, when its training program was perfected, its operations and identity manuals were complete, and its supply system was reorganized, Domino's decided to curtail the sale of large area franchises.

In place of the old area franchisees, where the terms of the agreement varied as to the number of outlets franchise holders could open and the specific services they must provide were vaguely defined, Domino's new multiunit franchise limited the holder to a maximum of five stores per contract, set a rigid timetable for store openings, and increased home office control over training, store operations, and supervision. Under the new contracts, Domino's agreed to pay the cost of site selection for the first shop and to allow the $29,500 franchise fee to cover all five stores. In return, the franchise holder agreed to open the five units at set intervals, with the last store to be opened just under two years of the first. In addition, the multiunit franchisee had to absorb the costs of site selection for all units after the first, for remodeling, and for advertising his or her grand opening.[65]

To ensure that multiunit franchisers were well versed in all of Domino's methods, the company required that they complete the now–fully developed employee selection and training program, including courses in site location, lease negotiation, and other subjects designed specifically for the multiunit franchisee. The company also had the right to approve all store managers and mandate their formal training by the home office. Finally, in a move to motivate store managers, Domino's required that they either own part of the outlet they managed or receive a percentage of its profits.[66]

Domino's shift to small multiunit franchises reflected abilities and concerns that were typical of a mature business-format franchiser. In the late 1960s, while trying to establish himself in the market, Monaghan willingly sacrificed a measure of control and profits for rapid expansion. By the late 1970s he no longer needed to rely as much on area franchisees and could supply franchisee services more efficiently in any case. More importantly, consolidation of control, training, advertising, operations, and supply not only guaranteed greater uniformity, but it also diminished the threat that any single franchisee or group of franchisees might become powerful enough to defy the parent company. Franchisee relations had been generally good since the revolt in 1971, but as Monaghan was doubtlessly aware, franchisees purchased much more than the right to use Domino's trade name and recipes. If his company was to continue to thrive, it was vital that Domino's, and not its area franchisees, provide the services that franchisees continually required.[67]

Conclusion

By 1979, when the company had nearly 300 stores in operation, Tom Monaghan attempted a second major expansion. Unlike in 1969, this time he achieved considerable success. Between 1979 and 1985, Domino's and its area franchisees opened over 2,500 outlets, or slightly more than one store per day. Monaghan could do this because in the years between 1969 and 1979 he had reoriented the company and developed an infrastructure that was capable of providing training, support, and supplies in high volume and at a relatively low cost. The key to his success in developing this support system was his ability to apply the principles of mass production to the creation of small business. After 1972 every major change in the structure of his company was intended to approximate economies of scale and scope, standardize the product, and coordinate its production and institutional support.[68]

In more general terms, Domino's and other franchise industry firms succeeded because of changes in the basic structure of the economy. With the creation of the modern economy came dozens of managerial innovations and specialized services designed to assist the large-scale enterprises that have dominated the American economic landscape during the twentieth century. These were the basic services that the business-format franchise provided small business owners. Because they typically did not use elaborate managerial tools such as cost accounting or inventory control systems and because they lacked the capital for specialized services such as professional advertising or specially designed outlets, small businesses were often thought to have little or no need for these services. As perceptive entrepreneurs came to realize in the 1950s, however, most of these services were neither irrelevant nor impractical for the small business owner if they could be provided at an affordable price.

The Franchise Industry and Domino's Pizza

The franchise contract provided the perfect tool for this purpose. By the 1950s product franchisees had already demonstrated that the franchise contract offered an invaluable organizational tool that was capable of combining large and small business into a single administrative unit. Through this unique form of organization, big business produced small businesses and in doing so did, in fact, create a system that combined the economic efficiency and security of big business with the independence of small business. Although substantial debate continues on exactly how independent this new breed of small business owner really is, the economic benefits of the franchise system are indisputable. Recently, more than one-half of all independent businesses have failed within five years. In contrast, fewer than 5 percent of franchised businesses have suffered the same fate.[69]

Conclusion

Between the 1860s and the 1950s two distinct types of franchise systems developed in the United States. The first, product franchising, had its origins in the 1840s, when the makers of complex and expensive manufactured goods began to modify the agency system to more effectively penetrate the expanding national market. The second, business-format franchising, first appeared in the 1920s but did not develop into an industry until the late 1950s, when shrewd entrepreneurs came to realize that because of the advantages it offered the potential business owner, the franchise could be marketed as a distinct product.

After examining five firms that have made extensive use of the franchise system, it is possible to reach some general conclusions in each of the following areas: the development of the franchise system in the American economy, the influence of traditional business practices in shaping modern large-scale enterprises, and the interaction of large and small businesses in the modern economy.

To begin with, product franchising was an outgrowth of the modern economy that developed as part of the search for more efficient ways of organizing and administering distribution by big business. As events at the McCormick Harvesting Machine Company and the I. M. Singer Company show, the makers of complex and costly manufactured goods such as reapers and sewing machines found that existing wholesalers were either unwilling or unable to distribute their products. In order to move their goods beyond a local market, these manufacturers did what business owners traditionally have done in similar cases: they established direct links with independent retailers who became their exclusive legal representatives in a particular area. Agency sales, as this method was called,

Conclusion

had several advantages that made it a logical choice for new firms trying to establish or expand their reach. McCormick and Singer, each of which lacked money and experience, were originally drawn to selling through agents because it was a cheap and effective way to tap the national market. By using agents whose duties were spelled out by contract, both firms gained at least nominal assurance that their goods would be sold at a uniform price and provided with maintenance and repair services. Agents offered these services at a cost far below that of establishing company-owned stores. Thus, in their early years of operation, the agency system allowed McCormick and Singer to concentrate the bulk of their time and scarce resources on the more complex problem of developing methods for high-volume, low-cost production.

Once McCormick and Singer reached high-volume production, it became necessary to modify the agency system to give them better control over the flow of goods and information through the firm. Here their paths diverged. At McCormick, improved coordination began with the creation of the Agency Department in 1859. By this time McCormick had made the transition from small firm to big business, and this subtly changed its relationship with dealers. To coordinate the distribution of the company's increased output, the Agency Department began to formalize dealer relations and to develop more uniform sales policies. By absorbing dealers partially into the administrative structure of the company, McCormick undermined the basic equality that had characterized the old agency relationship. Agents no longer bargained with the company on the terms of their contracts, nor did they have as wide a latitude in the operation of their business. But owing to the seasonal nature of McCormick's product line, which did not allow dealers to market the company's products exclusively, McCormick never developed a true franchise system because it never gained full control over its dealers' livelihood.

Singer abandoned agency sales for the same general reasons as McCormick, but Singer replaced agency with a very different type of distribution system. Once production shot up after 1856, Singer began to phase out agents in favor of a dual distribution system based on company-owned stores to serve the lucrative urban market and independent, but tightly controlled, agents in less fruitful areas. Once it became possible and profitable for dealers to specialize almost exclusively in the sale of Singer products, the company could establish rigid control over its dealers. This gave

Singer a powerful tool with which to control dealer actions by offering them the opportunity to earn steady profits in exchange for limiting their freedom of action as independent owners. Despite their differences, however, organizational changes at both Singer and McCormick were evolutionary, not revolutionary.

As America's economy matured, the nature of the franchise relationship became more elaborate and more clearly defined. The Ford Motor Company, for example, accomplished the transition in distribution from independent agents to franchised dealers very quickly, primarily because it made the leap from small to big business in the space of only a few years. Thus, Ford experienced the same types of pressures as McCormick and Singer much earlier in its existence. In the decade between the founding of the Ford Motor Company in 1903 and Henry Ford's introduction of mass production in 1913, revolutionizing the automobile industry, the firm created a large and well-coordinated distribution system based almost entirely on the use of franchised dealers. Like McCormick and Singer, Ford originally established its own connections with agents because existing wholesalers were unable to market its wares. In the days before the Model T, Ford felt little need to establish uniform standards of dealer performance and lacked the resources to monitor dealer actions closely in any case. As the company grew in size, however, it became necessary to take a greater interest in the operation of the outlets that sold its products. One of the reasons Ford could do this was that the nation's improved communications network made it relatively easy for the company to gather reliable information on markets and dealer operations quickly and continuously. This, in turn, reduced the company's dependence on the judgment of its independent agents and gave the home office the ability to formulate sales policies on a national scale, while Ford's considerable influence with its dealers guaranteed that its wishes would be carried out.

At Ford, the largely equal relationship of principal and agent came to be replaced by the symbiotic relationship of franchiser and franchisee—even before the company began mass production in 1913. Given its size, power, or virtually any other measure, Ford clearly had the ability to dictate to its dealers and it did not hesitate to use its power to set the boundaries of this new relationship. Nevertheless, as it eventually discovered, Ford depended on its dealers as much as they depended on the company.

Ultimately, this tension between the overwhelming power of the fac-

tory on the one hand and its dependence on the dealer force on the other
defined the boundaries of the product franchise. Until the late-1930s Ford
built its franchise program almost exclusively around making the most
of the advantages it held over dealers. This approach worked fairly well
when times were good, but it gave dealers little incentive to stay with the
company when profits slipped. One of the lessons Ford executives learned
from the Great Depression was that the long-term health of their business
depended on a strong and contented dealer force. In the late 1930s Ford
began to revamp its franchise system to give dealers some protection from
the power of the company and to increase the profitability of their operations. It did this by revising contracts to eliminate the threat of sudden
termination without cause and by creating mechanisms to tie the manufacturer and its dealers even more closely together. These mechanisms
took the form of operating and training manuals covering most phases of a
dealer's operations, elaborate administrative structures to oversee dealer
operations, and special organizations such as the Universal Credit Corporation to help dealers finance the purchase of Ford products and the Dealer
Policy Board to give dealers a voice in company affairs and to mediate
disputes between dealers and the company.

While Ford executives were busy building their distribution system,
oil refiners were adapting franchising to their own needs. Like earlier
product franchisers, refiners turned to the system when existing distributors proved unable to market their products. Refiners' use of franchising
marked a major expansion of the system. Gasoline was, by and large, a
generic good. Consumers could not readily tell the product of one refiner
from another and found it difficult to judge the impact of various brands
on the operation of their vehicles. In the oil industry, the special handling gasoline required led refiners to product franchising, but it was their
desire to create a distinct brand identity for their fuel that led them to develop business-format franchising. Because the successful sale of gasoline
required outlets constructed specifically for that purpose, refiners quickly
recognized that the outlet itself could be used to create a distinct image
for the gasoline it sold. As the point of contact between producers and
consumers, the gasoline station played a major role in influencing consumers' buying habits. When they recognized this, refiners such as the
Sun Oil Company began to take an active role in dealers' operations. Like
other product franchisers, Sun found itself tied closely to dealers whom

the public viewed as nearly synonymous with the company and, out of necessity, developed elaborate systems to control and assist the thousands of independent dealers that sold its products.

Sun, like most other refiners, achieved the high degree of uniformity it required by developing a system dealing with all aspects of station operation—from training and uniforms to advertising and equipment. In this way, acceptance of the refiners' system offered dealers the path of least resistance in organizing and operating their businesses. As an added incentive, refiners provided most of these specialized services to dealers at costs far lower than could be had from outside sources. This, together with dealer recognition of the importance of uniform standards of appearance and service, allowed refiners to remain legally independent of the dealers who sold their products while maintaining a strong influence over their operations.

The final change in the franchise system occurred in the late 1950s, when the well-publicized success of postwar franchisers such as McDonald's kicked off a "boom" that led to the development of franchising as an industry in and of itself. Unlike prewar franchisers, the majority of firms entering the field after World War II were business-format franchisers. The proven suitability of business-format franchising to the sale of generic goods and services vastly increased the areas where franchises could be used, but the greatest expansion took place after franchisers and the public came to regard the business-format franchise as a business opportunity. Because the franchisee bought a package of services that virtually guaranteed profitability, the product actually sold through the outlet became less important than the other parts of the package, and just about anything that could be sold through a specialized outlet could now be franchised.

The main reason for this new use of franchising was the maturation of the modern economy. In a business-format franchise, the parent company sells far more than just the right to use its trade name or distribute its products. What it really sells is a complete system, including an established name, training, and a host of professional services such as site selection, managerial assistance, and national advertising, all of which lay beyond the reach of the typical small business person. Most of these services were created to assist large-scale enterprises and did not exist in the traditional economy.

Conclusion

Social changes also contributed to the development of franchising. Its usefulness as a tool for establishing the brand identification of goods sold through specialized outlets was the major reason that sellers of generics turned to the system. Once the franchise became a product in its own right, the public preference for branded goods served to stimulate the sale of franchises as business opportunities. To the members of a society predisposed to prefer branded goods of uniform and proven quality over unique and unfamiliar products, franchising provided a logical alternative to building one's own business.

In order to build a strong identity and public acceptance of their product, business-format franchisers first needed some way to produce a consistently high-quality package of franchise services in volume. To do this, franchise industry firms adapted the principles of high-volume production to the manufacture of small businesses. At Domino's, for example, the introduction of distinctive outlets and standardized equipment not only helped create a uniform image for the company but also simplified and brought great economies to outlet remodeling. Through the College of Pizzarology, Tom Monaghan was able to apply batch production techniques to franchisee training, while home office control over advertising and organizational changes such as the introduction of the Corporate Area Representative allowed the home office to implement and coordinate promotions and other services for the benefit of the entire system.

As the case of Domino's also shows, the process of developing the internal infrastructure could be difficult. Like the founders of many early franchise industry firms, Monaghan began as a traditional small businessman and did not fully recognize that his new product, the Domino's Pizza shop, would require new methods of production. In 1969, when he made his first big move into franchising, he tried to manufacture franchises using informal craft production techniques. The results were nearly fatal. Domino's primitive franchise production system collapsed under the relatively modest goal of opening 100 stores in its first year. Domino's ended the year with less than one-half of its anticipated stores open; moreover, the confusion and expense from the effort left the company nearly bankrupt. Ten years later, however, Tom Monaghan once again started a major expansion that added over 1,500 outlets within five years without seriously straining Domino's ability to establish, equip, and supply its shops and recruit and train its franchisees. Monaghan could do this because by the late

1970s he had constructed an internal infrastructure capable of producing franchise services with the same type of efficiency and uniformity that his outlets produced pizza.

A secondary goal of this study was to determine the influence of traditional business practices on the organization of the large, modern firm. Based on my findings, traditional practices had a major impact—at least as far as the use of franchising is concerned. For the most part, existing methods of distribution were more adaptable to the needs of the modern business enterprise than were traditional methods of production. In each of the industries I examined, new production technologies led to tremendous increases in output. Before manufacturers could make effective use of these new technologies, however, they had to develop new methods of organization in order to provide the close control required to make these systems function smoothly. Fewer organizational changes took place in distribution because traditional practice allowed managers to achieve adequate regulation over the flow of goods through their systems.

Although manufacturers had sound economic reasons for adapting and integrating traditional methods into the organizations they developed to cope with the modern economy, other factors played a role in preserving traditional practices. The basic suitability of a modified version of the agency system accounts primarily for its adoption by manufacturers. Institutional inertia and legal changes also helped ensure its retention. Except in the case of Singer, where company-owned outlets always were significant, the marketing systems of the other firms studied were quickly dominated by franchise units. With each passing year, manufacturers found themselves more reliant on the dealers who sold their goods and were familiar with the organizations they had built. When conditions changed, producers' first reaction was always to modify rather than eliminate the franchise system.

As the Grangers' unsuccessful attempts to bypass McCormick's dealers in the 1870s and Fords' abortive moves into direct retailing in 1916 and 1933 show, once manufacturers became deeply committed to franchising, they were unwilling to disrupt their established channels of distribution despite compelling reasons to do so. In the 1870s one of the reasons McCormick refused to sell directly to Granger groups was the resistance he encountered from dealers' associations. By that time dealers were organized

Conclusion

so well that McCormick and other equipment makers were reluctant to risk their wrath even when faced with a potential consumer boycott. Likewise, at Ford, franchising was able to withstand the changes brought about by the introduction of mass production and the disruptions of the Great Depression because Ford had come to rely so heavily on dealers that the prospect of reorganizing its entire distribution system was less appealing than foregoing gains anticipated from a mixed system of company-owned and franchised outlets.

Legal changes also played a role in preserving the franchise system. In every industry but sewing machine manufacturing, legislation designed to correct perceived inequities in the franchise followed its arrival. One of the chief concerns of lawmakers was how to protect franchisees who, though legally independent, relied almost entirely on a single supplier. In order to protect the livelihood of franchisees, legislators defined the franchise relationship more clearly and made it more difficult for manufacturers to eliminate established dealers. Prompted by the National Automobile Dealers Association, legislators in the mid-1950s made it illegal for automakers to terminate or fail to renew dealers' contracts without "just cause." In the 1970s gasoline retailers and franchise industry firms received the same protection. The result has been to harden existing channels of distribution.

As the example of the petroleum industry shows, more general legal changes also contributed to the spread of the franchise system. The wave of antichain store legislation that swept the country in the 1930s made it prohibitively expensive for oil companies to own and operate more than a handful of the outlets that sold their products. Because refiners desired control over the entire outlet in order to promote their products, they were forced to develop franchise systems that ensured the voluntary cooperation of dealers in establishing uniform standards of appearance and service.

Taken as a whole, the development and persistence of product franchising suggests that, at least in distribution, the visible hand of management combined with—rather than superseded—traditional practices in controlling and coordinating the flow of goods through the firm. As a loose method of vertical integration, franchising left dealers significant freedom in such vital areas as purchasing, pricing, and day-to-day operations. Thus, while managers may set the general boundaries of dealers' behavior through the use of the franchise contract, the dealer, as a legally independent owner, is ultimately responsible for the operation of his or her business.

The final goal of this study was to ascertain the place of small business in the modern economy. Here, franchising provided perhaps the most extreme example of the interconnections between large and small business. In seeking to understand how small business operates in the modern economy, scholars have tended to stress the existence of a dual economy in which small business continues to thrive primarily by avoiding direct contact with its larger counterparts. As franchising's importance to the economy attests, however, avoidance was not the only or even the best path to success. Once the franchise industry brought big business into the production of small business and allowed the small business owner access to many of the efficiencies of big business, it greatly increased the small business owner's chances for survival.

Whereas the appearance of the franchise industry provided at least a partial solution to the economic problems of small business, the social effects of the professionalization of small business are less certain. On one hand, the economic advantages of business-format franchising are undeniable. The majority of independent small businesses fail within three years; in contrast, throughout the 1980s the nonrenewal rate for franchised businesses has been around 4 percent. On the other hand, economic security is not the only reason people seek small business ownership. The mechanisms that make franchise units so successful are not the property of the individual franchisee who uses them, and the franchisee's freedom of action is limited by the need to conform to the requirements of the system he or she is licensed to use. The question of just how independent franchisees actually were became the subject of a major debate during the 1960s and 1970s, and since then legislation has brought a greater measure of equity to a relationship that is by its nature unequal. Unequal does not necessarily mean unfair, however. On the whole, it appears that for a significant portion of the population, franchising provides an attractive balance between the need for security and the desire for independence.

Notes

1. For examples of writers who have confused the origin of the term *franchise* with the system it represents see Boorstin, *The Americans*, pp. 428–29; Vaughn, *Franchising Today, 1966–1967*, pp. 239–40; Dias and Gurnick, *Franchising*, p. 13; U.S. Department of Commerce, *Franchising in the Economy, 1985–1987*, p. 2. For the evolution of *franchise* as a legal term see *Words and Phrases*, s.v. "Franchise." *Words and Phrases* is a standard legal reference.

2. On the development of corporate law see Seavoy, "Public Service Origins" and "Laws to Encourage Manufacturing"; on the development of agency law see Gilmore, *Death of Contract*, chap. 1. Legally, franchising is a system that lies somewhere between two older contractual marketing methods: agency sales and vendor-vendee sales. At one extreme, agency contracts create a relationship whereby one firm acts as the employee of another. This type of arrangement is typically used by manufacturers who wish some say in the distribution of their goods but lack the expertise or resources to open company-owned outlets. To circumvent this problem, they contract with established distributors, who act as their legal representatives. As agents, these retailers are required to honor manufacturers' stipulations on conditions of sale, and, within reason, manufacturers are legally bound to honor the actions of their agents. At the other extreme lie vendor-vendee contracts. These are straight sales contracts, where one party agrees to sell and another to purchase. The relationship carries no legal obligations beyond this point, and manufacturers lose both control and obligation over the marketing of their products.

3. Other sources more directly interested in franchise development indicate that the term came into common use somewhat earlier. In *The Exclusive Agency*, a report published by the New York University Bureau of Business Research in

1923, the word *franchise* was used interchangeably with the term *exclusive agency* by businessmen responding to a survey on the advantages of the agency system. The Oakland Motor Car Company labeled its dealer agreement a franchise as early as 1908. The text of Oakland's agreement closely resembles that of a standard agency contract except that the distributor is defined as a "dealer," and the contract clearly states that it "does not in any matter delegate to the dealer the right or authority to transact any business for or in the name of the manufacturer." Chapter 1 of my study will show that functionally the franchise system developed even earlier. New York University Bureau of Business Research, *The Exclusive Agency*; Hewitt, *Automobile Franchise Agreements*, app. A.

4. For other definitions of franchising and comparisons to related methods of distribution see Donald Thompson, *Contractual Marketing Systems*; McCord, *Franchising Sourcebook*; Lewis and Hancock, *Franchise System of Distribution*. On the evolution of franchise law see Braun, "Policy Issues of Franchising," *Southwestern University Law Review*, pp. 155–73. Lawyers Cooperative Publishing, *American Jurisprudence*, a standard legal encyclopedia, has a 700-page entry on franchising listed under "Private Franchise Contracts." It presents a very comprehensive overview of the current state of the various branches of franchise law.

5. For examples of studies concerned with product franchising see Hewitt, *Automobile Franchise Agreements*; Jack, "Channels of Distribution"; Marx, "Development of the Franchise Distribution System."

6. On the appearance of early system franchisers see Henderson, "Franchising Yesterday"; "The Howard Johnson's Restaurants," *Fortune*; Hall, "Franchising"; Love, *McDonald's*; Kroc and Anderson, *Grinding It Out*; Sanders, *Life as I Have Known It*; Liles, *Oh Thank Heaven*.

7. The terms *modern* and *traditional* as they apply to the economy and the firm are used frequently throughout this study and may require some explanation. America's modern economy, which was firmly in place by the 1920s, is highly industrialized, has a well-developed national communication and transportation system, and is dominated by large firms that coordinate the flow of the majority of goods and services through the economy. The modern business enterprise is large, but organization rather than size is the most important feature dividing the traditional firm from its modern successor. The modern business enterprise contains many distinct operating units and is managed by a hierarchy of salaried executives. The traditional economy is based on labor-intensive production and distribution primarily for local or regional markets. In the traditional economy, the movement of goods and services is carried out through a complex web of small firms and is directed by market forces. Traditional business methods of organization are based on the principles of independent ownership of operating units, with coordination

between units determined by market forces and regulated by law or custom. For a more complete description of the modern economy see Chandler, *Visible Hand*.

8. On recent trends in the writing of business history see Galambos, "Technology, Political Economy, and Professionalization"; Brinkley, "Writing the History of Contemporary America"; Hidy, "Business History"; Chandler, "Business History." On the development of the modern economy see Chandler, *Visible Hand*.

9. On the structure of the modern economy and the split between large and small business see Averitt, *Dual Economy*.

10. The question of the relationship between large and small businesses shows up occasionally in the debate over the merits of the franchise system. For a number of different perspectives see U.S. Congress, Senate, *Impact of Franchising on Small Business* and *Impact upon Small Business of Dual Distribution*; Brown, *Franchising—Realities and Remedies*; Atkinson, *Franchising*; Tinney, "A Study of Contemporary Franchising"; Sklar, "Franchises and Independence."

CHAPTER ONE

1. This is one of the main themes in Chandler, *Strategy and Structure*, although Chandler focuses on the crises that brought about the development of new organizational structures. The most conspicuous attempt to combine traditional methods of organization with new methods of production was inside contracting. For a good description of McCormick's and Singer's experiences with this method of organization see Hounshell, *From the American System*, chaps. 2–4.

2. The United States had a total population of under 4 million in 1790, almost 13 million in 1830, and over 17 million in 1840.

3. For a good overview of the structure and operation of the traditional economy see Perkins, *The Economy of Colonial America*. For a detailed look at the colonial economy see McCusker and Menard, *The Economy of British America*. For an exceptionally well-done study of a single colonial and early American firm see Baxter, *House of Hancock*.

4. Landes, *Unbound Prometheus*, esp. chaps. 1–2; Deane, *First Industrial Revolution*; Chandler, *Visible Hand*, pp. 244–53. For a detailed look at preindustrial technology see Gimpel, *Medieval Machine*.

5. For a good overview of the creation of the national market see Chandler, *Visible Hand*, pt. 2. Travel times have been taken from ibid., pp. 84–85. For a more intimate account of transportation development see Rubin, "Canal or Railroad?"

6. Porter and Livesay, *Merchants and Manufacturers*, remains the best overall survey of changes in marketing during this period.

7. Dublin, *Women at Work*, gives a detailed look at factory life and the problems of establishing an early manufacturing business. On the difficulties in working out production problems at Singer, McCormick, and Ford see Hounshell, *From the American System*, chaps. 2, 4, and 6 respectively.

8. Porter and Livesay, *Merchants and Manufacturers*, chaps. 8–9; Chandler, *Visible Hand*, chap 9. Before the United States could develop a true national market, it was necessary to destroy the trade barriers designed to protect local manufacturers at the expense of large "foreign" corporations headquartered in other states. Although the U.S. Constitution gave the federal government the power to "regulate Commerce with foreign nations, and among the several states," internal trade barriers in the form of discriminatory taxes and licensing fees remained a significant barrier to interstate trade until national firms such as Singer successfully challenged the states in a series of legal battles during the last quarter of the nineteenth century. For a good treatment of the changing legal environment see Cochran and Miller, *Age of Enterprise*, chap. 8; Hurst, *Law and Markets*. For an excellent account of the breakdown of legal barriers to a national market see McCurdy, "American Law and the Marketing Structure of the Large Corporation."

9. Glenn Porter, *Rise of Big Business*, pp. 45–53; Porter and Livesay, *Merchants and Manufacturers*, chaps. 10–11. For a theoretical look at the forces that drove manufacturers see Norton, "Empirical Investigation of Franchising as an Organizational Form."

10. "The Manufacturers Agent as a Channel of Distribution," *Harvard Business Review*. See also New York University Bureau of Business Research, *The Exclusive Agency*, for a brief discussion of the faults and merits of the agency system.

11. "The Manufacturers Agent as a Channel of Distribution," *Harvard Business Review*; New York University Bureau of Business Research, *The Exclusive Agency*.

12. Hutchinson, *McCormick*, vol. 1, gives the best description of McCormick's early years. For other accounts see Conard, "Evolution of the Harvesting Machine"; McCormick, *Century of the Reaper*; Casson, *McCormick*.

13. On the formation of International Harvester see Kramer, "Harvesters and High Finance."

14. Hutchinson, *McCormick*, 1:195, 212; McCormick, "What 71 Years of Business Have Taught Us," p. 658.

15. Hutchinson, *McCormick*, 1:214–15, 221; C. H. McCormick to Wm. S. McCormick, April 2, 1845, May 15, 1845, 2A, box 1, file: McCormick, C. H., and Others, Cyrus McCormick Collection, State Historical Society of Wisconsin, Madison (hereafter cited as MC/SHSW); *Ohio Cultivator*, July 15, 1845, p. 64.

16. C. H. McCormick to Wm. S. McCormick, August 6, 1845, 2A, box 1, file: McCormick, C. H., and Others, MC/SHSW; *Ohio Cultivator*, April 15, 1847, p. 64.

17. Hutchinson, *McCormick*, 1:209–11; Ardrey, "Harvesting Machine Industry."

18. Quotation from Hutchinson, *McCormick*, 1:194–95.

19. For a good description of the first reaper war see Hutchinson, *McCormick*, vol. 1, chaps. 7–8; C. H. McCormick to Robert McCormick, May 3, 1845, October 13, 1845, 2A, box 1, file: McCormick, C. H., and Others, MC/SHSW. On the spread of the reaper throughout the Midwest see *Ohio Cultivator*, October 1, 1846, p. 147, July 15, 1852, p. 211.

20. In the spring of 1847, for example, Leander McCormick went to Cincinnati to oversee production at C. A. Brown's shop as his paid employee. C. H. McCormick to Leander McCormick, January 6, 1847, 2A, box 1, file: McCormick, C. H., and Others, MC/SHSW. See also C. H. McCormick to Wm. S. McCormick, August 6, 1845, ibid.

21. C. H. McCormick to Wm. S. McCormick, August 6, 1845, 2A, box 1, file: McCormick, C. H., and Others, MC/SHSW. See also C. H. McCormick to Wm. S. McCormick, August 10, 1845, ibid. For published warnings about the poor quality of the machines produced by McCormick's licensees and McCormick's response, see *Ohio Cultivator*, July 15, 1848, p. 108, and February 15, 1847, p. 29.

22. "Supreme Court of the United States No. 176, Cyrus H. McCormick, Appellant, vs. Charles M. Gray and Wm. B. Ogden," and "Cyrus H. McCormick with Ogden and Jones" (sales agreement) (quotation), 2A, box 1, file: Gray and Ogden, 1849, MC/SHSW.

23. "Supreme Court of the United States No. 176, Cyrus H. McCormick, Appellant, vs. Charles M. Gray and Wm. B. Ogden," 2A, box 1, file: Gray and Ogden, 1849, and "Cyrus H. McCormick to Miller, Wingate & Co.," 2A, box 45, file: McCormick, C. H., 1860, MC/SHSW; Hounshell, *From the American System*, p. 161.

24. On the development of McCormick's sales organization see Hutchinson, *McCormick*, vol. 1, chaps. 14–15; McCormick, "What 71 Years of Business Have Taught Us," pp. 654–59. For a good account of McCormick's overseas operations see Carstensen, *American Enterprise in Foreign Markets*.

25. One of McCormick's most active traveling agents was James T. Griffin. Griffin not only helped develop the American market for the company but also assisted McCormick in establishing the European sales organization. For a detailed description of the domestic duties of traveling agents see the correspondence between Griffin and McCormick, 2A, box 45, files: Griffin, J. T., MC/SHSW.

26. Contract with Abner Thompson for State Agency (Pennsylvania), 1A, box 4,

file: 1852, McCormick, C. H., MC/SHSW; Contract with Thomas Patterson for New York and southeastern Canada, ibid. The above-mentioned files also contain routine correspondence between the company and state agents, which describes their duties in detail. Wm. S. McCormick to Jas. Henry, January 1860, April 1860, 1A, box 16, file: 1860, McCormick, Wm. S., MC/SHSW.

27. "Agency Record, 1857–1868," 3X (4 vols.), MC/SHSW.

28. Contract between C. H. McCormick and D. R. Burt, 1853, 1A, box 4, file: 1853, McCormick, C. H.; Wm. S. McCormick to Jas. Henry, March 3, 1860, box 15, file: 1860, McCormick, C. H., and Bros.—both in MC/SHSW.

29. Occasionally, agents did not even have facilities in which to store machines. See, for example, Underhill and Bourland to C. H. McCormick and Bros., March 31, 1859, 2X, box 26, file: 1859, MC/SHSW. During the harvest season the company handled repair services by sending out factory experts to assist farmers and agents during the harvest. After the harvest, owners had to send their machines to the factory if they wished McCormick to handle the repairs. Richard Morrow (agent for Piqua, Ohio) to C. H. McCormick, April 8, 1854, 2X, box 45, file: 1854, MC/SHSW.

30. For examples of McCormick's willingness to grant agencies without any investigation of the applicant see D. Staples to C. H. McCormick, April 30, 1854, 2X, box 4, file: 1854, MC/SHSW. One reason that no reliable data exist on the number of McCormick agents is that he used subagents extensively in the early years. Compare, for example, the "Agency Record, 1857–1868," 3X, MC/SHSW, which lists scores of agents for each state of the Midwest in 1860, with "Sales in 1860," 1A, box 15, file: 1860, McCormick, C. H., MC/SHSW, which lists approximately twenty agents per state.

31. For an enlightening discussion of the changing nature of generic goods and the requirements of advertising nongeneric goods see McDean, "Beatrice." By the early twentieth century relatively simple and inexpensive pieces of farm equipment, such as mowers, had become generic goods as patent rights expired and farmers gained a greater understanding of mechanized farm implements. For the development of this process see U.S. Bureau of Corporations, *Farm-Machinery Trade Associations*, chap. 5. On the same sort of personal relationship in the mail order business see Tedlow, *New and Improved*, pp. 270–71.

32. Order for reaper, 2A, box 45, file: 1854, MC/SHSW; Facsimile of instructions for assembly and operation of McCormick reaper, 1858, in Hutchinson, *McCormick*, 1:358; Letter to general agents, August 18, 1880, General Letters and Circulars Sent to Agents, 3X (bound vol.), MC/SHSW.

33. The same general conditions applied to McCormick's overseas operations. For a solid treatment of McCormick's agency system in Russia see Carstensen, *American Enterprise in Foreign Markets*.

34. Circular letters to agents, 1859 and 1860, "Out-going Correspondence: To Shepherd and Polk (agents), 1857–1863," 3X, vol. 85 (scrapbook), MC/SHSW.

35. Ibid.

36. Hounshell, *From the American System*, p. 161; List of general agents (1880s), "General Letters and Circulars Sent to General Agents, 1879–1883" (scrapbook), 3X, item 67, no box, no file, MC/SHSW.

37. U.S. Bureau of Corporations, *Farm-Machinery Trade Associations*, chap. 1; Federal Trade Commission, *Report . . . on the Causes of High Prices of Farm Implements*, chap. 1; Broehl, *John Deere's Company*, pt. 2.

38. Hutchinson, *McCormick*, vol. 2, chap. 14.

39. U.S. Bureau of Corporations, *Farm-Machinery Trade Associations*, esp. chap. 5.

40. Most works on the early history of the sewing machine industry deal primarily with technological developments. For several good examples of this type see Godfrey, *International History of the Sewing Machine*; Cooper, *History of the Sewing Machine*; Hounshell, *From the American System*, chaps. 2–3. For more general accounts see Parton, "History of the Sewing Machine"; Ewers, *Sincere's History*. For accounts dealing directly with Singer see Jack, "Channels of Distribution"; Brandon, *Capitalist Romance*.

41. Brandon, *Capitalist Romance*, chaps. 2–3; Parton, "History of the Sewing Machine"; Ewers, *Sincere's History*, chap. 2. By the time he invented a sewing machine Singer might well have had at least two families to support. Not counting an earlier wife to whom he was still married, Singer quickly established three other families shortly after moving to New York. For a brief description of the more colorful and complex features of Singer's private life see Brandon, *Capitalist Romance*, chap. 8.

42. Brandon, *Capitalist Romance*, p. 43.

43. Parton, "History of the Sewing Machine," pp. 534–38.

44. Boston *Daily Times*, November 7, 1850, quoted in Brandon, *Capitalist Romance*, p. 51. In 1853 Singer produced only 810 machines. Hounshell, *From the American System*, p. 89.

45. Brandon, *Capitalist Romance*, chap. 3; Jack, "Channels of Distribution," 118–22. Samples of Singer's early contracts can be found in the Singer archives in Madison—see files: Correspondence, Legal and Domestic, 1851–77 (box 155), and "Abstract of All Assignments on Record . . . Blodgett & Lerow" (box 189), Singer Manufacturing Company Collection, Singer Archives, State Historical Society of Wisconsin, Madison (hereafter cited as SA/SHSW).

46. Jack, "Channels of Distribution," pp. 118–19.

47. Contracts, box 155, files: Correspondence, Legal and Domestic, 1851–77, SA/SHSW. These files contain over three dozen contracts between Singer and

early rights holders. Almost all are from 1851 or 1852. The same files contain only two contracts that included the right to make and sell Singer's machine. "Memorandums of Disposal of Old Territorial Right and Agreements with Various Agents before the Year 1856," box 223 (bound vol.), SA/SHSW. I discovered no evidence that either licensee actually produced any machines.

48. Contracts, box 155, files: Correspondence, Legal and Domestic, 1851–77, SA/SHSW.

49. Jack, "Channels of Distribution," p. 119.

50. Brandon, *Capitalist Romance*, pp. 51–52; Jack, "Channels of Distribution," pp. 119–21; Contracts, box 155, files: Correspondence, Legal and Domestic, 1851–77, SA/SHSW.

51. On the development of the sewing machine combination, see Cooper, *History of the Sewing Machine*, pp. 38–41

52. Jack, "Channels of Distribution," pp. 122–25; Hounshell, *From the American System*, p. 89. On Singer's move into the production of consumer machines see Brandon, *Capitalist Romance*, pp. 116–19.

53. Contracts with Robert Kene[?] and John Stromenger, box 225, file: 1851, SA/SHSW; Jack, "Channels of Distribution," pp. 118–25.

54. Contract with Walter Bennett, box 225, file: 1857 and Contract with Gray and Parker, box 155, file: 1851–77—both in SA/SHSW; Brandon, *Capitalist Romance*, pp. 124–26. The contract with Parker and Gray ran against the general trend in Singer's expansion. In 1863 Singer sold his Syracuse branch to Parker and Gray for $1,000 plus the cost of the stock on hand. Singer usually preferred to use company-owned branches in large eastern cities. Like his arrangements with other large agencies, Singer's contract with Parker and Gray was for two years. Contracts with local agents were of indefinite duration and could be terminated without cause by either party. See Contract, box 231, file: Business Documents, Misc., SA/SHSW.

55. Contract, box 231, file: Business Documents, Misc., SA/SHSW. These files also contain samples of the contracts used by Singer's major competitors. No significant difference existed between the local agency contract used by Singer and its competition. Jack, "Channels of Distribution," gives a detailed account of how the agents' inability to provide adequate credit resulted in close ties with the company.

56. Jack, "Channels of Distribution," pp. 130–31.

57. Ibid., pp. 122–25; *Singer & Co.'s Gazette* quoted in Brandon, *Capitalist Romance*, p. 130; Contract with William Bennett, box 225, file: 1857, SA/SHSW.

58. Circular memorandum, November 1861, box 189, file: 1861, SA/SHSW (quotation). For historians who have overestimated the amount of control Singer exercised during the years it was establishing itself on the national market see

Chandler, *Visible Hand*, pp. 303–7; Porter and Livesay, *Merchants and Manufacturers*, pp. 194–95; Hounshell, *From the American System*, pp. 89–90.

59. Price list, box 189, file: 1866, and "Meeting of the Agents of the Singer Manufacturing Company," box 191, file: 1877, SA/SHSW.

60. For a good summary of Singer's reorganization see Chandler, *Visible Hand*, pp. 303–7.

61. For a good description of Singer's overseas operations, see Davies, " 'Peacefully Working to Conquer the World.' " See also "Meeting of the Agents of the Singer Manufacturing Company," box 189, file: 1877, SA/SHSW.

62. "Suggestions to Central Offices," box 231, file: 1878 (quotation), and Summary of Branch Activity, 1867–73, vol. 223, SA/SHSW.

63. "Suggestions to Central Offices," box 231, file: 1878, SA/SHSW.

64. Ibid. The status of general agents was no less certain. The company had never made any distinction between company-owned stores and general agencies. Some of the "agents" at this meeting were in fact agents of the company in a legal sense, while others were branch managers.

65. "Instructions to Managers of Branch Offices" and "Appendix," box 191, file: 1878, SA/SHSW. The company's accounting methods made no distinction between company-owned branches and dealers. Machines were invoiced to branches and dealers at a set price, and payments were credited to their accounts.

66. Circular announcing establishment of traveling examiners' system, box 172, file: 1882, SA/SHSW.

67. "Examiners Reports," boxes 170–76, filed by year, "General Meeting," box 231, file: 1885, and "To the General Agents of the Singer Manufacturing Company," box 231, file: 1885, SA/SHSW.

68. See, for example, "Examiners Report" on Milwaukee, Wis., July 6, 1881; on Cincinnati, Ohio, August 4, 1881; and on Pittsburgh, Pa., June 8, 1881—all in box 170, file: 1881, SA/SHSW.

69. "Examiners Report" on Baltimore, Md., March 10, 1881, box 170, file: 1881, SA/SHSW.

70. "Copy of Circular Letter Dated December 18, 1882," box 231, file: 1882, and "To the General Agents of the Singer Manufacturing Company," box 231, file: 1885, SA/SHSW.

71. "To the General Agents of the Singer Manufacturing Company," box 231, file: 1885, SA/SHSW.

72. Ibid.

73. Ibid.; "Copy of Circular Letter Dated December 18, 1882," box 231, file: 1882, SA/SHSW. For examples of various types of Singer contracts from the 1880s see box 231, files: 1881–87, and "Exhibit 'A'," box 150, file: Misc. Domestic Correspondence, SA/SHSW. On the training of canvassers see "General Instruc-

tions for Special Agents," "Special Instructions for Supervising Canvassers,'" and "Canvassers' Manual of Instructions," box 233, various files, SA/SHSW.

74. For representative works on the franchise debate of the 1960s see, for example, Curry et al., *Partners for Profit* and Brown, *Franchising: Trap for the Trusting.* For an insightful critique of the social concerns about franchisee independence see Ghent, *Our Benevolent Feudalism.* For a more scholarly treatment see Sklar, "Franchises and Independence."

CHAPTER TWO

1. On the shift from a developing to an industrial economy see Rostow, *Process of Economic Growth,* esp. chap. 12; Averitt, *Dual Economy.* On the development of organizational and managerial structures see Chandler, *Visible Hand.*

2. On the development of the railroad see Chandler, *Visible Hand,* chap. 5. All statistics were taken from U.S. Bureau of the Census, *Historical Statistics of the United States.* On the trucking industry see Childs, *Trucking and the Public Interest.* On the influence of motor vehicles in urban areas and the urban economy see Preston, *Automobile Age Atlanta.*

3. On the development of mass production at Ford see Hounshell, *From the American System.*

4. Chandler, *Visible Hand,* chap. 7, gives a good overview of the origins and development of the mass retailer. For works dealing specifically with the development of the mass market see Strasser, *Satisfaction Guaranteed,* and Tedlow, *New and Improved.*

5. For a general history of the chain store see Lebhar, *Chain Stores in America.* On mail order and the development of Sears see Worthy, *Shaping an American Institution,* and Tedlow, *New and Improved,* chap. 5. For a social history of the department store see Benson, *Countercultures.*

6. Sears & Roebuck did market its own automobile from 1905 through 1910 but apparently could not make a success of the venture. See Nevins and Hill, *Ford: The Times,* p. 409.

7. Two other changes—the rise of the business press and the appearance of trade associations—also made important but more indirect contributions to improved communications in the early twentieth century. By 1910 over half a dozen mass circulation periodicals devoted to the auto industry were in print, while by 1917 both manufacturers and dealers had strong national trade associations. On the rise of the business press see Peterson, *Magazines in the Twentieth Century.* On the rise of trade associations see Hawley, *The Great War*; Chandler, *Visible Hand,*

chap. 6. By 1914 Ford was making routine use of "night letters" and telegraphed reports for daily updates on sales; see, for example, "January Branch Letter #20," January 24, k9k2 [1912], accession (hereafter acc.) 509, box 1, file: 1912, and "Charlotte Branch," December 1914, acc. 509, box 2, file: 1914, Ford Motor Company Collection, Ford Archives, Edison Institute, Dearborn, Mich. (hereafter cited as FA/EI).

8. For an extremely well-put-together study of internal communications and office technology in large firms see Yates, *Control through Communication*, esp. chaps. 1–3. Mills, *White Collar*, chap. 8; Anderson, "Gender, Class, and Culture," chap. 1.

9. Yates, *Control through Communication*. These new tools were sometimes not well understood by managers. On the use and misuse of cost accounting see Gregory Thompson, "Misused Product Cost Accounting." Thompson's article appears in the Autumn 1989 issue of the *Business History Review*, which is devoted to the development of managerial tools for big business.

10. Chandler, *Strategy and Structure*, esp. chaps. 2–3.

11. On advertising see Pope, *The Making of Modern Advertising*. Scientific management also developed into an industry in its own right—see Nelson, *Taylor*. The development of systematic management and complex organizational structures can also be included in the supporting infrastructure of big business. I chose to separate them because managerial and organizational innovations were necessary to the creation of big business, and institutions like modern advertising grew to serve big business once it had come to dominate the modern economy.

12. Galambos, *Public Image of Big Business*, esp. chap. 3; Hawley, *The New Deal*, Introduction; Dicke, "Public Image of American Small Business."

13. Hofstadter, *Age of Reform*, p. 23; U.S. Bureau of the Census, *Historical Statistics of the United States*.

14. Warner, *Streetcar Suburbs*; Preston, *Automobile Age Atlanta*; Mills, *White Collar*, pt. 1; Wiebe, *Search for Order*.

15. On the creation of the consumer culture see Sussman, *Culture as History*; Galbraith, *Affluent Society*, esp. chap. 1; Potter, *People of Plenty*. As Potter points out, one of the unique features of American society has always been an assumption of abundance. Prior to industrialization, however, Americans thought of abundance more in terms of resources than goods. This commonly held belief that American resources were nearly inexhaustible contributed significantly to the culture of consumption that developed after industrialization.

16. Sinclair Lewis, *Babbitt*, pp. 8, 23. On the impact of the automobile on American culture see Fink, "Three Stages of American Automobile Consciousness."

17. "Branch Histories," acc. 429, box 1, FA/EI.

18. Hewitt, *Automobile Franchise Agreements*, p. 10. On the early development of the auto industry see Seltzer, *Financial History of the American Automobile Industry*; Fink, *Car Culture*.

19. U.S. Bureau of the Census, *Historical Statistics of the United States*; Seltzer, *Financial History of the American Automobile Industry*, p. 21.

20. Hewitt, *Automobile Franchise Agreements*, chap. 2. See also Chandler, *Giant Enterprise*.

21. David Hounshell, *From the American System*, chap. 6.

22. Hewitt, *Automobile Franchise Agreements*, chaps. 3–4.

23. Nevins and Hill, *Ford: The Times*, chap. 11; "Suggested Retail Prices (List Prices)," AR-65-90 "P," Ford Industrial Archives, Redford, Mich. (hereafter cited as FIA). The most comprehensive work on the Ford Motor Company remains Nevins and Hill's three-volume history: *Ford: The Times*; *Ford: Expansion and Challenge*, and *Ford: Decline and Rebirth*. See also David Lewis, *Public Image of Henry Ford*; Burlingame, *Ford*; Hounshell, *From the American System*, chaps. 6–7; Wik, *Ford*.

24. Nevins and Hill, *Ford: The Times*, chap. 13.

25. Ibid., chaps. 16, 18–19.

26. Nevins and Hill, *Ford: Expansion and Challenge*.

27. Nevins and Hill, *Ford: The Times*, chap. 16; Hounshell, *From the American System*, chap. 6.

28. Ibid., pp. 249–51.

29. Seltzer, *Financial History of the American Automobile Industry*, pp. 19–21.

30. "Reminiscences of William L. Hughson," pp. 5–6, FA/EI; Ford Motor Company, *Ford Dealer Story*, pp. 4–7; "Reminiscences of Charles H. Bennett," pp. 38–40, FA/EI.

31. James Couzens to Chas. E. Fay, October 18, 1905, AR-65-7, box 1, file: Boston Branch, and James Couzens to Thomas Hay, November 5, 1905, AR-65-7, box 1, file: Chicago Branch, FIA. See also Tedlow, *New and Improved*, pp. 130–35.

32. "Reminiscences of John H. Eagal, Sr.," pp. 14–17 (quotation, p. 14), FA/EI.

33. James Couzens to Chas. E. Fay, October 18, 1905, AR-65-7, box 1, file: Boston Branch, FIA; "Reminiscences of C. C. Housenick," p. 5, and "Reminiscences of Arnold File: Sammis," pp. 5–6, FA/EI.

34. Nevins and Hill, *Ford: The Times*, pp. 249–50, 342. See also "Reminiscences of Arnold File: Sammis," pp. 7–8, FA/EI.

35. "Reminiscences of John H. Eagal, Sr.," p. 12, FA/EI.

36. Quoted in Nevins and Hill, *Ford: The Times*, p. 249.

37. Ibid., pp. 342–45; "Branch Histories," acc. 429, box 1, FA/EI.

38. James Couzens to Chas E. Fay, October 18, 1905, AR-65-7, box 1, file: Bos-

ton Branch, and James Couzens to Thomas Fay, November 5, 1905, AR-65-7, box 1, file: Chicago Branch, FIA.

39. Because I uncovered no standardized contracts in Ford records written prior to 1908 and because several early dealers state in their reminiscences that they operated without a contract, I assume that Ford did not use standardized contracts before that time.

40. Ford did revise its dealer contracts to give dealers a greater measure of equality in 1936, when the company liberalized its dealer policy, but these changes did not fundamentally alter the dealers' duties. For representative dealer contracts see "Dealer's Agreement," [1909], acc. 297, box 2, file: L-36, "Ford Sales Agreement," acc. 76, box 35, file: 1917, "Sales Agreement," acc. 78, box 24, file: 1934, and "Mercury 8 Sales Agreement," acc. 449, box 6, file: 1939, FA/EI.

41. "Dealer's Agreement," [1908–9], acc. 296, box 2, file: L-36, FA/EI. The language in Ford's franchise contract remained almost unchanged until 1938. After 1938 the company began to include justifications for some provisions and generally made them more understandable to laymen, but it did not alter the intent of the contract or the obligations of the dealer.

42. Ford eliminated territorial restrictions from its contracts in 1920 as part of its response to the recession of that year, although it effectively limited a dealer's market area by confining dealers to "one and only one place of business" in later contracts. This change was probably made to protect smaller dealers from being dominated by larger ones. The company also specifically prohibited new dealers in any territory where the existing dealer was taking his full quota, had recently erected new buildings, or already had profitable branches. "Elimination of Territory Lines and Appointment of Additional Dealers" (3 separate letters with the same title and date), December 1, 1920, acc. 78, box 89, file: December 1920, and "Infringements and Forfeiture of Deposit," March 2, 1914, acc. 509, box 2, file: March 1914, FA/EI. Later both of these restrictions were declared to be illegal restraints of trade and were removed from contracts.

43. "1911 Dealer's License and Agreement, 1912," acc. 74, box 28, and "Memo," December 1911, acc. 509, box 1, file: December 1914, FA/EI; "Advertising Program for 1926," AR-66-18, box 1, FIA.

44. Dealers were required to submit monthly sales reports until 1911, when weekly reports were introduced. "Letter—Dallas Branch," March 12, 1914, acc. 509, box 2, file: March 1914, FA/EI. Ford switched to ten-day reports in 1920. "Ten-Day Reports," October 15, 1920, acc. 78, box 89, file: October 1920, FA/EI.

45. "Dealer Agreement," acc. 297, box 2, file: L-36, FA/EI; Hewitt, *Automobile Franchise Agreements*, pp. 37 (quotation), 75. As Hewitt points out in chapters 3 and 4, the courts were not always willing to allow this denial.

46. "Branch Histories," acc. 429, box 1, FA/EI; Nevins and Hill, *Ford: The*

Times, p. 479; "Memo," November 24, 1914, acc. 509, box 2, file: November 1914, FA/EI.

47. Nevins and Hill, *Ford: The Times*, pp. 400–409; "Branch Letter," September 22, 1913, acc. 509, box 1, file: September 1913, and "Sales," August 13, 1914, acc. 509, box 2, file: August 1914, FA/EI; Harry Porter, "Sales Methods That Net $1,000,000 a Week." Aside from the dealers and subdealers who made up the bulk of Ford's dealer system, the company also had a small number of special dealers located in branch cities who were not expected to provide repair service and, as a result, received a slightly lower discount.

48. Hewitt, *Automobile Franchise Agreements*, p. 18.

49. "The Manufacturers Agent as a Channel of Distribution," *Harvard Business Review*, p. 98 (quotation); Seltzer, *Financial History of the American Automobile Industry*, chap. 2. "Automobiles II—The Dealer," *Fortune*, gives a good account of dealer operations and factory/dealer relations.

50. Nevins and Hill, *Ford: The Times*, p. 644; "Minutes of Operating Committee," March 7, 1916, acc. 85, box 1, FA/EI. On the similarities of marketing practices in the sewing machine, farm equipment, and auto industries see Livesay, "Nineteenth-Century Precursors to Automobile Marketing." There is no evidence to suggest that Ford's marketing system was based on either Singer's or McCormick's; rather, it seems that all three faced similar problems, especially in their early years.

51. "Minutes of Operating Committee," March 7, 1916, acc. 85, box 1, FA/EI.

52. "Minutes of Operating Committee" and "Minutes of Executive Committee," March 20, 1916, July 14, 1916 (quotation), acc. 85, box 1, FA/EI. In the summary of the discussion over the staffing of these new branches, the executive committee made an interesting point about the differences between Ford's retail managers and dealers when it decided that local dealers "would not make suitable Branch Managers. The reason given was that they, having worked for themselves for so many years, would not feel like tying themselves down and working for the Ford Motor Company." "Minutes of Executive Committee," August 1, 1916. For the reaction of the press see "Ford Co. Adds 34 Branches," *Automobile*; "Ford to Drop Retail Sales," *Automobile*; "Ford Salesmen Form Agencies," *Automobile*; "Ford Agencies Increase Rapidly in Every City," *Automobile*.

53. For the scant discussion on ending branch sales see "Minutes of Executive Committee," January 22, 1917, acc. 85, box 1, FA/EI.

54. "Sales," June 22, 1914, acc. 509, box 2, file: June 1914; "Memo," August 4, 1914, acc. 509, box 2, file: August 1914; and "Sales Memo," acc. 509, box 2, file: April 1915, FA/EI (quotation).

55. On the industry's reaction to Ford's move into and out of retailing see "Ford

to Drop Retail Sales," *Automobile*; "Ford Salesmen Form Agencies," *Automobile*; "Ford Agencies Increase Rapidly in Every City," *Automobile*; "Many Copy Ford's Sales Plan," *Automobile*.

56. Nevins and Hill, *Ford: Expansion and Challenge* and *Ford: Decline and Rebirth*, provide the most detailed account of these years.

57. Sloan, *My Years with General Motors*, p. 284 (quotation); Nevins and Hill, *Ford: Decline and Rebirth*, chap. 5; "Branch Organization Adjustments," February 21, 1933, acc. 78, box 21, and "Branch Personnel," May 19, 1936, acc. 502, box 14, FA/EI.

58. Perhaps the best example of Ford's harsh treatment of dealers and the resentment this created was his decision to load his dealers with cars to make them help dig the company out of its huge debt in 1920–21. Apparently this action, described below, attracted no public notice at the time. Once Ford went into a decline in the late 1920s, however, a number of highly critical articles about it appeared in the national press.

59. Nevins and Hill, *Ford: The Times*, p. 479; "Memorandum on Representation," [1937], acc. 449, box 6, FA/EI. For another estimate on the number of Ford dealers see Tedlow, *New and Improved*, pp. 137–38.

60. "Minutes of Operating Committee," March 8, 1916, acc. 85, box 1, FA/EI; "Sales # 18 (General)," September 16, 1926, AR-66-18, box 2, FIA.

61. "Ford Motor Company" (dealer inspection form), November 4, 1921, and "Dealers Questionnaire," acc. 76, box 35, FA/EI; "Uniform Accounting Principles for Dealers," February 1, 1927, AR-66-18, box 1, FIA.

62. Nevins and Hill, *Ford: Expansion and Challenge*, pp. 161–66; "Concentration on Retail Sales," November 4, 1920, acc. 78, box 910, FA/EI. On the press reaction to Ford's financial crisis of the early 1920s in the late twenties see Sprague, "Confessions of a Ford Dealer"; Forbes, "Why Our Articles on Henry Ford Are Being Published"; "Ford Dealers Rebel," *Business Week*.

63. National Automobile Chamber of Commerce, *Facts and Figures*.

64. "National Automobile Dealers Association Started," *Automobile*; Federal Trade Commission, *Report on the Motor Vehicle Industry*, chap. 10; "Discontinuing of City Dealers' Associations," May 4, 1922, acc. 78, box 89, FA/EI; "Meetings of City Dealers," September 16, 1926, AR-66-18, box 2, FIA; Sloan, *My Years with General Motors*, chap. 16.

65. Nevins and Hill, *Ford: Expansion and Challenge*, p. 465; "Branch Letter," March 4, 1914, acc. 509, box 2, file: March 1914, and "Minutes of Operating Committee," August 12, 1916, acc. 85, box 1, FA/EI.

66. "Dealers' Monthly Requirements," March 3, 1933, acc. 454, box 3, file: Branch Organization, 1933, FA/EI.

67. "Ford Stores," *Business Week*; "To All Ford Dealers," October 24, 1932, acc. 78, box 21, and Edsel Ford to P. A. Williams, January 3, 1933, acc. 572, box 13, FA/EI.

68. "Unit Automobile Sales by Retail Outlets of Ford Motor Company and Affiliates, 1927–1937," acc. 33, box 49, FA/EI.

69. "Memorandum on Representation," acc. 449, box 6, FA/EI; Marx, "Development of the Franchise Distribution System."

70. "Definite Sales Plan," July 21, 1933, acc. 509, box 10, FA/EI.

71. "Memorandum, Dealer Problems," December 23, 1937, "Memorandum," June 14, 1938, "Sales Department," 1940[?], and "Branch Organization," May 15, 1940, acc. 449, box 6, FA/EI.

72. "Ford Revises Dealer Franchise," *Business Week*; "Sales Agreement" 1938, acc. 449, box 6, FA/EI.

73. "Department Communication": T. W. Skinner to J. R. Davis, [ca. 1937], box 449, file 2, FA/EI.

74. On General Motors's wartime relations with its dealers see Sloan, *My Years with General Motors*, pp. 295–98; "Letter to All Dealers," February 20, 1942, acc. 545, box 4, file: Dealers, FA/EI. For dealer activities during the war see "Automobile Dealers Offset Lack of Cars," p. 2.

75. On Ford's postwar reorganization and dealer reaction see "Rebirth of Ford," *Fortune*.

76. Baird, "Ford Post-War Plans"; U.S. Congress, Senate, *Automobile Marketing Practices*, pp. 975–76.

77. Baird, "Ford 'College' Trains Dealers" and "Ford Post-War Plans," pp. 74, 77. See also Baird, "All About Ford's New Sales Tool"; U.S. Congress, Senate, *Automobile Marketing Practices*, p. 977.

78. "Holding Company," August 16, 1949, AR-68-27, box 2, "Executive Communication," June 21, 1956, AR-66-31, box 8, and "Ford Motor Company Franchise Policies" (quotation), 1955, AR-66-33, box 3, FIA. The first hearing, held by the Senate Subcommittee on Antitrust and Monopoly, met in late 1955 to investigate General Motors. The second investigation was held by the Senate Subcommittee on Interstate Trade and Commerce. For a good summary of both see Macaulay, *Law and the Balance of Power*, p. 76.

79. See, for example, L. W. Smead to C. E. Bowie and C. J. Seyffer (memorandum), November 10, 1955, on "Oklahoma Automobile Dealers Association Convention"; "Executive Communication," March 29, 1957 (summary of meeting with NADA officials), AR-66-31, box 9, FIA; "Auto Industry Closes Its Ranks," *Business Week*.

80. U.S. Congress, Senate, *Hearings on Automobile Dealer Franchises*. For an enlightening summary of General Motors's factory/dealer relations see "Memo-

randum Regarding General Motors Dealer Relationships: Suggestions as to What Might Be Done," A. P. Sloan to W. S. Carpenter, January 13, 1956, acc. 542, box 856-D, Walter S. Carpenter Papers, Hagley Museum and Library, Wilmington, Del. For Sloan's personal assessment on the motives for the 1955 hearings and how General Motors should react see "RE: Government Study on General Motors," A. P. Sloan to Donaldson Brown, December 15, 1955, acc. 1334, box 5, F. Donaldson Brown Papers, Hagley Museum and Library, Wilmington, Del.

81. U.S. Congress, Senate, *Automobile Marketing Practices*, pp. 970–84, 997.

82. Ibid., pp. 973, 997. See also the statements of Alfred P. Sloan and Frederick J. Bell (former vice-president of NADA) during the Senate Subcommittee on Antitrust and Monopoly's investigation of General Motors in *Hearings on Automobile Dealer Franchises*.

83. U.S. Congress, Senate, *Automobile Marketing Practices*, pp. 978–80.

84. For a good summary of the Federal Automobile Dealers Franchise Act see "Private Franchise Contracts" in Lawyers Cooperative Publishing, *American Jurisprudence*, pp. 478–583.

85. Macaulay, *Law and the Balance of Power*, pp. 92–107; "Auto Dealers Win," *Business Week*; "Auto Dealers Get Their Chance," *Business Week*.

CHAPTER THREE

1. Lovejoy, "Chain Filling Stations" (quotation, p. 21); Williamson et al., *Age of Energy*, pp. 194, 222.

2. Barger, *Distribution's Place*, p. 134. For a good description of the tensions created by the rise of big business in the oil industry and refiners' administrative responses see Chandler, *Strategy and Structure*, chaps. 1, 4. On the link between professional advertising and the rise of big business see Pope, *The Making of Modern Advertising*.

3. Pope, *The Making of Modern Advertising*; Tipper, *New Business*, p. 13. See also Cherington, *Advertising Book*, esp. pt. 1.

4. Williamson, *Age of Energy*, pp. 214–41; "Money to Be Made," *National Petroleum News*.

5. Williamson, *Age of Energy*, p. 219; *Federal Trade Commission v. Sinclair Refining Company*, 261 U.S. 463.

6. Barger, *Distribution's Place*, p. 134; McLean and Haigh, *Growth of the Integrated Oil Companies*, chap. 9.

7. Logan, *Stabilization in the Petroleum Industry*, app.; Williamson, *Age Of Energy*, p. 204.

8. Williamson, *Age of Energy*, pp. 206–30, 481–88; McLean and Haigh, *Growth of the Integrated Oil Companies*, pp. 102–9.

9. McLean and Haigh, *Growth of the Integrated Oil Companies*, chap. 9.

10. On the history of Sun see Giebelhaus, *Business and Government in the Oil Industry*; Johnson, *The Challenge of Change*.

11. "The Company's Founder," *Our Sun*.

12. Giebelhaus, *Business and Government in the Oil Industry*, chap. 2; Gliddens, *Standard Oil Company*, p. 3.

13. Giebelhaus, *Business and Government in the Oil Industry*, chap. 2; "The Story of Sun," *Our Sun*, pp. 17–19.

14. Giebelhaus, *Business and Government in the Oil Industry*, chap. 2; "The Story of Sun," *Our Sun*, pp. 17–19.

15. Giebelhaus, *Business and Government in the Oil Industry*, pp. 28–31; "The Story of Sun," *Our Sun*, pp. 18–19.

16. "The Story of Sun," *Our Sun*, pp. 18–19.

17. Gliddens, *Standard Oil Company*, pp. 2–7; Giebelhaus, *Business and Government in the Oil Industry*, pp. 25–31.

18. "The Story of Sun," *Our Sun*, pp. 17–21.

19. Giebelhaus, *Business and Government in the Oil Industry*, 53–55; "The Story of Sun," *Our Sun*, pp. 20–21; Prentiss, *Ford Products*, 1:79.

20. U.S. Congress, Temporary National Economic Committee (hereafter cited as TNEC), *Investigation of Concentration of Economic Power*, p. 7189.

21. McLean and Haigh, *Growth of the Integrated Oil Companies*, p. 104; Giebelhaus, *Business and Government in the Oil Industry*, pp. 69–79; "Remember the Pump with Arms?" *Our Sun*.

22. "Sun Oil," *Fortune* (quotation); Williamson, *Age of Energy*, pp. 444–45; U.S. Congress, TNEC, *Investigation of Concentration of Economic Power*, pp. 8, 791.

23. McLean and Haigh, *Growth of the Integrated Oil Companies*, chaps. 9–10; American Petroleum Institute, *Petroleum-Industry Hearings*, p. 103.

24. "Money to Be Made," *National Petroleum News*, pp. 112–17; Williamson, *Age of Energy*, pp. 221–27.

25. Gliddens, *Standard Oil Company*, pp. 174–77; McLean and Haigh, *Growth of the Integrated Oil Companies*, pp. 268–69; Jakle, "The American Gasoline Station." See also Fanning, "Gasoline Filling Stations Big Item."

26. "The Story of Sun," *Our Sun*, pp. 22–23; "40 Years' Growth in the Oil Industry, 1926," p. 19, acc. 1317, box 710, file: "40 Years' Growth in the Oil Industry," SOCC/HML.

27. *Federal Trade Commission v. Sinclair Refining Company*, 261 U.S. 463; "Instructions for Marketing Gasoline," p. 4, acc. 1317, box 910, and "Service Station Costs," acc. 1317, box 55, file: "Sun Oil Company-Properties, SOCC/HML; Phillips, "Jobbers Invite Trouble," p. 38 (quotation); McLean and Haigh, *Growth of*

the Integrated Oil Companies, pp. 267–68; Williamson, *Age of Energy,* pp. 482–83.

28. "Instructions For Marketing Gasoline," pp. 15–18, acc. 1317, box 910, SOCC/ HML.

29. Ibid., p. 3; "Brief for the Sun Oil Company," acc. 1317, box 909, SOCC/HML.

30. "Instructions for Marketing Gasoline," acc. 1317, box 910, SOCC/HML.

31. Ibid., p. 8. On the development of a company-designed advertising campaign see "Sales and Advertising Bulletin," September 21, September 23, and October 26, 1920, "Newspaper Electros on Free Crankcase Service," acc. 1317, box 909, file: Sunoco Motor Oils—S & A Bulletins—Agents, SOCC/HML.

32. "Instructions for Marketing Gasoline," p. 3, acc. 1317, box 910, and "Brief for the Sun Oil Company," pp. 79–88, acc. 1317, box 909, SOCC/HML.

33. U.S. Congress, TNEC, *Investigation of Concentration of Economic Power,* pp. 7210–12.

34. Ibid., p. 8674; Jakle, "The American Gasoline Station." For a good description of the rationale for station uniformity, which mirrors the main arguments put forward by later business format franchisers, see Halbert, "Certified Service Stations."

35. Federal Trade Commission, "Report on Prices, Profits, and Competition," pp. 255–59; Williamson, *Age of Energy,* pp. 481–88.

36. Federal Trade Commission, "Report on Prices, Profits, and Competition," pp. 255–59; Williamson, *Age of Energy,* pp. 481–88. On the debate over the merits of lease and license, or lease and agency, as it was sometimes called, see "Ring Their Door-Bells," *Petroleum Age;* Green, "California Companies Leasing Stations to Individual Operators"; Guthrie, "Leasing Oil Company Stations to Operators Is Successful"; Stafford, "Why One Jobber Finds Agency Outlets Better than Company Stations."

37. *Federal Trade Commission v. Sinclair Refining Company,* 261 U.S. 463; Black, "Exclusive Dealer Devices."

38. Federal Trade Commission, *Report on Prices, Profits, and Competition* and *Lease and Agency Agreements;* "Baker's Views on Lease and Agency," *National Petroleum News;* "Lease and Agency Called Subterfuge," *National Petroleum News;* Petty, "Lease and Agency Held Legal."

39. Giebelhaus, *Business and Government in the Oil Industry,* pp. 75–79, 150–52.

40. "Sun Oil Company," pp. 6–7, acc. 1317, box 58, and "Trial Highlights," October 11, 1955, acc. 1317, box 912, file: "Trial Highlights 1–12," SOCC/HML.

41. Giebelhaus, *Business and Government in the Oil Industry,* pp. 75–79; "The Story of Sun," *Our Sun,* pp. 22–23.

42. "Remember the Pump with Arms?" *Our Sun,* pp. 11–12; "Sun Oil Com-

pany," p. 7, acc. 1317, box 58, SOCC/HML. On concerns over the safety of gasoline see, for example, Ross, "Standard Oil's Death Factory"; Hamilton, "What Price Safety?"

43. "G-606" and "G-608," acc. 1317, box 904, file: G-503/G-868, and S. B. Eckert to Paul Hadlick, April 1, 1935, acc. 1317, box 916, file: S & A Bulletin 11A, SOCC/HML.

44. For a nearly complete sample of the various types of distributor contracts used by Sun from 1928 through 1947 see acc. 1317 (legal, antitrust), vol. 902, SOCC/HML.

45. "Manual of Instruction and Information for Sun Oil Company Service Station Salesmen," acc. 1317, box 694, SOCC/HML.

46. "To Our Dealers. . . ." *Sunoco Diamond.* Nearly every issue of the *Diamond* stresses the community of interest between the company and its dealers or suggests ways to improve a dealer's business that would also increase the uniformity of Sun's dealer network. See, for example, "You Have 14,000 Partners"; "Rip the Blindfold from Blind Records"; "She Don't Look Like the Same Gal"; "Lubrication Showcase"; "These Ads . . . Yours for the Asking"; "Sunoco's New Merchandising Program."

47. McLean and Haigh, *Growth of the Integrated Oil Companies,* p. 104.

48. Stafford, "Motorists Prefer One-Brand Stations."

49. On industry reaction to antichain legislation see "Chain Store Taxes Are Menace," *National Petroleum News*; "U.S. Supreme Court Gives States Power," *National Petroleum News*; Berringer, "Indiana Standard." On more recent evaluations of antichain legislation see McLean and Haigh, *Growth of the Integrated Oil Companies,* pp. 289–301; Williamson, *Age of Energy,* pp. 705–8. A third view—that refiners dropped company-owned stations to avoid the social security tax and other New Deal innovations—also exists. For a good summary of this opinion see Black, "Exclusive Dealer Devices."

50. Lee, *Anti–Chain-Store Tax Legislation,* pp. 5–9.

51. Ibid., pp. 15–16.

52. *Fox v. Standard Oil Company of New Jersey,* 55 S. Ct.; Berringer, "Indiana Standard."

53. *Fox v. Standard Oil Company of New Jersey,* 55 S. Ct.; Berringer, "Indiana Standard."

54. M. H. Leister to F. S. Cannon, February 13, 1935, file: Circular Letters, "Forms to Be Used for Contracting Sunoco Dealers and Leasing Property for All States Where *NO* Gasoline Chain Store Tax Is in Effect" and "Forms to Be Used for Contracting Sunoco Dealers and Leasing Property in States Where Gasoline Chain Store Tax Is in Effect," acc. 1317, box 911, SOCC/HML; "Effect of Former

Company-Operated Stations on Salesmen's Routing," October 28, 1936, acc. 1317, box 916, file: S & A Bulletin—11A, SOCC/HML.

55. John Moffett to S. B. Eckert, April 3, 1936, acc. 1317, box 916, file: S & A Bulletin—11A, SOCC/HML.

56. W. C. Pew to J. O. Craig et al., July 31, 1939, and W. C. Pew to Mr. Plumb, December 8, 1939, acc. 1317, box 916, file: S & A Bulletin—11A, SOCC/HML.

57. *United States v. Sun Oil Company*, 176 F. Supp. 715, pp. 732–33.

58. Ibid.

59. Ibid.

60. Ibid. See also "Analysis of Sun Oil Company's Growth, 1937–1947," acc. 1317, box 58, file: Sun Oil Company, and "Summary of Operations, Motor Products Department, 1948–1960," acc. 1317, box 693, SOCC/HML.

61. Glassey, "Sun Oil's 'Dynafuel' "; Sun Oil Company, "Annual Report, 1944," p. 4, and "Annual Report, 1945," p. 9, Hagley Library, Wilmington, Del.

62. "General Subjects No. 181," January 19, 1939, acc. 1317, box 910, file: Sales and Advertising Bulletin, SOCC/HML; "Modernize Your Office!" *Sunoco Diamond*; "Station Out of Date?" *Sunoco Diamond*.

63. *Standard Oil Company of California et al. v. United States*, 337 U.S. 293; *Richfield Oil Corporation v. United States*; *United States v. Sun Oil Company*, 176 F. Supp. 715.

64. *Standard Oil Company of California et al. v. United States*, 337 U.S. at 314.

65. *United States v. Sun Oil Company*, 176 F. Supp. 715.

66. U.S. Department of Commerce, *Statistical Abstract of the United States*, 1978 and 1989. The PMPA attracted very little attention from the industry press or the business press generally. Although the law was very comprehensive in its treatment of the franchise relationship, it corresponded fairly well to existing practice in the industry. This probably accounts for the lack of interest in its passage. For a look at most of what the press did have to say about the PMPA see "Oil Majors Retreat," *Business Week*; "Shhhh! Carter Signs Dealer-Day Bill," *National Petroleum News*; "Jobbers Get Unexpected Dealer-Day Support," *National Petroleum News*. On the debate over the passage of the PMPA see U.S. Congress, House, *Petroleum Marketing Practices*.

CHAPTER FOUR

1. "The Howard Johnson Restaurants," *Fortune*, pp. 84–86. See also Langdon, *Orange Roofs*, pp. 46–53.

2. "The Howard Johnson Restaurants," *Fortune*, p. 86.

3. Ibid., p. 94.

4. Ibid.

5. Ibid., pp. 84, 94. For a good discussion of Johnson's design department see Langdon, *Orange Roofs*, pp. 47–51.

6. "The Howard Johnson Restaurants, *Fortune*, pp. 94–96 (quotation, p. 96).

7. On the standardization of roadside food services see Belasco, "Toward a Culinary Common Denominator." For a more general treatment of the homogenization of travel see Boorstin, *The Image*, chap. 7. For a more personal view see Monninger, "Fast Food." For a sociological perspective on the lure of the chain restaurant see Kottak, "Rituals at McDonald's."

8. By 1955 the service sector was the largest single contributor to the GNP. U.S. Bureau of the Census, *Historical Statistics of the United States.*

9. Ibid.; Mayer, "Small Business," pp. 332–94.

10. Hawley, *The New Deal*; Fisher and Whitley, *Big Business as the People See It.*

11. Mayer, "Small Business," pp. 332–49; Zeigler, *Politics of Small Business.*

12. Riesman, *Lonely Crowd*; Mills, *White Collar*; Whyte, *The Organization Man*; Wilson, *Man in the Gray Flannel Suit.* Politically, the most tangible expression of the fate of the small business owner was the formation of the Small Business Administration in 1953. Because of the symbolic importance of the small business person, virtually all major political debates over the economy since the 1930s included at least lip service to the need to preserve small business. On the political debate over small business see Zeigler, *Politics of Small Business.*

13. Bunzel, *The American Small Businessman.* See also Bunzel, "General Ideology of the American Small Businessman"; Chinoy, *American Workers.*

14. Quoted in Burck, "Franchising's Troubled Dream World," p. 121. On the idea of franchising as a method of combining the security of big business with the independence of ownership see, for example, Curry et al., *Partners for Profit*; Dias and Gurnick, *Franchising.* Business-format franchising can also be seen as part of the consumer culture. On the development of the consumer culture see Fox and Lears, *Culture of Consumption.*

15. "Franchise Selling Catches On," *Business Week.* For examples of the articles that contributed to the franchise boom see Fleming, "Franchises"; Clark, "You Can Be Your Own Boss"; "Get a Franchise?" *Changing Times*; "The Everlasting Dream," *Newsweek.* For a good example of franchisers' growing awareness of the development of franchising as a distinct industry see Hooker, "The Story of Minnie Pearl."

16. On the emergence of franchising as an industry see Kursh, *Franchise Boom.* For a listing of many of the hundreds of firms that now service the franchise

industry in what appears to be every conceivable way see *The 1989 Franchise Annual.*

17. Kursh, *Franchise Boom*, pp. 194–201; "Franchise Selling Catches On," *Business Week*, pp. 90–93; International Franchise Association, *Looking Back* and *Directory of Membership, 1986–1987*, pp. 6–23. On the development of the International Center for Franchise Studies see Babcock, "Past, Present, and Future." For a good overview of the IFA's role in the formation of franchise law see Rudnick, *Decade of Franchise Regulation.*

18. Hancock and Lewis, *Franchise System.* For a good overview of the development of franchise law see Braun, "Policy Issues of Franchising"; Rudnick, *Decade of Franchise Regulation*; Santoni, "Franchising."

19. *Standard Oil Company of California et al. v. United States*, 337 U.S. at 314; *United States v. Sun Oil Company*, 176 F. Supp. 715.

20. *Susser v. Carvel Corporation*, 206 F. Supp. 636.

21. *Seigel v. Chicken Delight, Inc.*, 448 F.2d 43.

22. *Principe v. McDonald's Corporation*, 631 F.2d 303 at 311.

23. for a good overview of state franchise laws and the FTC rulings see Santoni, "Franchising."

24. For a highly detailed description and analysis of the rationale behind franchise legislation see Braun, "Policy Issues of Franchising." For a brief summary of the main provisions of the FTC rule see *The 1989 Franchise Annual*, pp. H49–H52.

25. For a summary of the various state laws see *The 1989 Franchise Annual*, pp. H59–H60. For a more detailed discussion see Glickman, *Franchising.*

26. On the overall development of Domino's see Monaghan and Anderson, *Pizza Tiger*; Domino's Pizza, Inc., *25-Year History* (hereafter cited as "Internal History"). For less comprehensive accounts see "Michigan Campus Spawns a Pizza King," *Michigan Business*; Brickley, "'Pizza Tiger' Tom Monaghan."

27. "Internal History," p. 1; Monaghan and Anderson, *Pizza Tiger*, pp. 60–61; "Michigan Campus Spawns a Pizza King," *Michigan Business.*

28. Monaghan and Anderson, *Pizza Tiger*, pp. 62–63.

29. Ibid., chaps. 4–5.

30. Ibid., pp. 58, 99–101.

31. "Internal History," p. 3. On the development of the fast-food industry see Love, *McDonald's*, chap. 3. The entire issue of the *Journal of American Culture* 2 (Fall 1979) is devoted to "the rise of mass-produced foods"; it takes a broad approach, dealing not only with fast food but also with changes in related areas such as food-processing technology and the social impact of mass-produced food.

32. "A Quarter Century in Review: A Chronology of Events in the History of Domino's Pizza, Inc.," Domino's Pizza Corporate Archives, Ann Arbor, Mich.

(hereafter cited as DA). Domino's archives were established in 1986, but as of June 1987, when the research for this project was completed, few of the holdings had been cataloged. As a result, it was impossible to include either box or file locations for Domino's corporate records. These archives were closed in 1989.

33. Monaghan and Anderson, *Pizza Tiger*, pp. 105, 110–11; "A Quarter Century in Review," p. 3, DA.

34. "Internal History," p. 2.

35. Ibid., p. 5; Monaghan and Anderson, *Pizza Tiger*, p. 63.

36. Monaghan and Anderson, *Pizza Tiger*, p. 77; "Michigan Campus Spawns a Pizza King," *Michigan Business*.

37. Monaghan and Anderson, *Pizza Tiger*, p. 110; "Domino's Pizza Franchise Agreement," August 3, 1967, DA.

38. "Michigan Campus Spawns a Pizza King," *Michigan Business*; Monaghan and Anderson, *Pizza Tiger*, pp. 125–26.

39. Monaghan and Anderson, *Pizza Tiger*, p. 136; Tom Monaghan to Wendell Smith, March 26, 1969, and Monaghan to J. Richard Lumpe, April 23, 1970, DA.

40. "The Domino Story," DA.

41. "Michigan Campus Spawns a Pizza King," *Michigan Business*.

42. Monaghan and Anderson, *Pizza Tiger*, chaps. 9–10.

43. "Internal History," pp. 23, 26; "Defendants' Post-Trial Memorandum," p. 7, DA. For a concise description of the crash of 1969 see Raffio, "Domino's Pizza," pp. 98–99.

44. "Internal History," pp. 24–26, DA; Monaghan and Anderson, *Pizza Tiger*, p. 148.

45. Monaghan and Anderson, *Pizza Tiger*, pp. 154–57. See also Ray Foresman to Robert Seymour, October 12, 1972 (company buy-out of rebellious franchisees), DA.

46. Monaghan and Anderson, *Pizza Tiger*, pp. 137–38.

47. Dave Kilby (Florida-area franchisee) to Tom Monaghan, April 9, 1975, Tom Monaghan to Dave Kilby, April 14, 1975, "Domino's Pizza Distributor Agreement," April 1970, and "Domino's Pizza, Inc. (DPI) Area Distributor's Agreement," 1973, DA.

48. "Domino's Pizza Distributor Agreement," April 1970, p. 2, and "Domino's Pizza, Inc. (DPI) Area Distributor's Agreement," 1973, p. 2 (quotation), DA.

49. Raffio, "Domino's Pizza," p. 99; "Pizza Franchises for Sale," *Pepperoni Press* (Domino's company newspaper); Monaghan and Anderson, *Pizza Tiger*, pp. 162–65.

50. "In the United States District Court for the Northern District of Georgia, Atlanta Division, *Amstar v. Domino's Pizza Inc.*, Civil Action No. C75–1895A, Defendant's Post-Trial Memorandum," p. 7, DA.

51. Monaghan and Anderson, *Pizza Tiger*, pp. 171–73; "College of Pizzarology," *Pepperoni Press*; "Executive Team Meeting, Training Department Report," October 30, 1978, DA.

52. "Executive Team Meeting, Training Department Report," November 13, 1978, DA.

53. Tom Monaghan to David Seltz, April 28, 1975, DA; "Pizza Franchises for Sale," *Pepperoni Press*.

54. Monaghan and Anderson, *Pizza Tiger*, pp. 174–78.

55. Dave Kilby to Tom Monaghan, April 9, 1975, Tom Monaghan to Dave Kilby, April, 14, 1975, "Synopsis of Meeting between Area Franchisee Multiple Management Group and the DPI Executive Team," September 28, 1979, "Executive Team Meeting Minutes," December 19, 1979, pp. 3–5, and David Kilby to Executive Team, "Inter-Office Memo" on "Franchise Policies," October 3, 1979, DA.

56. "DPI, BOD Meeting Minutes," November 27, 1979, pp. 4–6, and "Corporate Area Representative Manual," [1980], DA.

57. "Tom Monaghan Fact Sheet," p. 2, DA; "Pizza Franchises for Sale," *Pepperoni Press*. Examples of Domino's franchise literature are in "Domino's Pizza, Inc., Operations Manual," [1979], DA. Typical requests for franchise information and the company response are Oscar Schreiber (franchise director, 1978–79) to Doris Brennan, May 18, 1978, and Oscar Schreiber to Mary Carden, February 28, 1978, DA.

58. "Franchising—Status Report" (memorandum), October 2, 1978, "Executive Team Meeting—Training Department Report," October 30, 1978, "Executive Team Meeting—Training Department Report," November 13, 1978, "Domino's Pizza, Inc., Operations Manual," [1979], and "Domino's Pizza, Inc., Identity Manual," [1979], DA.

59. "Domino's Pizza, Inc. (DPI), Area Distributor's Agreement," p. 5, and "Franchise Offering Circular for Prospective Franchisees Required by the State of Michigan," [1978], p. 11, DA.

60. "Group 243 Design, Report on Status of Work for Domino's Pizza, Inc.," November 11, 1975, "243 Site Selection Agreement," various dates since 1979, "Group 243 Design, Inc., Report on Status of Work for Domino's Pizza," various dates in 1978–79, and "Executive Team Meeting," December 11, 1978, p. 1, DA.

61. "Uniform Franchise Offering Circular," 1975, 1978, 1980, 1985, DA.

62. Monaghan and Anderson, *Pizza Tiger*, chaps. 14–15; *Amstar Corporation v. Domino's Pizza, Inc.*, 615 F.2d 252. On franchisee concern over the loss of the Domino's name see "Monthly Report [on Franchisee Operations] for November 1979—Sue Pagniano," and Joe Romono to Dick Mueller (memorandum), November 1979, DA.

63. Monaghan and Anderson, *Pizza Tiger*, chap. 15; [Group 243], "Special Memo to DPI," January 18, 1980, DA.

64. Raffio, "Domino's Pizza," pp. 102–3.

65. "Group Pilot Project," [1978], "Executive Team Minutes," January 18, 1980, p. 8, and "Area Franchise Policy," [1980], DA.

66. "Area Franchise Policy," [1980], DA.

67. Raffio, "Domino's Pizza," p. 102; "Synopsis of Meeting between Area Franchise Multiple Management Group and DPI Executive Team," September 28, 1979, DA.

68. "Domino's Pizza Chronology," pp. 5–8, DA.

69. U.S. Department of Commerce, *Franchising in the Economy*, p. 14.

Bibliography

This bibliography is organized as follows:
Business Records
Government Records
Legal Cases Cited
Books, Articles, and Theses

BUSINESS RECORDS

Domino's Pizza Records, Domino's Pizza Corporate Archives, Ann Arbor, Mich. (Domino's archives were disbanded in 1989.)

Ford Motor Company Collection, Ford Archives, Edison Institute, Henry Ford Museum and Greenfield Village, Dearborn, Mich., and Ford Industrial Archives, Redford, Mich.

Cyrus H. McCormick Collection, State Historical Society of Wisconsin, Madison.

Singer Manufacturing Company Collection, Singer Archives, State Historical Society of Wisconsin, Madison.

Sun Oil Company Collection, Hagley Museum and Library, Wilmington, Del.

GOVERNMENT RECORDS

Federal Trade Commission. *Report of the Federal Trade Commission on the Causes of High Prices of Farm Implements.* Washington, D.C.: Government Printing Office, 1920.

————. *A Report on Prices, Profits, and Competition in the Petroleum Industry.* Washington, D.C.: Government Printing Office, 1928.

Bibliography

————. *Lease and Agency Agreements in the Petroleum Industry.* Washington, D.C.: Government Printing Office, 1933.

————. *Report on the Motor Vehicle Industry.* Washington, D.C.: Government Printing Office, 1940.

National Recovery Administration. *Codes of Fair Competition.* Vol. 1. Washington, D.C.: Government Printing Office, 1933.

U.S. Bureau of the Census. *Census of Distribution: Retail Chains.* Washington, D.C.: Government Printing Office, 1933.

————. *Historical Statistics of the United States: Colonial Times to 1970.* Washington, D.C.: Government Printing Office, 1976.

U.S. Bureau of Corporations. *Farm-Machinery Trade Associations.* Washington, D.C.: Government Printing Office, 1915.

U.S. Congress. House. Subcommittee on Energy and Power, Committee on Interstate and Foreign Commerce. *Petroleum Marketing Practices.* 94th Cong., 2d sess. Washington, D.C.: Government Printing Office, 1978.

————. Senate. Subcommittee on Antitrust and Monopoly, Committee on the Judiciary. *Hearings on Automobile Dealer Franchises.* 84th Cong., 1st sess. Washington, D.C.: Government Printing Office, 1956.

————. Senate. Subcommittee of the Committee on Interstate and Foreign Commerce. *Automobile Marketing Practices.* 84th Cong., 2d sess. Washington, D.C.: Government Printing Office, 1956.

————. Senate. Subcommittee no. 4, Select Committee on Small Business. *The Impact upon Small Business of Dual Distribution and Related Vertical Integration.* 88th Cong., 1st sess. Washington, D.C.: Government Printing Office, 1963.

————. Senate. Select Committee on Small Business. *Impact of Franchising on Small Business.* 91st Cong., 2d sess. Washington, D.C.: Government Printing Office, 1970.

————. Temporary National Economic Committee. *Investigation of Concentration of Economic Power—Hearings Before the Temporary National Economic Committee.* 76th Cong., 3d sess. Washington, D.C.: Government Printing Office, 1941.

U.S. Department of Commerce. *Statistical Abstract of the United States.* Washington, D.C.: Government Printing Office, 1978 and 1989.

————. *Franchising in the Economy, 1985–1987.* Washington, D.C.: Government Printing Office, 1987.

Bibliography

LEGAL CASES CITED

Amstar Corporation v. Domino's Pizza, Inc., 615 F.2d 252 (1980).

Federal Trade Commission v. Sinclair Refining Company, 261 U.S. 463 (1923).

Fox v. Standard Oil Company of New Jersey, 55 S. Ct. (1935).

Principe v. McDonald's Corporation, 631 F.2d 303 (1980).

Richfield Oil Corporation v. United States, 343 U.S. 922 (1951).

Seigel v. Chicken Delight, Inc., 448 F.2d 43 (1971).

Standard Oil Company of California et al. v. United States, 337 U.S. 293 (1949).

Susser v. Carvel Corporation, 206 F. Supp. 636 (1962).

United States v. Sun Oil Company, 176 F. Supp. 715 (1959).

BOOKS, ARTICLES, AND THESES

American Petroleum Institute, comp. *Petroleum-Industry Hearings before the Temporary National Economic Committee.* New York: American Petroleum Institute, 1942.

Anderson, Mary Christine. "Gender, Class, and Culture: Women Secretarial and Clerical Workers in the United States, 1925–1955." Ph.D. dissertation, Ohio State University, 1986.

Ardrey, R. L. "The Harvesting Machine Industry." *Scientific American Supplement* no. 1407 (December 20, 1902): 22545.

Atkinson, Jeff. *Franchising: The Odds-On Favorite.* Chicago: International Franchise Association, 1968.

"Auto Dealers Get Their Chance to Oppose 'One-Sided' Franchise Deals." *Business Week*, June 30, 1956, p. 81.

"Auto Dealers Win." *Business Week*, August 20, 1956, p. 34.

"Auto Industry Closes Its Ranks." *Business Week*, February 2, 1957, pp. 25–26.

"Automobile Dealers Offset Lack of Cars by Concentrating on Service and War Work." *Automotive War Production*, January 1944, p. 2.

"Automobiles II—The Dealer." *Fortune*, October 1931, pp. 38–43+.

Averitt, Robert T. *The Dual Economy: The Dynamics of American Industry Structure.* New York: W. W. Norton, 1968.

Babcock, Cheryl. "International Center for Franchise Studies: Past, Present, and Future." *Franchising World* 19 (May/June 1987): 36–39.

Baird, D. G. "All About Ford's New Sales Tool: Marketing Research." *Sales Management* (March 1, 1948): 44–6+.

———. "Ford 'College' Trains Dealers in the ABC's of Profit-Making." *Sales Management* (July 15, 1946): 56+.

Bibliography

————. "Ford Post-War Plans: Improved Car, More Dealers, Basic Pay of Salesmen." *Sales Management* (January 15, 1945): 71+.

"Baker's Views on Lease and Agency." *National Petroleum News* 25 (August 2, 1933): 20.

Barger, Harold. *Distribution's Place in the American Economy since 1869.* Princeton, N.J.: Princeton University Press, 1955.

Baxter, William. *The House of Hancock.* Boston: Harvard University Press, 1945.

Belasco, Warren. "Toward a Culinary Common Denominator: The Rise of Howard Johnson's, 1952–1940." *Journal of American Culture* 2 (Fall 1979): 503–18.

Benson, Susan Porter. *Countercultures: Saleswomen, Managers, and Customers in the American Department Store.* Chicago: University of Illinois Press, 1988.

Berringer, E. L. "Indiana Standard Begins Leasing All Iowa Service Stations." *National Petroleum News* 27 (May 29, 1935): 24-H.

Black, Forrest. "Exclusive Dealer Devices in the Marketing of Petroleum Products." *Georgetown Law Journal* 29 (Winter 1940): 439–59.

Blackford, Mansel. *Pioneering a Modern Small Business: Wakefield Seafood and the Alaska Frontier.* Greenwich, Conn.: JAI Press, 1979.

Boas, Max, and Steve Chain. *Big Mac: The Unauthorized Story of McDonald's.* New York: E. P. Dutton, 1976.

Boorstin, Daniel. *The Image.* New York: Atheneum, 1961.

————. *The Americans: The Democratic Experience.* New York: Random House, 1973.

Brandon, Ruth. *A Capitalist Romance: Singer and the Sewing Machine.* Philadelphia: J. B. Lippincott, 1977.

Braun, Ernest. "Policy Issues of Franchising." *Southwestern University Law Review* 14 (November 2, 1984): 155–273.

Brickley, Homer. " 'Pizza Tiger' Tom Monaghan." *Toledo Blade Sunday Magazine,* June 20, 1987, pp. 8–18.

Brinkley, Alan. "Writing the History of Contemporary America." *Daedalus* 113 (Summer 1984): 121–41.

Broehl, Wayne G., Jr. *John Deere's Company: A History of Deere and Company and Its Times.* New York: Doubleday, 1984.

Brown, Harold. *Franchising: Trap for the Trusting.* Boston: Little, Brown, 1970.

————. *Franchising—Realities and Remedies.* New York: Law Journal Press, 1973.

Bunzel, John. "The General Ideology of the American Small Businessman." *Political Science Quarterly* 70 (March 1955): 87–102.

————. *The American Small Businessman.* New York: Knopf, 1962.

Bibliography

Burck, Charles G. "Franchising's Troubled Dream World." *Fortune*, March 1970, pp. 116–21+.

Burlingame, Roger. *Henry Ford: A Great Life in Brief.* New York: Knopf, 1955.

Carstensen, Fred V. *American Enterprise in Foreign Markets: Studies of Singer and International Harvester in Imperial Russia.* Chapel Hill: University of North Carolina Press, 1984.

Casson, Herbert N. *Cyrus Hall McCormick: His Life and Work.* Chicago: A. C. McLurg, 1909.

"Chain Store Taxes Are Menace to Oil Industry Stations." *National Petroleum News* 24 (February 12, 1932): 36.

Chandler, Alfred D., Jr. "The Beginnings of 'Big Business' in American Industry." *Business History Review* 33 (Spring 1959): 1–31.

———.*Strategy and Structure: Chapters in the History of the Industrial Enterprise.* Cambridge: MIT Press, 1962.

———. *Giant Enterprise: Ford, General Motors, and the American Automobile Industry.* New York: Harcourt, Brace and World, 1964.

———. *The Visible Hand: The Managerial Revolution in American Business.* Boston: Harvard University Press, 1977.

———. "Business History: What Is It About?" *Journal of Contemporary Business* 10, no. 3 (1981): 47–66.

Cherington, Paul T. *The Advertising Book, 1916.* New York: Doubleday, 1916.

Childs, William R. *Trucking and the Public Interest: The Emergence of Federal Regulation, 1914–1940.* Knoxville: University of Tennessee Press, 1985.

Chinoy, Eli. *American Workers and the American Dream.* Garden City, N.Y.: Doubleday, 1955.

Clark, Blake. "You Can Be Your Own Boss." *Reader's Digest* 75 (September 1959): 221–25. (Condensed from *Today's Living*, August 16, 1959.)

Cochran, Thomas C., and William Miller. *The Age of Enterprise.* Rev. ed. New York: Harper, 1961.

"College of Pizzarology." *Pepperoni Press*, October 7, 1973, p. 3.

"The Company's Founder." *Our Sun* 26 (Summer/Autumn 1961): 11–13.

Conard, Howard. "Evolution of the Harvesting Machine." *The National Magazine*, August 1890, pp. 594–605.

Cooper, Grace Rogers. *History of the Sewing Machine.* Washington, D.C.: Government Printing Office, 1968.

Curry, A. H.; et al. *Partners for Profit: A Study of Franchising.* New York: American Marketing Association, 1966.

Davies, Robert B. "'Peacefully Working to Conquer the World': The Singer Manufacturing Company in Foreign Markets, 1854–1889." *Business History Review* 18 (Autumn 1969): 299–325.

Bibliography

Davisson, Charles, and Herbert Taggart. *Financial and Operating Characteristics of Automobile Dealers and the Franchise System.* Ann Arbor: University of Michigan, 1974.

Deane, Phyllis. *The First Industrial Revolution.* 2d ed. New York: Cambridge University Press, 1979.

Dias, Robert, and Stanley Gurnick. *Franchising.* New York: Hastings House, 1969.

Dicke, Thomas S. "The Public Image of American Small Business Portrayed in the American Periodical Press, 1900–1938." M.A. thesis, Ohio State University, 1983.

Dominguez, Henry. *The Ford Agency: A Pictorial History.* Osceola, Wis.: Motorbooks International, 1981.

Domino's Pizza, Inc. *Domino's Pizza: 25-Year History.* Ann Arbor, Mich.: Domino's Pizza Inc., 1985.

Douglas, Diane. "The Machine in the Parlor: A Dialectical Analysis of the Sewing Machine." *Journal of American Culture* 5 (September 1982): 20–29.

Doyel, Tommy Terry. "The Economic Outlook for Small Business Franchising." Ph.D. dissertation, University of California, Los Angeles, 1971.

Dublin, Thomas. *Women at Work: The Transformation of Work and Community in Lowell, Massachusetts, 1826–1860.* New York: Columbia University Press, 1979.

"The Everlasting Dream—Be Your Own Boss." *Newsweek*, February 12, 1962, pp. 68–70.

Ewers, William. *Sincere's History of the Sewing Machine.* Phoenix: Sincere Press, 1970.

Fanning, N. O. "Gasoline Filling Stations Big Item." *Oil and Gas Journal*, March 20, 1924, p. 106.

Fink, James J. "Three Stages of American Automobile Consciousness." *American Quarterly* 24 (October 1972): 451–73.

———. *The Car Culture.* Cambridge: MIT Press, 1975.

Fisher, Burton, and Stephen Whitley. *Big Business as the People See It.* Ann Arbor: University of Michigan, Institute for Social Research, 1951.

Fishwick, Marshall, ed. "FOCUS: The World of Ronald McDonald." *Journal of American Culture* 1 (Summer 1978): 336–471.

Fleming, Eugene D. "Franchises: Big New Frontier for Small Business." *Cornet*, July 1961, pp. 37–41.

Forbes, B. C. "Why Our Articles on Henry Ford Are Being Published." *Forbes* 19 (May 15, 1927): 15–19.

"Ford Agencies Increase Rapidly in Every City." *Automobile* 35 (August 24, 1916): 300.

Bibliography

"Ford Co. Adds 34 Branches." *Automobile* 35 (July 27, 1916): 161.

"Ford Dealers Rebel; Many Leave Ranks." *Business Week*, April 2, 1930, p. 9.

"Ford to Drop Retail Sales." *Automobile* 35 (August 17, 1916): 255+.

Ford Motor Company. *The Ford Dealer Story*. Dearborn, Mich.: Ford Motor Company, 1953.

"Ford Revises Dealer Franchise." *Business Week*, February 18, 1939, p. 23.

"Ford Salesmen Form Agencies." *Automobile* 35 (August 17, 1916): 291.

"Ford Stores." *Business Week*, December 21, 1932, p. 8.

"Franchise Selling Catches On." *Business Week*, February 6, 1960, p. 90+.

Fox, Richard, and T. J. Lears, eds. *The Culture of Consumption: Critical Essays in American History, 1880–1980*. New York: Pantheon, 1983.

Galambos, Louis. *The Public Image of Big Business, 1880–1940*. Baltimore: Johns Hopkins, 1975.

————. "Technology, Political Economy, and Professionalization: Central Themes of the Organizational Synthesis." *Business History Review* 57 (Autumn 1983): 471–93.

Galbraith, John Kenneth. *The Affluent Society*. Boston: Houghton Mifflin, 1958.

"Get a Franchise? . . . Way to go into Business for Yourself." *Changing Times* 13 (May 1959): 7–11.

Ghent, W. J. *Our Benevolent Feudalism*. New York: Macmillan, 1902.

Giebelhaus, August W. *Business and Government in the Oil Industry*. Greenwich, Conn.: JAI Press, 1980.

Gilmore, Grant. *The Death of Contract*. Columbus: Ohio State University Press, 1974.

Gimpel, Jean. *The Medieval Machine: The Industrial Revolution of the Middle Ages*. New York: Holt, Rinehart, and Winston, 1976.

Glassey, Frank. "Sun Oil's 'Dynafuel' to Be Sold at Modern Age Stations." *National Petroleum News* 38 (November 7, 1945): 68–69.

Glickman, Glayds. *Franchising*. New York: Matthew Bender, updated as necessary.

Gliddens, Paul. *Standard Oil Company (Indiana): Oil Pioneer of the Middle West*. New York: Appleton-Century-Crofts, 1955.

Godfrey, Frank. *An International History of the Sewing Machine*. London: Robert Hale, 1982.

Green, William. "California Companies Leasing Stations to Individual Operators." *National Petroleum News* 19 (May 4, 1927): 95–96.

Guthrie, V. B. "Leasing Oil Company Stations to Operators Is Successful." *National Petroleum News* 21 (March 20, 1929): 68–78.

Halbert, W. K. "Certified Service Stations Is Texas Co. Plan for Closer Tieup with Dealers" *National Petroleum News* 19 (June 15, 1927): 20–22.

Bibliography

Hall, William P. "Franchising—New Scope for an Old Technique." *Harvard Business Review* 42 (January/February 1964): 60–72.

Hamilton, Alice. "What Price Safety? Tetra-ethyl Lead Reveals a Flaw in Our Defenses." *Survey* 54 (June 15, 1925): 333–34.

Hancock, Robert, and Edward Lewis. *The Franchise System of Distribution.* Washington, D.C.: Government Printing Office, 1963.

Hawley, Ellis. *The New Deal and the Problem of Monopoly.* Princeton, N.J.: Princeton University Press, 1966.

————. *The Great War and the Search for a Modern Order.* New York: St. Martin's Press, 1979.

Henderson, Ernest, Sr. "Franchising Yesterday." In *Franchising Today, 1966–1967,* edited by Charles Vaughn, pp. 239–44. San Francisco: Matthew Bender, 1967.

Hewitt, Charles Mason, Jr. *Automobile Franchise Agreements.* Homewood, Ill.: Richard D. Irwin, 1956.

Hidy, Ralph. "Business History: A Bibliographic Essay." In *Recent Developments in the Study of Business and Economic History: Essays in Memory of Herman E. Krooss,* edited by Paul Uselding. Greenwich, Conn.: JAI Press, 1977.

Hidy, Ralph, and Muriel Hidy. *Pioneering in Big Business, 1882–1911: History of Standard Oil Company (New Jersey).* New York: Harper, 1955.

Hofstadter, Richard. *The Age of Reform.* New York: Knopf, 1955.

Hooker, John Jay. "The Story of Minnie Pearl." In *Franchising Today,* edited by Charles Vaughn, pp. 131–39. Lynbrook, Mass.: Farnsworth Publishing, 1970.

Hounshell, David. *From the American System to Mass Production, 1800–1932.* Baltimore: Johns Hopkins, 1984.

"The Howard Johnson's Restaurants." *Fortune,* September 1940, pp. 82+.

Hurst, James. *Law and Markets in United States History.* Madison: University of Wisconsin Press, 1982.

Hutchinson, William T. *Cyrus Hall McCormick.* 2 vols. New York: D. Appleton-Century, 1930 and 1935.

International Franchise Association. *Looking Back: Looking Ahead, an IFA 25th Anniversary Retrospective as Seen by IFA's Past Presidents.* Washington, D.C.: International Franchise Association, 1985.

————. *Directory of Membership, 1986–1987.* Washington, D.C.: International Franchise Association, 1986.

Jack, Andrew B. "The Channels of Distribution for an Innovation: The Sewing-Machine Industry in America, 1860–1865." *Explorations in Entrepreneurial History* 9 (Winter 1956/1957): 113–41.

Bibliography

Jakle, John. "The American Gasoline Station, 1920–1970." *Journal of American Culture* 1 (Fall 1978): 521–42.

James, Marquis. *The Texaco Story: The First Fifty Years, 1902–1952.* N.p.: The Texas Co., 1953.

"Jobbers Get Unexpected Dealer-Day Support." *National Petroleum News* 70 (January 1978): 36–37.

Johnson, Arthur. *The Challenge of Change: The Sun Oil Company, 1945–1977.* Columbus: Ohio State University Press, 1983.

Jones, Fred. *Middlemen in the Domestic Trade of the United States, 1800–1860.* Urbana: University of Illinois, 1973.

Kottak, Conrad. "Rituals at McDonald's." *Natural History* 87 (January 1978): 74–83.

Kramer, Helen. "Harvesters and High Finance." *Business History Review* 38 (Autumn 1964): 283–301.

Kroc, Ray, and Robert Anderson. *Grinding It Out: The Making of McDonald's.* Chicago: Henry Regnery, 1977.

Kursh, Harry. *The Franchise Boom: The New Revised Edition.* Englewood Cliffs, N.J.: Prentice-Hall, 1968.

Landes, David. *The Unbound Prometheus: Technological Change and Industrial Development in Western Europe from 1750 to the Present.* New York: Cambridge University Press, 1969.

Langdon, Philip. *Orange Roofs, Golden Arches: The Architecture of American Chain Restaurants.* New York: Knopf, 1986.

Lawyers Cooperative Publishing. *American Jurisprudence.* 2d ed. Vol. 62B. Rochester, N.Y.: Lawyers Cooperative Publishing, 1990.

"Lease and Agency Called Subterfuge to Circumvent Clayton Law." *National Petroleum News* 24 (February 25, 1931): 27–30.

Lebhar, Godfrey M. *Chain Stores in America, 1859–1962.* 3d ed. New York: Chain Store Publishing Corporation, 1963.

Lee, Maurice. *Anti–Chain-Store Tax Legislation.* Chicago: University of Chicago Press, 1939.

Lewis, David. *The Public Image of Henry Ford.* Detroit: Wayne State University Press, 1976.

Lewis, Edwin, and Robert Hancock. *The Franchise System of Distribution.* Washington, D.C.: Government Printing Office, 1963.

Lewis, Sinclair. *Babbitt.* New York: Harcourt, Brace, Jovanovich, 1922.

Liles, Allen. *Oh Thank Heaven! The Story of the Southland Corporation.* Dallas: The Southland Corp., 1977.

Livesay, Harold. "Nineteenth-Century Precursors to Automobile Marketing in the United States." In *Development of Mass Marketing*, [Proceedings of the Fuji Conference], edited by Klo Okochl and Kolchl Shimokawa, pp. 39–52. Tokyo: Tokyo University, 1980.

Logan, Leonard, Jr. *Stabilization in the Petroleum Industry*. Norman: University of Oklahoma Press, 1930.

Love, John F. *McDonald's: Behind the Arches*. New York: Bantam, 1986.

Lovejoy, F. W. "Chain Filling Stations to Be the Development of the Future." *National Petroleum News* 16 (June 9, 1926): 21.

"Lubrication Showcase." *Sunoco Diamond* 8 (August 1939): 11.

Luxenberg, Stan. *Roadside Empires*. New York: Viking, 1985.

Macaulay, Stuart. *Law and the Balance of Power*. New York: Russell Sage, 1986.

McCord, Jim., ed. *The Franchising Sourcebook*. New York: Practicing Law Institute, 1970.

McCormick, Cyrus. *The Century of the Reaper*. Boston: Houghton Mifflin, 1931.

———, ed. "What 71 Years of Business Have Taught Us." *System: The Magazine of Business* 30 (October 1916): 654–59.

McCurdy, Charles W. "American Law and the Marketing Structure of the Large Corporation, 1875–1890." *Journal of Economic History* 38 (September 1978): 631–49.

McCusker, John J., and Russell R. Menard. *The Economy of British America, 1607–1789*. Chapel Hill: University of North Carolina Press, 1985.

McDean, Harry C. "Beatrice: The Historical Profile of an American-Styled Conglomerate." In *American Business History: Case Studies*, edited by Harry C. Dethloff and C. Joseph Pusateri, pp. 381–412. Arlington Heights, Ill.: Harlan Davidson, 1987.

McLean, John, and Robert Haigh. *The Growth of the Integrated Oil Companies*. Boston: Harvard University Press, 1954.

"The Manufacturers Agent as a Channel of Distribution." *Harvard Business Review* 6 (October 1927): 95–101.

"Many Copy Ford's Sales Plan." *Automobile* 35 (October 12, 1916): 599.

Marx, Thomas G. "The Development of the Franchise Distribution System in the U.S. Automobile Industry." *Business History Review* 59 (Autumn 1985): 465–74.

Mayer, Kurt. "Small Business as a Social Institution." *Social Research* 14 (September 1947): 332–49.

"Michigan Campus Spawns a Pizza King: Domino's, Inc., Opens a Store a Week." *Michigan Business* 1 (June 28, 1969): no pp.

Mills, C. Wright. *White Collar: The American Middle Classes*. New York: Oxford University Press, 1951.

"Modernize Your Office!" *Sunoco Diamond* 10 (January 1941): 15.

Bibliography

Monaghan, Tom, and Robert Anderson. *Pizza Tiger*. New York: Random House, 1986.

"Money to Be Made: The Oil-Marketing Story." *National Petroleum News* 61 (February 1969): 111–30.

Monninger, Joseph. "Fast Food." *American Heritage* 39 (April 1988): 68–69.

National Automobile Chamber of Commerce. *Facts and Figures of, by, and for the Automobile Industry*, April 1919, p. 12.

"National Automobile Dealers Association Started." *Automobile* 35 (May 31, 1917): 1032.

Nelson, Daniel. *Frederick W. Taylor and the Rise of Scientific Management*. Madison: University of Wisconsin Press, 1980.

Nevins, Allen, and Frank Hill. *Ford: The Times, the Man, the Company*. New York: Scribner, 1954.

———. *Ford: Expansion and Challenge: 1915–1933*. New York: Scribner, 1957.

———. *Ford: Decline and Rebirth: 1932–1962*. New York: Scribner, 1962.

New York University Bureau of Business Research. *The Exclusive Agency*. New York: New York University, 1923.

Nolen, Herman Christian. "Chain Store Taxation." Ph.D. dissertation, Ohio State University, 1937.

Norton, Seth. "An Empirical Investigation of Franchising as an Organizational Form." *Journal of Business* 61 (April 1988): 197–218.

Ohio Cultivator. Various years, no titles. (See notes for specific dates.)

"The Oil Majors Retreat from the Gasoline Pump." *Business Week*, August 7, 1978, pp. 50–51.

Parton, James. "History of the Sewing Machine." *The Atlantic* 19 (May 1867): 527–44.

Pashigian, Bedros. *The Distribution of Automobiles: An Economic Analysis of the Franchise System*. Englewood Cliffs, N.J.: Prentice-Hall, 1961.

Perkins, Edwin. *The Economy of Colonial America*. New York: Columbia University Press, 1980.

Peterson, Theodore. *Magazines in the Twentieth Century*. Urbana: University of Illinois Press, 1964.

Petty, A. M. "Lease and Agency Held Legal in Principle, Lease and Licence Is Questioned." *National Petroleum News* 27 (April 24, 1935): 35–36+.

Phillips, W. B. "Jobbers Invite Trouble by Helping Incompetents into Business." *National Petroleum News* 15 (October 31, 1923): 38.

"Pizza Franchises for Sale." *Pepperoni Press*, February 8, 1978, no pp.

Pope, Daniel. *The Making of Modern Advertising*. New York: Basic Books, 1983.

Porter, Glenn. *The Rise of Big Business, 1860–1910*. New York: Thomas Y. Crowell, 1973.

Porter, Glenn, and Harold Livesay. *Merchants and Manufacturers: Studies in the Changing Structure of Nineteenth-Century Marketing.* Baltimore: Johns Hopkins University Press, 1971.

Porter, Harry. "Sales Methods That Net $1,000,000 a Week." *System: The Magazine of Business* 31 (May 1917): 509–17.

Potter, David. *People of Plenty.* Chicago: University of Chicago Press, 1954.

Prentiss, Don C. *Ford Products and Their Sale.* 6 vols. Detroit: Franklin Press, 1923.

Preston, Howard. *Automobile Age Atlanta: The Making of a Southern Metropolis, 1900–1935.* Athens: University of Georgia Press, 1979.

Raffio, Ralph. "Domino's Pizza." *Restaurant Business* 83 (January 1, 1884): 95–105.

"Rebirth of Ford." *Fortune,* May 1947, pp. 81–89+.

"Remember the Pump with Arms?" *Our Sun* 26 (Spring 1961): 11–13.

Rice, James. *The Franchising Phenomenon.* Ann Arbor, Mich.: Institute for Continuing Legal Education, 1969.

Riesman, David. *The Lonely Crowd: A Study of the Changing American Character.* New Haven, Conn.: Yale University Press, 1950.

"Ring Their Door-Bells—They'll Ring Your Cash Register." *Petroleum Age,* February 1, 1927, p. 30.

"Rip the Blindfold from Blind Records." *Sunoco Diamond* 1 (May 1934): 14.

Ritzer, George. "The 'McDonaldization' of Society." *Journal of American Culture* 6 (September 1983): 101–7.

Ross, M. "Standard Oil's Death Factory." *Nation* 119 (November 26, 1924): 561–62.

Rostow, W. W. *The Process of Economic Growth.* 2d ed. New York: W. W. Norton, 1962.

Rubin, Julius. "Canal or Railroad? Imitation and Innovation in the Response to the Erie Canal in Philadelphia, Baltimore, and Boston." *Transactions of the American Philosophical Society* 51 (November 1961).

Rudnick, Lewis. *A Decade of Franchise Regulation.* Washington, D.C.: International Franchise Association, 1978.

Sanders, Harlan. *Life as I Have Known It Has Been Finger Lickin' Good.* Carol Stream, Ill.: Creation House, 1974.

Santoni, Roland. "Franchising: A Critical Assessment of State and Federal Regulation." *Creighton Law Review* 14, no. 1 (1980): 67–97.

Seavoy, Ronald E. "Laws to Encourage Manufacturing: New York Policy and the 1811 General Incorporation Statute." *Business History Review* 46 (Spring 1972): 85–95.

———. "The Public Service Origins of the American Business Corporation." *Business History Review* 52 (Spring 1978): 30–60.

Seltzer, Lawrence H. *A Financial History of the American Automobile Industry*. New York: Houghton Mifflin, 1928.

"She Don't Look Like the Same Gal [station renovation]." *Sunoco Diamond* 4 (May 1936): 8–10.

"Shhhh! Carter Signs Dealer-Day Bill into Law." *National Petroleum News* 70 (August 1978): 15–16.

Sklar, Fred. "Franchises and Independence." *Urban Life* 6 (April 1977): 33–52.

Sloan, Alfred P. *My Years with General Motors*. Garden City, N.Y.: Doubleday, 1964.

Soltow, James. "Origins of Small Business: Metal Fabricators and Machinery Makers in New England, 1890–1957." *Transactions of the American Philosophical Society*, n.s. 55 (December 1965).

Sprague, Jessie Rainsford. "Confessions of a Ford Dealer." *Harper's Magazine* 155 (June 1927): 26–35.

Stafford, Roger. "Motorists Prefer One-Brand Stations; Dealers Say They Boost Gallonage." *National Petroleum News* 23 (February 4, 1931): 83–84.

———. "Why One Jobber Finds Agency Outlets Better than Company Stations." *National Petroleum News* 22 (October 22, 1930): 65.

"Station Out of Date? You'd Better Renovate!" *Sunoco Diamond* 19 (February 1949): 10–13.

Staudt, Thomas A. *The Manufacturer's Agents as a Marketing Institution*. Washington, D.C.: Government Printing Office, 1952.

"The Story of Sun." *Our Sun* 26 (Summer/Autumn 1961): 17–23.

Strasser, Susan. *Satisfaction Guaranteed: The Making of the American Mass Market*. New York: Pantheon, 1989.

"Sunoco's New Merchandising Program." *Sunoco Diamond* 16 (May/June 1944): 16–17.

"Sun Oil." *Fortune*, February 1941, pp. 51–53+.

Susman, Warren. *The Culture as History: The Transformation of American Society in the Twentieth Century*. New York: Pantheon, 1984.

Tedlow, Richard S. *New and Improved: The Story of Mass Marketing in America*. New York: Basic Books, 1990.

"These Ads . . . Yours for the Asking." *Sunoco Diamond* 12 (September 1942): 21–22+.

Thompson, Donald, ed. *Contractual Marketing Systems*. Lexington, Mass.: D. C. Heath, 1971.

———. *Franchise Operations and Antitrust*. Lexington, Mass.: D. C. Heath, 1971.

Bibliography

Thompson, Gregory. "Misused Product Cost Accounting in the American Railroad Industry." *Business History Review* (Autumn 1989): 510–54.

Tinney, Terry Jack. "A Study of Contemporary Franchising, with Particular Emphasis on Factors Leading to the Repurchase of Fast-Food Service Franchises." Ph.D. dissertation, North Texas State University, 1972.

Tipper, Harry. *The New Business*. Garden City, N.Y.: Doubleday, 1914.

"To Our Dealers. . . ." *Sunoco Diamond* 1 (May 1934): inside front cover.

"U.S. Supreme Court Gives States Power to Tax Chains Out of Business." *National Petroleum News* 27 (January 16, 1935): 7–8.

Vaughn, Charles, ed. *Franchising Today, 1966–1967*. San Francisco: Matthew Bender, 1967.

———. *Franchising Today*. Lynbrook, Mass.: Farnsworth Publishing, 1970.

Warner, Sam Bass, Jr. *Streetcar Suburbs: The Process of Growth in Boston, 1870–1900*. 2d ed. Boston: Harvard University Press, 1978.

———. "Why One Jobber Finds Agency Outlets Better than Company Stations." *National Petroleum News* 22 (October 22, 1930): 65.

Whyte, William, Jr. *The Organization Man*. New York: Simon and Schuster, 1955.

Wiebe, Robert. *The Search for Order, 1877–1920*. New York: Hill and Wang, 1967.

Wik, Reynold. *Henry Ford and Grass Roots America*. Ann Arbor: University of Michigan Press, 1972.

Williamson, Harold F., et al. *The American Petroleum Industry: The Age of Energy, 1899–1959*. Evanston, Ill.: Northwestern University Press, 1963.

Wilson, Sloan. *The Man in the Gray Flannel Suit*. New York: Simon and Schuster, 1955.

Worthy, James. *Shaping an American Institution*. Urbana: University of Illinois Press, 1984.

Yates, JoAnne. *Control through Communication: The Rise of System in American Management*. Baltimore: Johns Hopkins, 1989.

"You Have 14,000 Partners." *Sunoco Diamond* 4 (September 1936): back cover.

Zeigler, Harmon. *The Politics of Small Business*. Washington, D.C.: Public Affairs Press, 1961.

Zunz, Olivier. *Making America Corporate, 1870–1920*. Chicago: University of Chicago Press, 1990.

Index

Neidlinger, George, 41

Ohio Cultivator, 19
Oil industry, 85–86, 89–90; marketing
    structure, 87–90, 95, 96–97, 99–100,
    153; equipment loans, 96–97, 100;
    exclusive dealers, 98–99; dealer con-
    tracts, 105–6; and antichain legisla-
    tion, 107–9; conditions in 1970s, 114.
    See also Service stations; Sun Oil
    Company
Olds, Ransom E., 55
Olean, N.Y., 91

Parker and Gray (Singer agents), 166
    (n. 54)
Penn Fuel Company, 91–92
Peoples Natural Gas Company, 92
Petroleum industry. *See* Oil industry
Petroleum Marketing Practices Act
    (PMPA) of 1978, 114, 115, 179 (n. 66)
Pew, J. Howard, 93, 94, 102
Pew, Joseph N., 90–93
Pew, Robert C., 92
Phelps, Orson C., 33, 34
Pipeline certificates, 90
Pittsburgh, Pa., 91, 92
Pizza Dispatch, 145–46
Principe v. McDonald's Corporation,
    129. *See also* McDonald's Corpora-
    tion
Product franchising: defined, 3; ori-
    gins, 3–4, 150; company/dealer
    relations, 115. *See also* Franchising;
    specific firms and industries

Rockelman, Fred, 63

Scientific management, 169 (n. 11)

Sears & Roebuck, 50
Seigel v. Chicken Delight, Inc., 129,
    146
Seltz Franchise Developments, 141
Service industries, 119, 123, 124. *See
    also* Economy, modern
Service stations, 86, 88, 89, 94–96
Sewing machine: durability, 32–33,
    38–39; prices in 1850s, 35. *See
    also* I. M. Singer Company
Sewing machine combination, 36–37
Seymour, Chappell & Company, 19
Singer, Isaac M., 32–34, 95, 121; and
    failure of Merritt Players (theater
    group), 33. *See also* I. M. Singer
    Company
Singer & Phelps, 34
Small business: relationship with big
    business, 5–6, 32, 46–47, 88, 107,
    115–16, 118–19, 125–26, 148–49,
    158; and McCormick, 32; post–World
    War II interest in, 124–26
Spindletop, Tex., 93
Sprague, Reginald, 120
Standard Oil Company, 91, 92, 96, 99,
    100, 106
Standard Stations case, 113, 114
Sun Oil Company (New Jersey), 9–10,
    153–54; origins, 90–94; production
    of manufactured gas, 92–93; move
    into lubricants, 93; Sunoco trade-
    mark, 93; decision to market gaso-
    line, 93–95; marketing strategy, 93–
    95, 102–3, 109–11; marketing struc-
    ture, 95; company-owned stations,
    96; cost of establishing outlets, 96,
    97; number of stations, 96, 102, 112;
    Blue Sunoco, 97, 102–3, 106; rela-
    tions with dealers, 97–98, 104, 106,

.